Power of Paradox

mastering the Borland database

Francis Botto

SIGMA PRESS – Wilmslow, United Kingdom

First published in 1990 by

Sigma Press, 1 South Oak Lane, Wilmslow, Cheshire SK9 6AR, England.

British Library Cataloguing in Publication Data

A CIP catalogue record for this book is available from the British Library.

ISBN: 1-85058-208-4

Typesetting and design by

Sigma Hi-Tech Services Ltd

Printed in Malta by
Interprint Ltd.

Distributed by

John Wiley & Sons Ltd., Baffins Lane, Chichester, West Sussex, England.

Preface

Paradox is a formidable relational database accompanied by the sort of documentation which leaves no stone unturned.

With this inescapable fact in mind, *Power of Paradox* is written to bridge the gap between the Users' Guides and the real world.

In so far as using computers is concerned, the real world is a strange and mysterious place. Users' Guides often tell you things which you do not need to know, skip items you should know, and sometimes they become so detached from practicality they are left to gather dust.

Now that I have told you the main objective in writing *Power of Paradox,* I can advise you on how to use it. Or can I? Realising that the author is not bound to be the best person to do this, I have consulted a number of real users (like you!), ranging from novices to database veterans. Briefly, these are my findings:

There was a blanket approval to skip hands-on sessions which did not fit in with overall requirements. The majority of users consulted seemed to think that *Power of Paradox* could be used both as a reference manual, and read from start to finish as a book. Entering all records contained in the example tables was deemed to be unnecessary; one or two records was thought to be adequate. Finally, some users kept *Power of Paradox* open at the Appendix for a source of quick reference while working.

Happy reading!

Francis Botto

1990, Swansea

Acknowledgements:

The author wishes to thank the following:

Denis Moran, Managing Director of Borland International (UK), for his invaluable suggestions after reading the initial outline.

Graham Beech, Publisher, for granting total freedom with regard to the contents of *Power of Paradox*.

Keene Communications Ltd., London, for supplying the software for this project.

Fleetwood Mac for their uncompromising perseverance in producing rock music for adults.

People who decline to comment on the author's name.

Paradox Version 3 and 3.5

Users of Version 3 can now upgrade to Version 3.5, with some advantages in terms of performance and functionality. Because of its upwards compatability with Paradox 3, users of the new version will find *Power of Paradox* to be equally useful to them.

With the exception of the modified installation procedure (see Appendix), everything contained in *Power of Paradox* applies to both versions 3 and 3.5.

Contents

1

Introducing Databases

1.1 Introduction

The belief that information storage has grown parallel to the proliferation of computers is by no means unfounded. Beyond the understandable migration of existing information to computer databases, it seems that the desire to store more and more computer data cannot be quelled. On the surface, this implies that computers are constantly finding new niches, while a deeper and more cynical analysis suggests that we might be storing information for the sake of it, and becoming so-called *technology victims*.

As necessary in medieval times, and long before that, information storage is by no means a by-product of the computer age. The Domesday Book of 1086, commissioned by King William I, perhaps illustrates a medieval database of invaluable and easily-accessible facts about the land. Computers have merely made the process of information storage more efficient and more flexible, as the Domesday Book of 1985 duly confirms. This contemporary, high-tech Domesday Book provides a survey of the land, where cities, towns, streets, landmarks, and familiar scenes can be viewed instantly on a personal computer using an interactive laser disc system developed by Philips.

Mundane information such as everyday records in the shape of (birth, marriage and death) certificates, diaries, ships' log-books and even books, is, essentially, a hallmark of civilisation. Its absence naturally leads to confusion and, sometimes, the unanswerable. For instance, the lack of information about William Shakespeare, particularly with regard to schooling and manuscripts, has led a small, but growing, number of people to relegate the name of this literary giant to nothing more than a pseudonym. Sceptics believe that a will which bears the signature, William

Shakespeare, tells of a person who could barely sign his own name, while believers insist that it was probably signed on his death bed.

Away from such mysteries, information which pertains to trading and economic activity is also important, if not invaluable. Information which relates to global trading and economic activity is constantly analysed in hope of finding hidden trends. In some quarters, it is used to generate long-wave cycles, or 'Kondratieff' waves as referred to in a book of that name which emanated from Russia in about 1920. Showing upswings and downswings of economic activity, these roughly confirm that recessions of one kind or another occur every 50 years or so, when the last 200 years of industrialisation and global trading are considered. To go back farther is not possible as there is simply not enough information!

For the sake of interest, Figure 1.1 shows some of the better known Kondratieff waves. Notice how these coincide exactly with the troughs and peaks of the original Kondratieff wave. Needless to say, many economists regard conclusions drawn from such waves as being *non sequitur*.

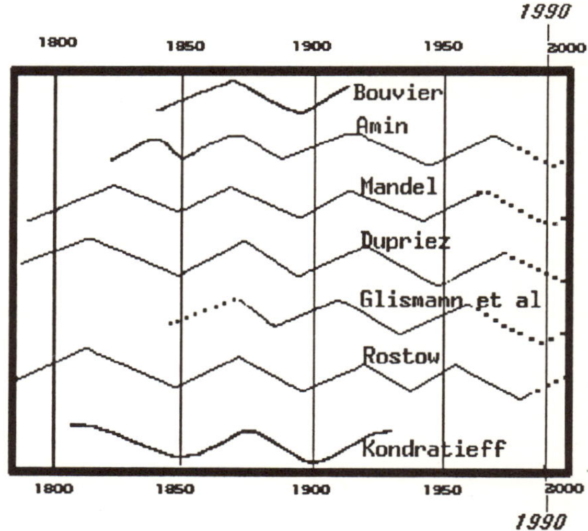

Figure 1.1: Kondratieff Waves

Today, of course, the bulk of stored information is directly associated with trade, commerce and, needless to say, bureaucracy. As you read this, you can be sure that your name is stored on literally hundreds, if not thousands, of computer systems. And it is not just banks, building societies, credit companies and the Civil Service that utilise this information. Information about yourself might be being processed for simple marketing techniques where companies target you with junk mail.

As a Paradox user, your information may fall into a number of categories, ranging from conventional business applications to research of varying kinds. Whatever information you store, it will be placed at your fingertips. This will make better use of your time, help make your company more competitive, and generally help you manage your information in otherwise impossible ways. If you are just beginning to gather, or to store, information, you could not have started at a more exciting time, nor with a better database.

1.2 What is a Database?

In simple terms, a database is best described as an electronic filing system which replaces the filing cabinet and possibly the secretary or clerk, too; it is used to both store and provide easy access to information. This is achieved by storing information in files which are separated into records, where records are further divided into fields. For example, take a look at the simple file shown in Figure 1.2.

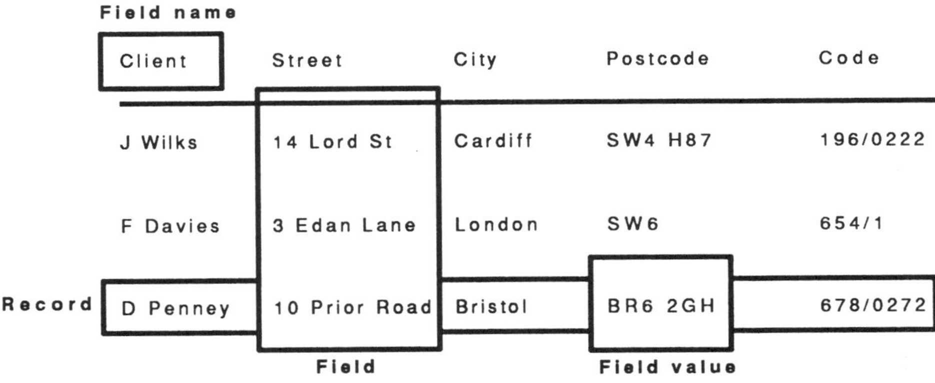

Figure 1.2: Simple database file

The simplest type of database is known as a *flat file* database in that no single file can be related or linked to another. Such a database is not relational (see Section 1.4). Flat file databases are now considered extremely limited to the extent where many feel that they should be avoided for other than basic database applications. However, they are less expensive, and are often chosen for this reason.

Paradox 3 is an relational database management system (RDBMS) which stretches the database concept far beyond the primitive flat file genre. Besides helping you store and retrieve information, it also permits you to interrogate your information where reference can be made to a number of tables of data. Later, when you get to grips with Paradox, you will realise that the database definition in this section could be regarded as an insult.

1.3 Origins of Databases

When personal computers began to spread throughout industry and commerce in the late 70s, the potential for information storage and retrieval was quickly realised. At that time, database programs were confined to large mainframe computers. One such database was JPLDIS, written by Jeb Long, a programmer at the Pasadena Jet Propulsion Laboratory – A NASA contractor of impeccable background. This database was exported to the personal computer by Wayne Ratliff, a programmer with another NASA contractor. After initially doing this to perform some mundane office chore, he hit upon the idea of marketing and selling the program under the instantly forgettable name, Vulcan. Sales were disappointing.

In the latter half of 1980, Wayne Ratliff's meeting with George Tate marked the beginning of relationship which was to change their lives. George Tate and Hal Lashlee had just started a software distribution business which was to become the famous name, Ashton-Tate. They decided to market and sell Vulcan under the name dBase II; this was thought to better manifest the purpose of the program. Dbase became a resounding success and was duly refined into dBase III in 1984, dBase III Plus in late 1985, and dBase IV in April 1988.

It is well known that Wayne Ratliff and George Tate had a special relationship – as successful partnerships often do. When George Tate suddenly died of a heart attack in June 1984, the seeds for a split were sown; Wayne Ratliff moved over to Migent before the release of dBase IV, and began work on another database program called Emerald Bay which, so far, has wielded nothing like the high profile dBase and Paradox 3 enjoy.

Based upon the large market uncovered by Ashton Tate, numerous other database programs have since emerged. Programs like DataPerfect, DataEase, Q&A, are just some of the packages that make up a highly competitive market.

1.4 Relational Databases

Using databases, the computer monitor is like a small keyhole through which you are trying to view the contents of a room – not that the author is given to peeping through keyholes! This tunnel vision, as it were, is particularly noticeable when using flat file databases; it is hard to gain an overall picture of how information might be linked. Even if the monitor screen were the size of a desktop, the difficulty of interrogating, and determining what relates to what, would be lessened by an almost unnoticeable degree.

A partial answer is provided by the relational database concept, in that it is possible to view and edit information which emanates from entirely different tables. (In relational-database parlance, files are referred to as tables.) Suppose, for example, you wanted to view information which stems from a number of different tables. You could easily do this using Paradox by simply filling in query forms, and indicating what you want to see. Querying is fully discussed in Chapter 7.

The relational database, however, was not developed so as to remedy the limited amount of information that can be displayed on a monitor screen. Indeed this is a welcome offshoot, however insignificant people may think it is. The rationale behind the development of the relational database was a practical one: to give rise to a database which could produce receipts, invoices, form letters, reports/summaries, and so forth which need not be confined to single tables.

More precisely, the relational database can be used to implement vital links between tables of data; thus while information is entered it is not shrouded in a kind of 'staccato', where everything seems detached, but embroiled with logical relationships.

Figure 1.3 shows a simple invoice which extracts data from two tables.

```
*******************************************************************************
*                              I N V O I C E                                  *
*******************************************************************************
ABC Technical Services, 3 Bowers Street, London WE7.  Tel 01 542 675412


Company: Brett Ltd
         John Sawyer
         7 Virginia Road
         Bristol

Amount: 1,050.00

Date: 10.04.90

*******************************************************************************
```

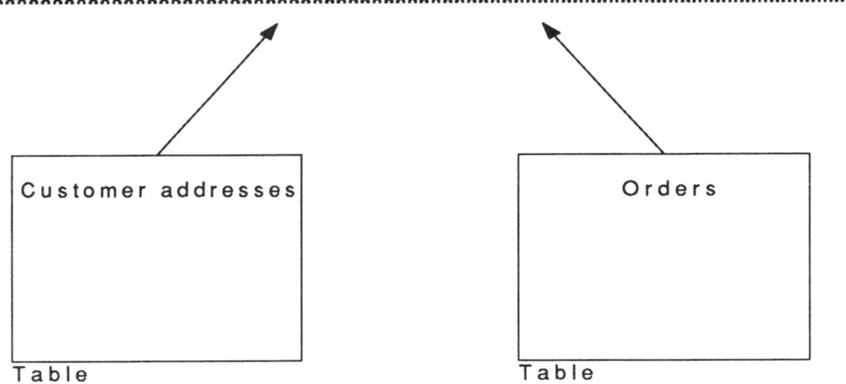

Figure 1.3: Invoice

As you progress through *Power of Paradox* the relational database concept will become clearer.

1.5 What is Paradox?

Paradox epitomizes all that a modern database should be. It is fully relational, able to produce graphs at a single keystroke, it has its own database application language called PAL (Personal Application Language), and it has a Personal Programmer which will enable you to generate applications without knowledge of programming.

The Personal Programmer is discussed in Chapter 11, showing how to taylor a Paradox application according to exact requirements.

Paradox is also non-procedural in that if you ask it, for example, to show you all your clients that have paid you in excess of £1,000, it does not need to be given a series of steps like many programming languages, but it will simply make the appropriate decisions to reach a result.

The basic requirement behind the development of Paradox was to produce a database which was both sophisticated and easy to use. This approach was thought to prise open a hole in the market. After all, it was noticeable that databases were either sophisticated and difficult to use, or they were simple (usually flat file) and of limited use.

The net result is a database which is menu driven, has an obliging help system, and, most important, is sophisticated. This is certainly a Paradox.

2

Installing Paradox 3

This chapter takes you through the process of installing Paradox 3. If you have installed Paradox (including the sample tables), you can progress to Chapter 3 without loss of continuity. Though this chapter unavoidably duplicates much of Chapter 3 *Installing Paradox* in the Introduction Guide and Chapter 2 *Fundamentals* in the User's Guide, extra hints and tips are included.

Throughout *Power of Paradox,* keystrokes are shown like this: **G**. Where keys are pressed consecutively, they are separated by a forward slash: **E/Y**. Where keys are pressed simultaneously they are separated by a hyphen: **Ctrl-F1**. **Alt-F5/F10/I**, for example, indicates that the **Alt** and **F5** keys are first pressed together, then **F10** is pressed, followed by **I**.

Dos commands and data items are shown as: Enter **3 North Drive** which indicates that you simply type **3 North Drive** and then press **<Enter>**.

2.1 Making Room on Hard Disk

Preparing a system so as to begin installing an additional item of software can be a daunting task, particularly when the hard disk is bursting at the edges, so to speak. Paradox 3 requires 2 Mbytes (or 2,000 Kbytes) of hard disk space prior to installation. In addition, to ensure that the most complex of Paradox operations can be negotiated swiftly, 1 Mbyte of free disk space following installation is recommended.

It is possible to check how much free disk space is available from the C> Dos prompt (obtainable by entering C:). Entering **dir** lists all files and perhaps directories in the current directory. At the very bottom of the list will be a number. This number must be greater than 3000000 to indicate that more than 3 Mbytes of disk space is available. Anything less than this and it will be necessary to delete unwanted files, or to move files over to floppy disk(s), or to another hard disk (see Appendix).

Most users, however, will have at their disposal a program which provides facility to erase files, as well as copy and move them from one directory to another. For example, the Borland Sprint word processor has useful file management facilities, as do most other professional word processors such as WordPerfect, Microsoft Word and WordStar. It is also possible to manage files using personal organiser programs such as Borland's SideKick, for instance.

2.2 System Requirements

If using an IBM or compatible machine less than four years old, it will certainly support Paradox. However, for the record, you must have the following items:

❑ IBM PC, PC XT, PC AT, PS/2, or other IBM compatible machine

❑ One floppy disk drive, and one hard disk with at least 3 Mbytes of free disk space

❑ 512 Kbytes of RAM

❑ Dos 2 or higher

❑ A dot-matrix or laser printer to provide graphical output

❑ A number of formatted floppy disks so as to store or backup Paradox data files.

2.3 Installation

Before actually running the installation program, it needs to be said that the whole process is straightforward to the extent that you hardly need to be advised. Indeed Paradox is the easiest of databases to install – so you needn't worry about a thing, if you are worried, that is.

The installation program will present various options which will be described in due course. Wherever necessary, it will also prompt you to change disks, so this section omits such advice. Now to begin the installation procedure (At last! I hear you cry):

1. Ensure that a C> prompt is on screen. If not, enter **c:** in order to make your hard disk the current drive. Enter **cd** to change to the root directory.

2. From the Paradox disks, select the Installation/Sample Tables Disk and insert it into drive A.

3. Enter **a:install**

You will first encounter some notes about Paradox. Read these and proceed by pressing **<Enter>**. You will then be confronted by the Installation menu shown in Figure 2.1.

```
                      PARADOX INSTALLATION
 Please specify the installation type

 Choice   Description

 1)       Hard Disk Installation
 2)       Network Installation
 3)       Optional Software Installation
 4)       Quit

       <--- Your Choice
```

Figure 2.1: Installation menu

If your computer is not connected to other machines by way of a network of any kind, enter **1** to select Hard Disk Installation – the vast majority of users will make this selection.

Item 2, Network Installation, should be chosen if Paradox is to be used on a Local Area Network (or LAN). Item 3 on the menu, Optional Software Installation, is used to reinstall Paradox features following an initial installation. For example, to install the sample tables after Paradox 3 is installed, re-run the Installation program, select item 3 Optional Software Installation, then, choose Sample Tables from the Optional Software Installation menu, shown in Figure 2.3.

4. In response to the prompt: *Please enter SOURCE drive : A* type **<Enter>** in order to opt for the default drive A.

5. Respond to the prompt: *Please enter the DESTINATION drive : C* by typing **<Enter>** to opt for the default drive C.

6. In response to the prompt: *Please enter the directory in which to install PARADOX 3:* press <Enter>, yet again, to opt for the default Paradox 3 directory.

7. When confronted by the five country groups, as shown in Figure 2.2 overleaf,

select English International by entering **2**. This will ensure that number, date and sorting conventions are appropriate, and it will also cause the sample tables supplied with Paradox to be converted into an acceptable format. This is important, as Power of Paradox makes use of the sample tables.

```
PARADOX INSTALLATION
To properly install Paradox, you must specify one of the five country
groups below.  This will tell Paradox which date and number formats to
use and how to sort your alphabetic fields.  After Paradox has been
installed, you may change the date or number conventions by using the
Paradox Custom Configuration Program.

Choice   Description

1)       United States
            Appropriate to the United States
2)       English International
            Appropriate to English-speaking countries outside the U.S.
3)       European
            Appropriate to European countries such as France and Germany
4)       Swedish/Finnish
            Appropriate to Sweden and Finland
5)       Norwegian/Danish
            Appropriate to Norway and Denmark

      <--- Your Choice
```

Figure 2.2: Country groups

8. Insert System Disk 1 into drive A and press **<Enter>**.

You now have to establish your Paradox Personal Signature: First, enter your name; then your company name, if appropriate; enter the serial number written on the Installation Disk; finally, if you do not wish to access data on a network, enter **n**.

If you make a mistake, fields can be edited by pressing **up-** or **down-arrow-keys**, you can delete any field by pressing **Ctrl-<left-arrow-key>**.

Satisfied with the signature information, press **F2** to save it.

9. Continue to insert disks as prompted.

When you arrive at the Optional Software Installation menu shown in Figure 2.3, opposite, enter **1** to select Sample Tables.

Press **<Enter>** to choose the default path for the storage of Sample tables.

In turn select options 2 to 5 on the Optional Software Installation menu, each time selecting the default path.

```
═══════════════Optional Software Installation═══════════════
 Please specify the optional software you wish to install.

 Choice   Description

 1)       Sample Tables
             Sample Tables Installation
 2)       Sample Application
             Sample Application Installation
 3)       PPROG
             Paradox Personal Programmer Installation
 4)       Protect
             Paradox Protection Generator Installation
 5)       Data Entry Toolkit
             Data Entry Toolkit Installation
 6)       Exit
             End installation session

        <--- Your Choice
```

Figure 2.3: Optional Software Installation menu

Finally, enter: **6** to end the installation session. Read the end note and reboot your system by pressing **Ctrl-Alt-Del**.

2.4 Memory Problems during Installation

Though the installation procedure is unlikely to cause problems, setbacks can occur. The most obvious is where insufficient disk space has caused the installation program to terminate proceedings prematurely. Installation will also be abandoned where insufficient Ram is available.

Though few modern, IBM and compatible machines have less than 512K of Ram, older machines, particularly those based on the 8088 processor, might have inadequate memory. It is possible to fit extra Ram to almost all machines, sometimes chips can be inserted directly into the motherboard. An alternative solution is to add the appropriate memory card(s). Contact the manufacturer of your machine, or the dealer from which you purchased it, for more information.

The bottleneck of insufficient memory may also be encountered where a TSR (terminate and stay resident) or pop-up program is loaded prior to running the installation program. For example, programs like Sidekick can cause memory problems where a machine is equipped with less than an adequate amount of Ram. (Incidentally, if you encounter memory problems using Borland SideKick, particularly when running the Personal Programmer in Chapter 11, use the program Skinst to limit the size of the notepad, or use startup options which load a limited portion of the program – see SideKick manual.)

2.5 Loading Paradox

Following the successful installation of Paradox, it is only natural to learn how to load it. With a C> prompt on screen, ensure the current directory is Paradox3 by entering: **cd\Paradox3**. If an alternative directory name was used during installation, type the appropriate directory name. Finally, enter: **paradox3**.

The Paradox Personal Signature will appear for a short while until the opening Paradox screen signature Paradox screen and main menu appear as shown in Figure 2.4. More about that in the next chapter.

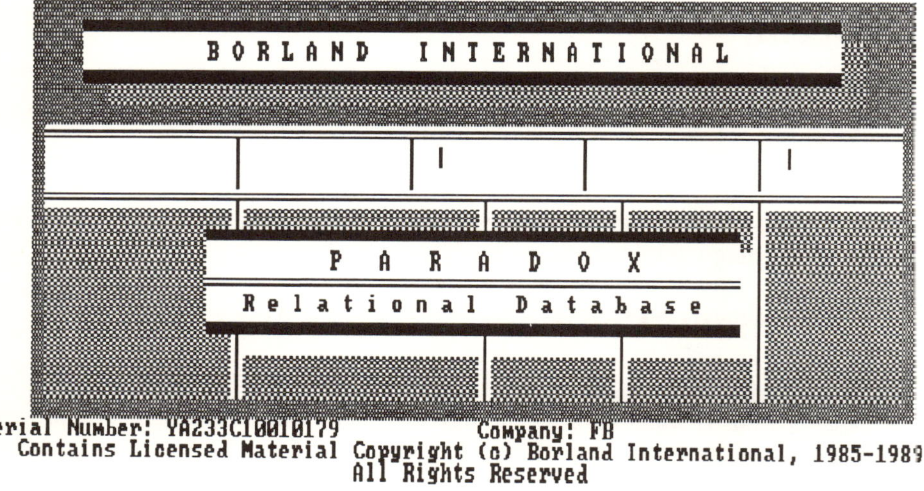

Figure 2.4: Paradox screen signature

To get out of Paradox, with the main menu on screen, press **E/Y.**

2.5.1 Loading Paradox Automatically

Invoking Paradox from the keyboard daily, can become a chore. However, it is possible to load Paradox, and other applications, automatically when a system is started. This can be achieved by modifying a batch file. Batch files are used to implement a number of Dos commands automatically. (Batch refers to the batch of Dos commands that are executed.) The batch file which we are going to modify is called the AUTOEXEC.BAT file. (You might find it easier to use an editor or a word processor which can handle Dos Text files.)

The following practice sessions address both the creation and modification of the AUTOEXEC batch file from Dos.

2.5.2 Hands-on Session – floppy disk users

This hands-on session shows you how to run Paradox automatically from floppy disk when you switch on your computer.

1. With the Dos prompt A> on the screen, and with your Dos startup disk in drive A, enter: **copy con autoexec.bat**.

You now have the ability to enter Dos commands which will be executed when your system is booted.

3. Enter the following lines:

```
c:
cd\paradox3
paradox3
```

4. Press **Ctrl-z** followed by **<Enter>** to save your AUTOEXEC file.

5. To put your adjustments to the test, press **Ctrl-Alt-Del** to reboot your system. You will find Paradox running without having to touch a single key.

2.5.3 Hands-on Session – hard disk users

This session shows you how to run Paradox automatically, when you switch on your computer, where Dos is in the root directory of your hard disk.

1. With the Dos prompt C> on the screen, enter: **cd** to resort to the root directory.

2. Enter: **copy con autoexec.bat**

You now have the ability to enter Dos commands which will be executed when your system is booted.

3. Enter the following lines :

```
c:
cd\paradox3
paradox3
```

4. Press **Ctrl-z** and then **<Enter>** to save your AUTOEXEC file

5. To put your adjustments to the test, press **Ctrl-Alt-Del** to reboot your system. You will find Paradox running without you having to touch a single key.

3

Paradox Overview

This chapter takes you on a whistle stop tour of the simplest Paradox capabilities and facilities. It briefly addresses the rationale behind its development and explains why, exactly, you are going to find it easy to use.

3.1 Paradoxical Paradox

Charles K Colton once said: *"Man is an embodied paradox, a bundle of contradictions."*

Those intent on making instant judgements, (like too many software reviewers), might regard Paradox as a contradiction, if not a bundle of contradictions – a database which is sophisticated and easy to use is a little hard to digest. This view perhaps stems from the consideration of other databases; those that are easy to use border on uselessness, while those that are sophisticated are sometimes *user-hostile*.

The contradiction, if there is one, pales when you realise how Borland (and a company called Ansa) achieved this feat called Paradox.

First, Paradox is menu driven. You can, therefore, exploit any of its powerful features by simply selecting menu items. Paradox menus are described in Section 3.4. Ease of use is further promoted by an extremely detailed Help system. F1, the so-called Help key, will assist with your initial efforts.

Help offered can be context sensitive, in that it will pertain to whatever you are doing at the time, or, the index can be used to select any topic of help required. For more information about the help system see Section 3.5.

3.2 Upgrading from Paradox 2

For those already familiar with Paradox 2, a particularly easy and enjoyable task lies ahead. Paradox 3 and 3.5 are very much its powerful big brothers. In addition to all the Paradox 2 features you have got used to, the latest versions offer significant improvements. The most important must be the inclusion of presentation graphics, with which data can be presented via a number of graph formats at a single keystroke. Figure 3.1 shows the stacked bar graph format.

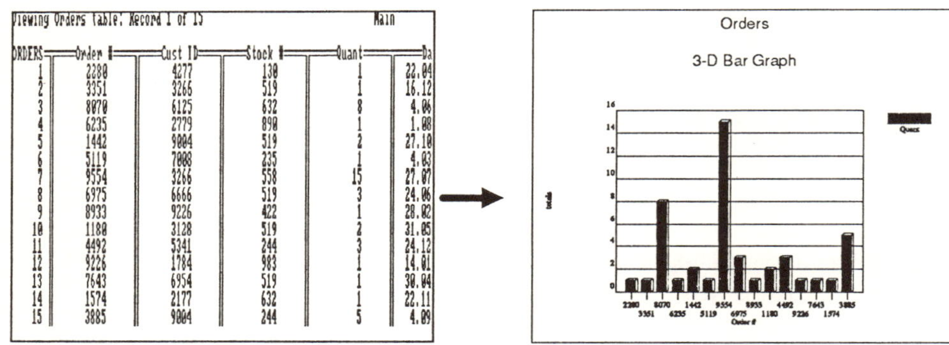
Viewing Orders table: Record 1 of 15 Main

ORDERS	Order #	Cust ID	Stock #	Quant	Da
1	2280	4277	130	1	22.04
2	3351	3266	519	1	16.12
3	8070	6125	632	8	4.06
4	6235	2779	890	1	1.08
5	1442	9004	519	2	27.10
6	5119	7008	235	1	4.03
7	9554	3266	558	15	27.07
8	6975	6666	519	3	24.06
9	8933	9226	422	1	28.02
10	1180	3128	519	2	31.05
11	4492	5341	244	3	24.12
12	9226	1784	983	1	14.01
13	7643	6954	519	1	30.04
14	1574	2177	632	1	22.11
15	3885	9004	244	5	4.09

Figure 3.1: Stacked bar graph

Graphs are fully discussed in Chapter 8.

3.3 How Data is Stored

Paradox data is stored in the form of tables, as shown in Figure 3.2. opposite

As you can see, tables are made up of records which are further divided into fields. Fields fall into four categories: *alphanumeric, date, currency* and *numeric.*

Access to Paradox tables is by no means restricted, it is possible to load a number of them. Understandably, loaded tables will not be shown simultaneously on screen as there is not enough room. The way Paradox gets round this is to load tables into a workspace, within which you can skip from one table to the next, instantly.

Using Paradox, the design of such tables is of paramount importance, if you are to manage your information efficiently, that is. However, it is possible to modify tables as your information requirements grow. In this respect Paradox will oblige your hindsight. The design, creation and modification of tables is discussed in Chapter 5.

Viewing Masterbk table: Record 1 of 128 Main

MASTERBK	Date	Employee	Customer	State	Home Group
1	21.08.87	Christiansen	Aberdeen	DC	Manners
2	20.10.89	Christiansen	Aberdeen	DC	Manners
3	20.10.89	Christiansen	Aberdeen	DC	Manners
4	5.05.88	Morris	McDougal	WA	Investment
5	15.08.88	Chambers	McDougal	WA	Manners
6	1.12.88	Morris	McDougal	WA	Investment
7	1.12.88	Morris	McDougal	WA	Manners
8	1.03.89	Morris	McDougal	WA	Sports
9	1.03.89	Morris	McDougal	WA	Manners
10	1.03.89	Morris	McDougal	WA	Investment
11	14.11.89	Christiansen	McDougal	WA	Travel
12	16.01.90	Christiansen	McDougal	WA	Travel
13	16.01.90	Christiansen	McDougal	WA	Investment
14	6.12.88	Morris	Bonnefemme	CA	Travel
15	4.08.89	Morris	Bonnefemme	CA	Sports
16	30.11.89	Kling	Bonnefemme	CA	Manners
17	30.11.89	Kling	Bonnefemme	CA	Travel
18	6.04.90	Christiansen	Bonnefemme	CA	Manners
19	16.05.90	Kling	Bonnefemme	CA	Manners
20	13.09.90	Morris	Bonnefemme	CA	Sports
21	29.02.88	Lee	Chavez	FL	Investment
22	13.07.88	Lee	Chavez	FL	Estate

Figure 3.2: Example of a Data Table

3.4 Paradox Menus

Paradox does not require you to memorise numerous key-combinations, as all features are freely available from its menus.

The main menu, or the top level menu, (shown in Figure 3.3) in which all other menus find their roots, is presented the moment Paradox is loaded.

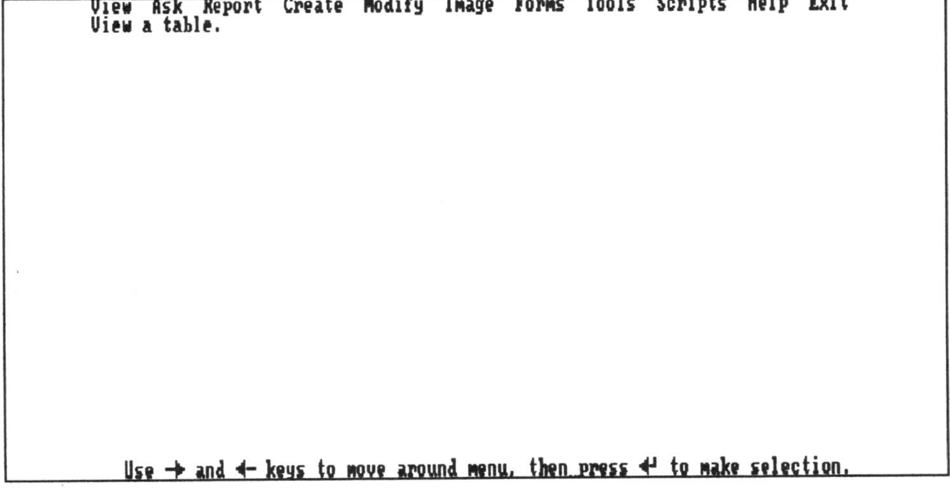

Figure 3.3: The main menu

Either of the following methods can be adopted to select menu items:

❑ Highlight the appropriate menu item using the **left-** and **right-arrow-keys** and press **<Enter>**;

❑ Press the key corresponding to the first letter of the menu item.

To cancel a menu selection, press **<Escape>**. To cancel all menu selections press F10 which causes the main menu to reappear.The following practice session shows how to use the View menu item.

The following practice session shows how to use the View menu item.

3.4.1 Hands-on Session

This hands-on session shows how to view the Customer sample table.

1. Press **V** to select View from the main menu.

2. Enter: **sample** to inform Paradox that you wish to viewone of the tables contained in the sample directory.

3. Press the **<right-arrow-key>** once to highlight the Customer table.

4. Press **<Enter>** to produce the Customer table shown in Figure 3.4.

Viewing Customer table: Record 1 of 33 Main ▲═

CUSTOMER	Cust ID	Last Name	Init	Street	City
1	1386	Aberdeen	F	45 Utah Street	Washington
2	1388	Svenvald	I	Gouvernment House	Reykjavik
3	1784	McDougal	L	4950 Pullman Ave NE	Seattle
4	2177	Bonnefemme	S	128 University Drive	Stanford
5	2579	Chavez	L	Cypress Drive	Palm Springs
6	2779	Fahd	S	The Palace	Riyadh
7	3128	Elspeth, III	R	1 Hanover Square	London
8	3266	Hanover	A	15 State Street	Dallas
9	3271	Massey	C	29 Aragona Drive	Oxon Hill
10	3771	Montaigne	L	30 Tauton Drive	Bellevue
11	4277	Matthews	R	P. O. Box 20336	Albuquerque
12	4335	Farouk	K	Hotel Cairo	Cairo
13	4480	Samuelson	F	Bull Run Ranch	Aurora
14	4485	Fischer	R	14 Willow Lane	Birmingham
15	4589	Leonardo	D	198 Via Canales	Rome
16	4700	Harris	J	Old Country Road	Atherton
17	4884	Anders	B	Jaktstigen 42	Lidingo
18	5341	Chevalier	R	392 Boulevard Raspil	Montpelier
19	5720	Helms	D	52 Brattle Street	Cambridge
20	5855	Chin	F	Hotel Orient	Jurong
21	6125	Hawes-Anderson	D	Waves Cottage	Palm Springs
22	6666	Matthews	J	1050 12th Street	San Francisc

Figure 3.4: Customer table

Notice that the cursor appears in the top left of the table, and along the upper edge of the screen are shown the table title, table size in terms of records, and directory name.

5. To erase the table from the screen, and clear it from the workspace, press **F8**.

Though, in this practice session, a menu selection was made by simply pressing the key corresponding to the first letter of the menu item, it is advisable to begin by making menu selections using the arrow keys together with the **<Enter>** key.

3.5 The Help Key

Few programs comprise Help systems which compare with that of Paradox. F1, the Help key, can reduce your reading time with regard to the Users' Guides. Bear in mind, however, that the Help system will only take you so far; when you become a more proficient you will need to resort to sections of the Users' Guides.

For context-sensitive help, that is information concerning a current task, simply press **F1**. To obtain Help screens concerning other topics, press **F1** twice and then select the appropriate item. Press **P** to return to Paradox. Try this for yourself.

3.6 Accessing Information

It is possible to see Paradox tables simply by selecting View and then choosing the appropriate table. Additionally, you can cycle between tables, or images as Borland likes to call them, when more than one image is loaded.

When tables expand, you soon outgrow the basic process of locating records using the arrow keys. Using Paradox, tables may contain many thousands of records, so how would you locate a particular one?

Paradox overcomes this problem by allowing you to interrogate your tables for specific items of information. For example, it will allow you to list records where, perhaps, customers have expended more than £100. Similarly, it lets you search for particular records using the Zoom feature. This is discussed in Chapter 4.

3.7 Presenting Data

Tables are fine in most circumstances. Sometimes, however, a table which contains much numeric data can be confusing, particularly when only a minute portion of it can be viewed on screen at a time.

Presenting tables graphically is a particularly powerful method of overcoming this inherent weakness. Paradox permits the generation of numerous graphs, ranging from standard bar graphs to pie graphs. These are discussed in Chapter 8.

3.8 More About the Menus

Paradox menus are arranged in such a way as to make their use intuitive. This makes Paradox particularly friendly to the first time user. It is important that you believe this fact as such faith will help you through the initial learning curve.

Consider the main menu shown in Figure 3.3. By pressing the left-and right-arrow-keys, it is possible to highlight individual menu items, causing a brief description to appear on the line below. To expedite the process of learning about the menu system, here is a concise explanation of what each item does:

View most often used, allows you to load tables into the workspace

Ask permits you to interrogate information by querying tables. This is achieved by filling in query forms (discussed in Chapter 7)

Report allows you to design, produce and print reports. Reports can be letters, invoices, tables, in fact anything that has to be printed (discussed in Chapter 10)

Create is used to design table structures (discussed in Chapters 5 and 6)

Modify permits tables to be edited, sorted and restructured (discussed in Chapter 5)

Image lets you resize and reformat a table, move to a field or record, select forms and generate graphs

Forms allows you to design or change forms (see Chapters 6 and 9)

Tools lets you rename tables, forms and reports; export and import data; copy and delete tables, forms, reports and scripts; speed up queries; add and subtract records; protect tables and scripts; lock and unlock tables; change directories; go to Dos (discussed on numerous occasions).

Scripts permits you to record and play scripts. These can range from simple macros, used to make keyboard recordings, to complete applications created using PAL or the Personal Programmer (discussed in Chapters 6 and 11)

Help gives context sensitive help, as well as help on chosen topics

Exit naturally lets you leave Paradox.

4

Beginning with Paradox

This chapter acquaints you with everyday tasks undertaken by the Paradox user. You will learn how to view tables, to move about tables, view forms, print a simple report, generate a graph and a great deal more.

For the benefit of readers that have begun Power of Paradox by delving into this chapter, the convention adopted with regard to key presses is as follows: keystrokes are shown like this: **G**. Keys pressed consecutively are separated by a forward slash: **E/Y**. Keys pressed simultaneously are separated by a hyphen: **Ctrl-F1**. **Alt-F5/F10/I**, for example, indicates that the **Alt** and **F5** keys are first pressed together, then **F10** is pressed, followed by **I**.

Dos commands and data items are shown as: enter **3 North Drive**, which indicates that you simply type **3 North Drive** and then press **<Enter>**.

Finally, before beginning, place the function key template on your keyboard. This will provide concise information as to what each function key does. More about such shortcuts later.

4.1 The Opening Screen

When Paradox is loaded, by entering:

```
cd\paradox3
paradox3
```

the 'signature' information first appears, followed by a bland, but uncluttered, screen showing the main menu as illustrated in Figure 4.1 on the next page.

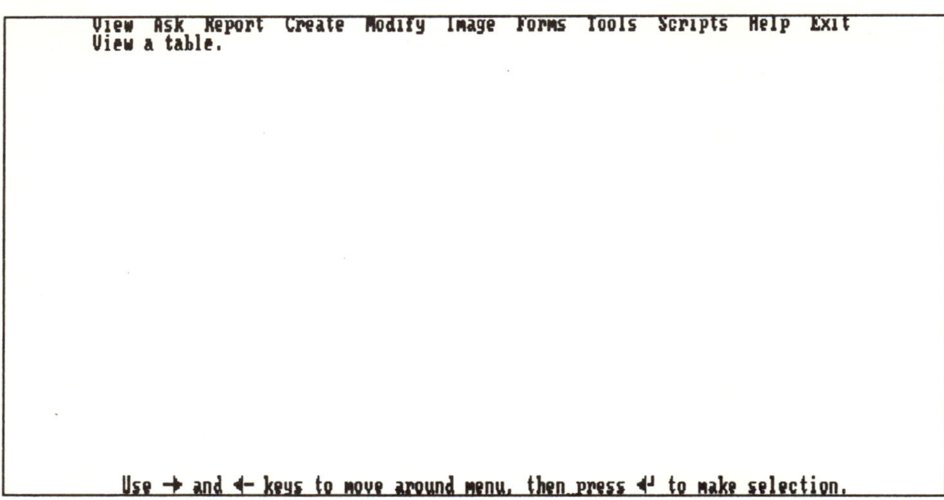
View Ask Report Create Modify Image Forms Tools Scripts Help Exit
View a table.

Use → and ← keys to move around menu, then press ↵ to make selection.

Figure 4.1: The Opening menu

Selections along the top of the screen, you will remember, constitute the main menu; the top level menu in which all others find their roots.

The workspace below the main menu is used to display tables, forms, reports and graphs. For the moment, we are concerned with tables. (Forms, reports and graphs are addressed in due course.) To recap, in Paradox parlance, tables on screen are referred to as images.

4.2 Viewing a Table

Tables form the backbone of Paradox; at the root of your information management there are always tables. They can be loaded one after another where it is possible to cycle from one to the next by invoking the up image and down image features.

The following hands-on session escorts you through the simple process of viewing and moving about one of the sample tables supplied with Paradox. If you have installed Paradox without the sample tables, refer to Chapter 2, Section 2.3.

4.2.1 Hands-on Session

This session shows how to view the Customer sample table, and is partially reproduced from the session in Chapter 3.

1. Press **V** to select View from the main menu.

2. Enter **sample** to inform Paradox that you wish to view one of the tables contained

in the Sample directory. It is important to remember that you can list the tables of any directory in this manner. Additionally, if **<Enter>** is pressed following the selection of View, a list of the tables in the current working directory is produced. Paradox3 is the default working directory.

Notice that the arrow to the right of the row of shown tables indicates that there are more. To move through these tables press **<right-arrow-key>**.

3. Using the arrow keys, highlight the Customer table.

4. Press **<Enter>** to produce the Customer table shown in Figure 4.2.

Viewing Customer table: Record 1 of 33 Main

CUSTOMER	Cust ID	Last Name	Init	Street	City
1	1386	Aberdeen	F	45 Utah Street	Washington
2	1388	Svenvald	I	Gouvernment House	Reykjavik
3	1784	McDougal	L	4950 Pullman Ave NE	Seattle
4	2177	Bonnefemme	S	128 University Drive	Stanford
5	2579	Chavez	L	Cypress Drive	Palm Springs
6	2779	Fahd	S	The Palace	Riyadh
7	3128	Elspeth, III	R	1 Hanover Square	London
8	3266	Hanover	A	15 State Street	Dallas
9	3271	Massey	C	29 Aragona Drive	Oxon Hill
10	3771	Montaigne	L	30 Tauton Drive	Bellevue
11	4277	Matthews	R	P. O. Box 20336	Albuquerque
12	4335	Farouk	K	Hotel Cairo	Cairo
13	4480	Samuelson	F	Bull Run Ranch	Aurora
14	4485	Fischer	R	14 Willow Lane	Birmingham
15	4589	Leonardo	D	198 Via Canales	Rome
16	4700	Harris	J	Old Country Road	Atherton
17	4884	Anders	B	Jaktstigen 42	Lidingo
18	5341	Chevalier	R	392 Boulevard Raspil	Montpelier
19	5720	Helms	D	52 Brattle Street	Cambridge
20	5855	Chin	F	Hotel Orient	Jurong
21	6125	Hawes-Anderson	D	Waves Cottage	Palm Springs
22	6666	Matthews	J	1050 12th Street	San Francisc

Figure 4.2: The sample Customer table

4.2.2 Clearing Images

Single images on screen, such as tables, can be erased from the workspace by pressing **F8** (Clear Image). You might like to try this. As you become a more proficient and a more demanding Paradox user, you will clear images on a regular basis. Pressing **Alt-F8** (Clear All) causes all images to be erased from the workspace.

4.3 Moving About a Table

Once displayed on screen, it is possible to move about a table using the arrow keys.

Try this for yourself. Swifter methods of moving the cursor are available: pressing **<Home>**, for example, moves to the first record of the table; **Ctrl-<Home>** moves to the first field or column; End moves to the last record; **Ctrl-End** moves to the last field or column. At this point it might be a good idea to try some of these methods on the sample Customer table.

Finally, it is possible to scroll a complete table left one screen by pressing **Ctrl-<left-arrow-key>**, and right one screen by pressing **Ctrl-<right-arrow-key>.**

4.4 Loading more than one Table

It is an everyday task for the Paradox user to load several tables. The number loaded at one time is limited only by the configuration of your system.

Loading another sample table involves repeating many of the steps listed in Hands-on Session 4.2.1. The following session clarifies matters.

4.4.1 Hands-on Session

Here, you are shown how to load another table, with the Customer table already on screen and in the workspace (see Hands-on Session 4.2.1)

1. Press **F10** to call up the main menu.

2. Press **V** to select View from the main menu.

3. Enter **sample** to inform Paradox that you wish to view one of the tables contained in the Sample directory.

4. Press **<right-arrow-key>** five times to highlight the Orders table.

5. Press **<Enter>** to produce the table shown in Figure 4.3. opposite.

Because the Orders table contains just 15 records, 4 records of the Customer table remain on screen. Notice that in the top right of the screen a small arrow pointing upward has appeared. This indicates that other images exist in the workspace, above the one shown on screen. If you will excuse the mixed metaphors (ie *keyhole* from Chapter 1), the screen is rather like a window which can be manipulated so as to view specific parts of a large workspace containing a number of different images.

4.5 Skipping from one Image to the Next

Paradox is extremely fast in terms of cycling from one image to the next. Pressing **F3** (Up Image) makes the image above the current one active. Similarly, **F4** (Down Image) makes the image beneath the current one active. Try both these actions for yourself.

Viewing Orders table: Record 1 of 15 Main ▲=

CUSTOMER	Cust ID	Last Name	Init	Street	City
19	5720	Helms	D	52 Brattle Street	Cambridge
20	5855	Chin	F	Hotel Orient	Jurong
21	6125	Hawes-Anderson	D	Waves Cottage	Palm Springs
22	6666	Matthews	J	1050 12th Street	San Francisc

ORDERS	Order #	Cust ID	Stock #	Quant	Dat
1	2280	4277	130	1	22.04.
2	3351	3266	519	1	16.12.
3	8070	6125	632	8	4.06.
4	6235	2779	890	1	1.08.
5	1442	9004	519	2	27.10.
6	5119	7008	235	1	4.03.
7	9554	3266	558	15	27.07.
8	6975	6666	519	3	24.06.
9	8933	9226	422	1	28.02.
10	1180	3128	519	2	31.05.
11	4492	5341	244	3	24.12.
12	9226	1784	983	1	14.01.
13	7643	6954	519	1	30.04.
14	1574	2177	632	1	22.11.
15	3885	9004	244	5	4.09.

Figure 4.3: Customer and Orders tables

A number of images in the workspace are best thought of as a stack of plates – each time you load an image it is slotted underneath. You can move up or down the stack by pressing **F3** (Up Image) and **F4** (Down Image).

When at the top of the stack, as it were, the arrow pointing up in the top right of the screen will disappear, while the arrow pointing down will indicate that images exist below the one shown on screen.

4.6 Using the Zoom Key

When an image is small, like the Orders table you previously loaded, it is extremely easy to locate any single record.

In the real world, tables of the size of some the sample ones exist only for a short while, as they soon grow. (Staggeringly, Paradox tables can contain up to two billion records!) Trying to locate a particular record in such large tables would take a considerable amount of time using the methods discussed in Section 4.3.

The Zoom key provides one solution to this problem by permitting you to locate a name, street, city or whatever by simply entering it. By the way, we have to call the name, street, city or whatever a field value, or simply a value.

The following hands-on session illustrates how to use the Zoom key.

4.6.1 Hands-on Session

Consider the Customer table and imagine, if you will, it is larger than it actually is, and you want to see the record of a customer with the surname, Smith.

1. Produce the Customer table on screen (see Hands-on Session 4.2.1).

2. Press **F10/I/Z** to produce the Zoom menu shown in Figure 4.4.

3. Press **V** to select Value. This initiates Paradox to search for a particular value in a field. Use the arrow keys to position the cursor in the Last Name field and press **<Enter>**.

4. Respond to the prompt Value: by entering: **Smith.** A brief search period will ensue, after which the Smith value will be found.

Field Record Value Main =▼
Move to a named field.

CUSTOMER	Cust ID	Last Name	Init	Street	City
1	1386	Aberdeen	F	45 Utah Street	Washington
2	1388	Svenvald	I	Gouvernment House	Reykjavik
3	1784	McDougal	L	4950 Pullman Ave NE	Seattle
4	2177	Bonnefemme	S	128 University Drive	Stanford
5	2579	Chavez	L	Cypress Drive	Palm Springs
6	2779	Fahd	S	The Palace	Riyadh
7	3128	Elspeth, III	R	1 Hanover Square	London
8	3266	Hanover	A	15 State Street	Dallas
9	3271	Massey	C	29 Aragona Drive	Oxon Hill
10	3771	Montaigne	L	30 Tauton Drive	Bellevue
11	4277	Matthews	R	P. O. Box 20336	Albuquerque
12	4335	Farouk	K	Hotel Cairo	Cairo
13	4480	Samuelson	F	Bull Run Ranch	Aurora
14	4485	Fischer	R	14 Willow Lane	Birmingham
15	4589	Leonardo	D	198 Via Canales	Rome
16	4700	Harris	J	Old Country Road	Atherton
17	4884	Anders	B	Jaktstigen 42	Lidingo
18	5341	Chevalier	R	392 Boulevard Raspil	Montpelier
19	5720	Helms	D	52 Brattle Street	Cambridge
20	5855	Chin	F	Hotel Orient	Jurong
21	6125	Hawes-Anderson	D	Waves Cottage	Palm Springs
22	6666	Matthews	J	1050 12th Street	San Francisc

Figure 4.4: The Zoom menu

4.7 More about Searching for Information

The Zoom feature can also be used to move the cursor to a record number or to a particular field. Selecting Field from the Zoom menu lists all fields in the current table. Choosing any of the shown fields results in the cursor being positioned appropriately. The following hands-on sessions run through both processes.

4.7.1 Hands-on Session – zooming in on a field

1. With the Customer table on screen (see Hands-on Session 4.2.1), press **F10** to call up the main menu.

2. Press **I** to select Image.

3. Press **Z** to choose Zoom.

4. Press **F** to select Field – this will allow you to zoom in on a field.

5. Using the arrow keys select the Country field. The cursor will then position itself amid the Country field.

4.7.2 Hands-on Session – zooming in on a record

1. Once again with the customer table on screen (see Hands-on Session 4.2.1), press **F10** to call up the main menu.

2. Press **I** to select Image.

3. Press **Z** to select Zoom.

4. Press **R** to select Record – this will allow you to zoom in on a record.

5. In response to the prompt, *Record number:*, enter **15.** The cursor will then position itself amid record number 15. Note, the cursor remains amid the field prior to moving to the record.

4.8 Using Wild Cards when Searching for Information

In Hands-on Session 4.6.1 values in a table were located by simply entering complete names. Besides being time consuming, this method requires that you know precisely the value for which you are searching. A solution to this problem lies in the use of wild card operators. These are used frequently in computing, particularly when filenames or particular items of information have to be located.

For anyone uncertain as to the purpose of wild cards, here is an explanation:

You may remember the controversy over the 1988 Seoul Olympics when athlete Seb Coe, having failed to qualify to represent Britain, was rumoured to have the possibility of a wild card entry. Well, in a nutshell, that sums up a wild card in computing, as it is an entity – usually a variable – bound by no rules.

Moving away from this analogy (and unashamed vagueness), Paradox wild cards, which operate under the characters @ and .., can be substituted for parts of field values. It is strange that the word vagueness should creep in here, as that is exactly what wild cards are meant to introduce.

Using Paradox the wild card operators are as follows:

@ masquerades as any single character

.. represents any sequence of characters

If, for example, it were necessary to search for the field value Leonardo, you could simply type L..O as a value. Equally, @eonardo would have the same effect.

Use of wild card operators is highly recommended; they will provide a fast route to your information. The following hands-on session shows how to use wild card operators.

4.8.1 Hands-on Session – using wild cards to search

Consider, once again if you will, the Customer table, and imagine that it is larger than it actually is, and you want to see the record associated with a customer of the surname Smith:

1. With the Customer table on screen (see Hands-on Session 4.2.1), press **F10**.

2. Press **I/Z** to produce the Zoom menu shown in Figure 4.4.

3. Press **V** to select Value. This tells Paradox to search for value in a field. Press the **right-** and **left-arrow-keys** as necessary to position the cursor amid the Last Name field, and then press **<Enter>**.

4. In order to locate the cursor beneath Smith, respond to the prompt *value:* by entering **S..h**.

A brief search period will ensue, after which the cursor is positioned amid the Smith value. (Incidentally, **Ctrl-Z** is a shortcut for Zoom, and **Alt-Z** can be used to find the next occurrence of a value.)

4.9 Creating Graphs

In terms of presenting data, graphs provide the professionalism required to impress your bank manager, boss or client.

Later, in Chapter 8, the presentation of Paradox Data will be discussed at length, but until then, let us grasp the basics by using the Customer table as an example.

4.9.1 Hands-on Session – generating a graph

1. With the Customer table on screen (see Hands-on Session 4.2.1), press **Ctrl-End** to position the cursor amid the Credit field. A golden rule when generating graphs is to position the cursor amid a numeric or currency field.

2. Press **F10** in order to call up the main menu.

3. Press **I** to select Image.

4. Press **G** to choose Graph.

5. Press **V** to select ViewGraph.

6. Press **S** to output the graph to the screen.

The graph shown in Figure 4.5 will then be produced. Notice how the Cust ID field values are used as X-axis categories. In your case, unlike those shown, X-axis categories will clash; Chapter 8 shows how to change the size of the offending titles.

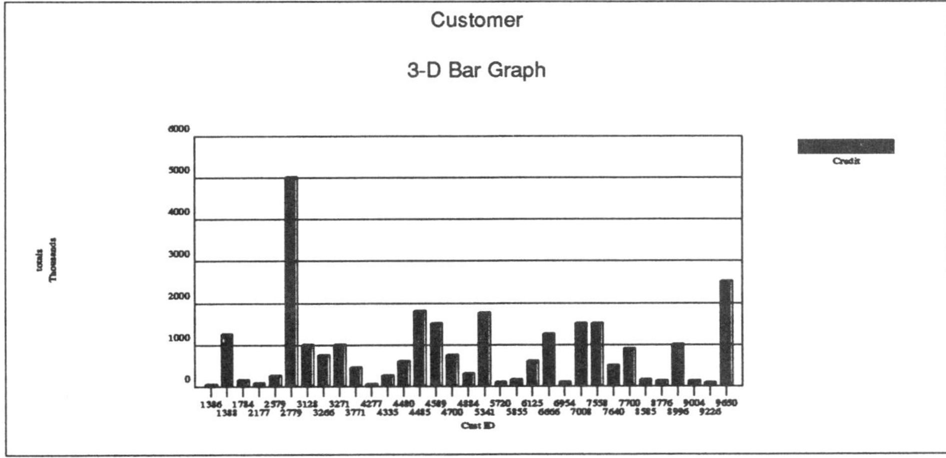

Figure 4.5: Bar graph (generated from Customer table)

Press any key to remove the graph.

4.9.2 Printing Graphs

Outputting a graph to the screen is fine for personal use, and, sometimes, for lectures and seminars on a small scale. However, when drafting reports or when you want to fax a graph, it is necessary to achieve a hardcopy. Printing the graph generated in the previous hands-on session involves a slight change in procedure.

The following hands-on session shows how to print the graph shown in Figure 4.5 and generated in Session 4.9.1.

4.9.3 Hands-on Session – printing a graph

1. With the Customer table on screen (see Hands-on Session 4.2.1), press **Ctrl-End** to position the cursor amid the Credit field.

2. Press **F10** in order to call up the main menu.

3. Press **I** to select Image.

4. Press **G** to choose Graph.

5. Press **V** to select ViewGraph.

5. With your printer on-line and available for printing, press **P** to print the graph.

If your graph did not print correctly (ie, was too large for the page, for example), certain printer settings have to be established. This is discussed in Chapter 8.

4.10 Forms

The tabular method of displaying values using columns and rows in tables, is not the only format by which data can be viewed and edited. Forms provide a useful alternative, where a free-form approach is adopted, permitting records to be displayed and edited in the manner shown in Figure 4.6.

Forms can be created and modified so as to suit exact requirements (see Figure 4.7). It is possible to attach up to 14 different forms to a single table. Forms are referred to as objects, where the table and its associated objects are collectively referred to as a family.

The following hands-on session shows how to display the standard, default form.

4.10.1 Hands-on Session – generating a form

1. With the Customer table on screen (see Hands-on Session 4.2.1) press **F10** in order to produce the main menu.

2. Press **I** to select Image.

3. Press **P** to choose PickForm.

4. Press **<Enter>** in order to select the standard (Paradox) form shown in Figure 4.6.

Viewing Customer table with form F: Record 2 of 33 Main ▲=▼

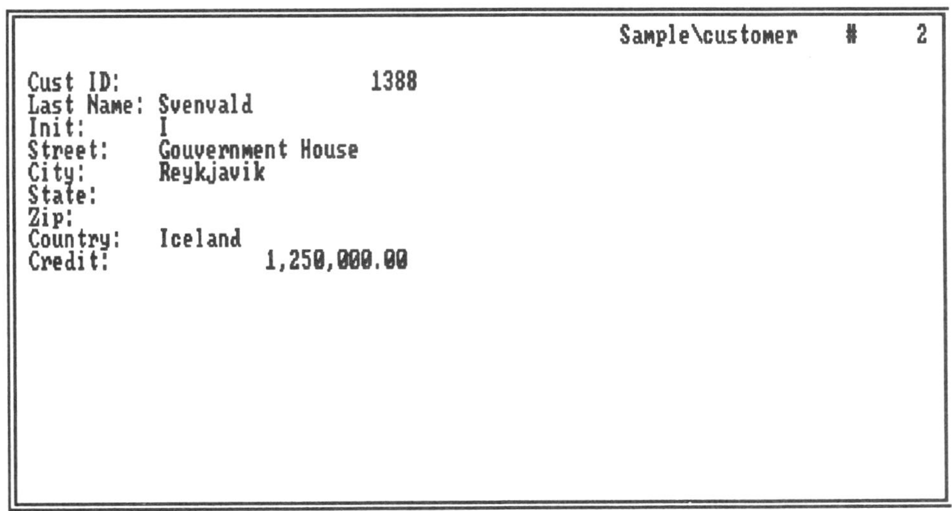

Figure 4.6: Standard form

Notice that the form basically contains all fields making up each record. Similar to tables, the appearance of the arrow shown in the top right of the screen, indicates that records are available above or below the current one.

Other records can be viewed by pressing the arrow-keys. For example, press **<down-arrow-key>** to move down through each field and ultimately through each record. Equally, you can move upwards through fields and records by pressing **<up-arrow-key>**.

5. Now we come to possibly one of the most useful shortcuts: instead of following stages 1 to 4, by pressing 4 keys, you could have simply pressed **F7** (Form Toggle). Press **F7** to return to the Customer table. Press **F7**, once again, and the standard form re-appears.

4.10.2 Selecting Forms

A table may have up to 14 custom forms associated with it. As such, it is natural to know how to invoke forms other than the standard one. The following hands-on session shows how to view a custom form associated with the Customer table.

4.10.3 Hands-on Session – selecting forms

1. With the Customer table on screen (see Hands-on Session 4.2.1) press **F10** in order to produce the main menu.

2. Press **I** to select Image.

3. Press **P** to select PickForm.

4. Press **1** in order to select the custom form shown in Figure 4.7.

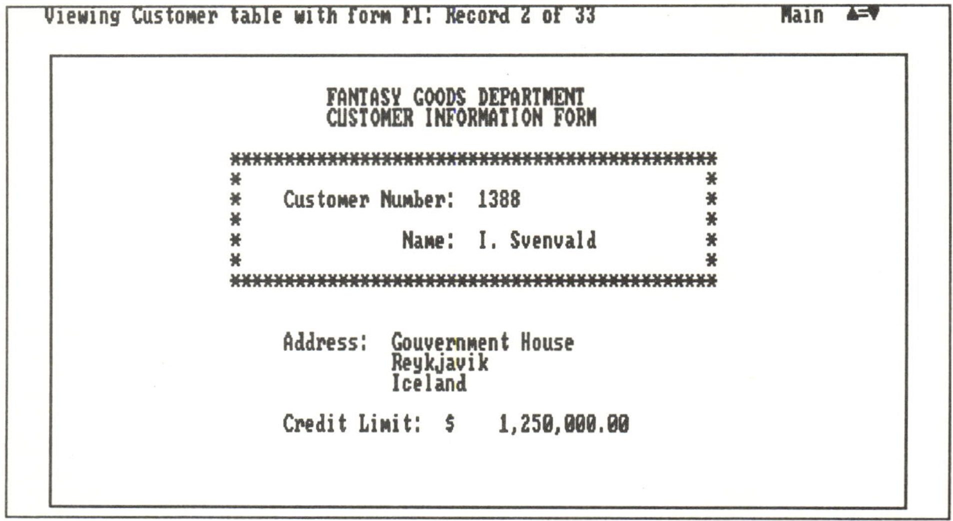

Viewing Customer table with form F1: Record 2 of 33 Main

FANTASY GOODS DEPARTMENT
CUSTOMER INFORMATION FORM

Customer Number: 1388

Name: I. Svenvald

Address: Gouvernment House
Reykjavik
Iceland

Credit Limit: $ 1,250,000.00

Figure 4.7: Custom form

When you now toggle between table and form by pressing **F7,** you will notice that the custom form returns. To view custom forms 2 and 3 repeat this hands-on session by selecting 2 and 3, in turn, at stage 4.

4.10.4 More on Moving about Forms

Apart from pressing the up- and down-arrow-keys to move about forms, there is a whole host of other swifter methods. Some of these are similar, if not the same, as those associated with moving about tables.

Pressing **<Home>**, for example, moves the cursor to the first record of the table; **Ctrl-<Home>** moves to the first field of a form; **<End>** moves to the last record of a table; **Ctrl-End** moves to the last field of a form. **PgUp** moves to the previous record and **PgDn** to the next; At this point it might be a good idea to try these methods on the sample Customer table.

4.11 Reports

In database parlance, a report means just one thing: achieving a printed copy of information. The need for reports is obvious, as at some time or other a printed document will be required, if only to provide written proof of stored information – *seeing is believing and there is always a boss or client to satisfy*. In Chapters 6 and 10, you will realise that Paradox reports can serve one of a number of purposes.

A report of any table currently on screen can be printed by pressing **Alt-F7** (Instant Report).

27.04.90 Standard Report Page 1

Cust ID	Last Name	Init	Street	City	State	Zip	Country	Credit
1386	Aberdeen	F	45 Utah Street	Washington	DC	20032		50,000.00
1388	Svenvald	I	Gouvernment House	Reykjavik			Iceland	1,250,000.00
1784	McDougal	L	4950 Pullman Ave NE	Seattle	WA	98105		150,000.00
2177	Bonnefemme	S	128 University Drive	Stanford	CA	94323		75,000.00
2579	Chavez	L	Cypress Drive	Palm Springs	FL	32938		250,000.00
2779	Fahd	S	The Palace	Riyadh			Saudi Arabia	5,000,000.00
3128	Elspeth, III	R	1 Hanover Square	London			England	1,000,000.00
3266	Hanover	A	15 State Street	Dallas	TX	75043		750,000.00
3271	Massey	C	29 Aragona Drive	Oxon Hill	MD	29902		1,000,000.00
3771	Montaigne	L	30 Tauton Drive	Bellevue	WA	98004		450,000.00
4277	Matthews	R	P. O. Box 20336	Albuquerque	NM	87234		50,000.00
4335	Farouk	K	Hotel Cairo	Cairo			Egypt	250,000.00
4480	Samuelson	F	Bull Run Ranch	Aurora	CO	89022		600,000.00
4485	Fischer	R	14 Willow Lane	Birmingham	MI	48011		1,800,000.00
4589	Leonardo	D	198 Via Canales	Rome			Italy	1,500,000.00
4700	Harris	J	Old Country Road	Atherton	CA	94322		750,000.00
4884	Anders	B	Jaktstigen 42	Lidingo			Sweden	300,000.00
5341	Chevalier	R	392 Boulevard Raspil	Montpelier			France	1,750,000.00
5720	Helms	D	52 Brattle Street	Cambridge	MA	02138		85,000.00
5855	Chin	F	Hotel Orient	Jurong			Singapore	150,000.00
6125	Hawes-Anderson	D	Waves Cottage	Palm Springs	FL	32382		600,000.00
6666	Matthews	J	1050 12th Street	San Francisco	CA	94232		1,250,000.00
6954	Mayor	K	48 Winding Way	Salt Lake City	UT	84108		100,000.00
7008	Simms	R	Box 13, RFD 2	Topeka	KS	66104		1,500,000.00
7558	Yee	L	2938 42nd Street	New York	NY	10032		1,500,000.00
7640	Raymond	S	398 Centre Street	Winnipeg	ON		Canada	500,000.00
7700	Connors	S	27 Portfolio Drive	Belair	CA	90026		900,000.00
8585	Sampson	L	29 Buena Vista Drive	Tiburon	CA	97992		150,000.00
8776	Weidner	R	56 Santa Ysbel	San Francisco	CA	94332		120,000.00
8996	Smith	J	Hotel Americain	Paris			France	1,000,000.00
9004	Ranier	T	8947 San Andreas	Klamath Falls	OR	97603		125,000.00
9226	Simpson	H	3 Pooks Hill	Dallas	TX	75211		75,000.00
9650	O'Hare	C	1 Airport Drive	Chicago	IL	60542		2,500,000.00

Figure 4.8: Standard (tabular) report format

With the Customer table on screen, press **Alt-F7** to output a report to your printer. The standard, tabular report shown in Figure 4.8 will be produced. (Network users: you may need to see your network administrator about how to send reports to a shared printer.)

4.12 Asking Questions

The notion that a database provides a means of information storage and retrieval undermines the very idea of modern packages such as Paradox. The modern database is much more than an automated filing system.

For example, say you have a number of tables that have grown to perhaps thousands of records. The information you have is readily available, but you really want to interrogate it. It is an inescapable fact that if you don't ask questions about your information, you are NOT managing it. Paradox, can be used to ask those hypothetical questions that you often wonder about.

Asking questions about your data is the most important aspect of using an information management tool like Paradox. In view of this, Chapter 7 is devoted entirely to this facet.

To appreciate the importance of interrogating your information, imagine for one moment you are the health and safety manager in a plant where numerous toxic substances are in daily use. You have been set the task of investigating why certain employees feel nauseous. You would probably implement the following tasks:

❑ List personnel that have complained of feeling nauseous

❑ Produce a list of these employees who work in the same area of the plant.

Finding the answer to such problems very often means adopting an iterative approach in which a series of questions are asked. Using Paradox, such individual 'questions' are answered by querying.

The following hands-on session shows how to perform a simple, but useful, query.

4.12.1 Hands-on Session

This session shows how to query the Customer table to produce a table containing only the Customer and Credit fields.

To ask Paradox to do this:

1. Press **Alt-F8** to clear all images.

2. Press **A** to select Ask.

3. Enter **sample**.

4. Select the Customer table. A query form will then appear.

5. Press **<right-arrow-key>** to position the cursor in the Cust ID field of the query form.

6. Press **F6** (Checkmark) to inform Paradox that this field pertains to your query.

7. Press the **<right-arrow-key>** four times to position the cursor in the City field.

8. Press **F6** (Checkmark) to inform Paradox that this field also pertains to your query.

(If you insert a checkmark in the wrong location, press **F6** once again.)

9. Press the **<right-arrow-key>** four times to position the cursor in the Credit field.

10. Press **F6** (Checkmark) to inform Paradox that this is another field you are interested in.

11. Press **F2** (Do-It!) to perform the query producing the Answer table shown in Figure 4.9.

Viewing Answer table: Record 1 of 33 Main ▲═

ANSWER	Cust ID	City	Credit
1	1386	Washington	50,000.00
2	1388	Reykjavik	1,250,000.00
3	1784	Seattle	150,000.00
4	2177	Stanford	75,000.00
5	2579	Palm Springs	250,000.00
6	2779	Riyadh	5,000,000.00
7	3128	London	1,000,000.00
8	3266	Dallas	750,000.00
9	3271	Oxon Hill	1,000,000.00
10	3771	Bellevue	450,000.00
11	4277	Albuquerque	50,000.00
12	4335	Cairo	250,000.00
13	4480	Aurora	600,000.00
14	4485	Birmingham	1,800,000.00
15	4589	Rome	1,500,000.00
16	4700	Atherton	750,000.00
17	4884	Lidingo	300,000.00
18	5341	Montpelier	1,750,000.00
19	5720	Cambridge	85,000.00
20	5855	Jurong	150,000.00
21	6125	Palm Springs	600,000.00
22	6666	San Francisco	1,250,000.00

Figure 4.9: Answer table

Using this simple technique it is possible to streamline tables showing only the required fields, which is particularly useful when dealing with large tables.

4.12.2 Hands-on Session – querying using an arithmetic operator

Just suppose you wanted to ask the simple question: how many customers from San Francisco have more than $100,000 credit?

1. Press **F8** to clear the Answer table and press **F10** to invoke the main menu.

2. Press **A** to choose Ask.

3. Enter **sample**.

4. Select the Customer table, once again. A query form will then appear.

5. Fill in the query form as shown in Figure 4.10, including the expression **>100000** in the Credit field.

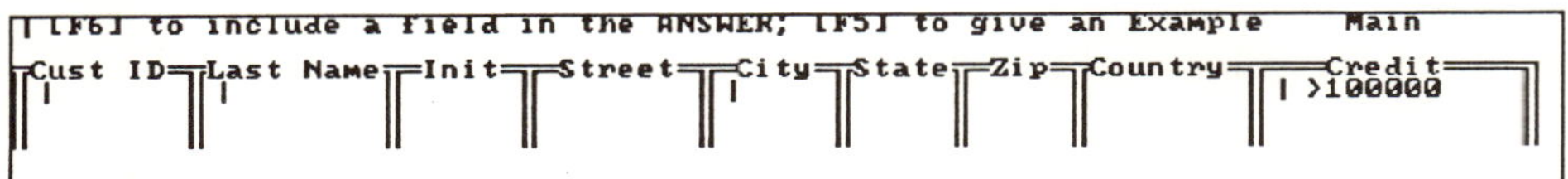

Figure 4.10: Query form

6. Press **F2** (Do-It!) to perform the query producing the Answer table shown in Figure 4.11.

Viewing Answer table: Record 1 of 27 Main

ANSWER	Cust ID	Last Name	City	Credit
1	1388	Svenvald	Reykjavik	1,250,000.00
2	1784	McDougal	Seattle	150,000.00
3	2579	Chavez	Palm Springs	250,000.00
4	2779	Fahd	Riyadh	5,000,000.00
5	3128	Elspeth, III	London	1,000,000.00
6	3266	Hanover	Dallas	750,000.00
7	3271	Massey	Oxon Hill	1,000,000.00
8	3771	Montaigne	Bellevue	450,000.00
9	4335	Farouk	Cairo	250,000.00
10	4480	Samuelson	Aurora	600,000.00
11	4485	Fischer	Birmingham	1,800,000.00
12	4589	Leonardo	Rome	1,500,000.00
13	4700	Harris	Atherton	750,000.00
14	4884	Anders	Lidingo	300,000.00
15	5341	Chevalier	Montpelier	1,750,000.00
16	5855	Chin	Jurong	150,000.00
17	6125	Hawes-Anderson	Palm Springs	600,000.00
18	6666	Matthews	San Francisco	1,250,000.00
19	7008	Simms	Topeka	1,500,000.00
20	7558	Yee	New York	1,500,000.00
21	7640	Raymond	Winnipeg	500,000.00
22	7700	Connors	Belair	900,000.00

Figure 4.11: Answer table

4.12.3 Renaming Answer tables

After querying, the resultant table is temporarily stored as Answer in the current directory. Each time a query operation is performed the existing Answer table is overwritten. Additionally, an Answer table is erased when you leave Paradox. Therefore, to retain an Answer table, you must change its name as soon as possible. The following hands-on session shows how to do this.

4.12.4 Hands-on Session – renaming tables

In the previous session a temporary Answer table was generated. This table can be retained by renaming it as follows:

1. Press **Alt-F8** to clear all images.

2. Press **T** to select Tools.

3. Press **R**, or **<Enter>**, to select Rename.

4. Press **T**, or **<Enter>**, to select Table.

5. Press **<Enter>** and choose the Answer table.

6. Enter a new name such as **cust**, for instance.

Remember, the Cust table will be in the working directory, ie Paradox3 directory. If a table with the new name already exists you will be given the option of cancelling the action.

A pathname can be included at stage 6 to write the table to another directory; for example, you could enter:

sample\cust

to write the table to the Sample directory.

5

Inputting Information

In the previous chapter, you were introduced to simple methods of interacting with Paradox so as to gain access to stored information. This chapter delves into the area of creating tables, and shows how to enter your own information. More importantly, here, you will become acquainted with the important subject of how your data is stored within Paradox. Topics addressed include creating tables, data-entry and editing, field types, key fields, forms for data entry, and restructuring tables.

5.1 Planning Ahead

So many people throughout industry and commerce, without professional advice or careful consideration, fail to analyse their database needs. The most frequent cause of this is a lack of awareness of what, exactly, a modern database such as Paradox is capable of; the user skips through the Introduction Guide, and sees the database as a simple program for storing and retrieving information in the form of neat tables and, then, delves in by inputting data willy-nilly. The outcome, more often than not, is a great deal of wasted time and effort.

Gathering information in a suitable form to build a database is by no means a specialist task, but merely one of common sense. Perhaps the most difficult part of the process is that which is assumed to be most obvious (as always!), ie what information do you really need to store?

For example, a personnel manager might cram a database with detailed employee records which contain irrelevant information. In the real world, information storage costs money, and will cause ANY computer system to run more slowly, so, it is only natural to store only what is absolutely necessary.

Then there is the matter of storing totally unrelated information in the same table, often causing the table to become too large for practical use. For instance, an employee record may contain such items as National Insurance number, ID number, job title, and then a rogue field which relates to a medical record. Flat file databases were, and are, infamous for this, often incorporating enormous files or tables containing all information under the sun.

As a relational database, Paradox frees the user from this hopeless dilemma because a table which is used to accommodate purely medical facts can easily be related to a table containing other employee information. Do not worry if you are at a loss here, we will get to these aspects in good time.

When trying to decide what information tables should contain, think about the immediate future. Soon you will have to lay your hands on that information, and later you will want to present it in the form of graphs and reports to give overall views of your information.

The easiest way to divide information into manageable tables is, ironically, to think back to before computers and to the days of paper: You have started a business and as always you soon begin to amass information. You have customer addresses, supplier addresses, along with accounts. Now you would hardly list customer addresses with supplier addresses, so, as expected, these have to occupy separate tables. In other words, consider tables as books or even pieces of paper, when deciding upon the form a database should take.

To summarise, just consider the following simple points and rules of thumb:

❑ Store information which is relevant – do not store part numbers, for instance, of supplied items where the supplier, date of purchase etc will suffice

❑ Tables should ideally address one topic of information, where all fields pertain to that topic

❑ If possible, tables should be kept to a manageable size, as should fields

❑ Ensure that you choose the correct field types. For example, don't use an alphanumeric field to accommodate dates or currency. You will learn more about field types later

❑ Where tables are to be related, they must contain a common field such as a serial number or name, for example

❑ Do not duplicate information unless absolutely necessary.

Though it is vitally important to consider in detail the manner in which information is stored, Paradox is, in fact, forgiving as it permits tables to be restructured. There is no shame in having to restructure tables – even the most competent database user will do so. At this early stage, it should be borne in mind that it will be difficult to structure tables to exact requirements. As a novice, you are unfamiliar with the ins and outs of the way data can be sorted, accessed, related and generally manipulated. You have to start somewhere, however, so here goes . . .

5.2 Backing up Data

Where a database forms the mainstay of a business or equally important enterprise, the loss of information through computer breakdown, user error, or perhaps sabotage can be catastrophic. Computer disasters occur all too frequently nowadays as more and more companies commit their information to computer. Even if a few hours keying-in is lost, time is wasted and money subsequently lost.

With regard to sabotage, there are a number of virus programs in circulation, the most potent of which can quite easily corrupt a significant amount of your database. Virus programs are not found on disks supplied by leading companies such as Borland, but are more likely to be found on copied disks. However, shareware and public domain (PD) software have had virus problems in the past. Keeping a system virus-free is simply matter of checking the origins of disks, and avoiding those which you are not absolutely sure of.

Paradox, however, to a great extent, lowers the risk of data loss by constantly saving tables and objects as they are updated. Based upon the speed of the user's typing, an interval between automatically saving data is set. (Data is backed up to the working directory.)

Though this all sounds ingenious, it is not the flawless safety net that it first appears; as all data is written to a single hard disk, an unwelcome virus program, or machine failure such as a head crash, could corrupt or, worse still, erase the contents of the hard disk. To be safe, data has to be backed up to a separate hard disk, or, where this is not possible, to floppy disk(s).

To backup a table and its family of objects, to floppy disk:

1. Press **T** to select Tools from the main menu.

2. Choose Copy, and press **T** to select Table.

This primes the copy feature to duplicate a table and its accompanying family.

3. Press **<Enter>** and select the table you wish to copy, provided the table you wish to copy resides in the working directory; if not, type the directory name before pressing **<Enter>**.

4. Enter the name of the table to which you want to copy the table – you can include directories and pathnames here. For example, if you want to copy the table to floppy disk you might use the prefix, **a:**.

5.2.1 Automatically Backing Up Data

To a limited extent, the Autosave feature can be modified using the Paradox Custom Configuration Program (or CCP). All that can be modified is the interval between auto saves, and even then, it cannot be set precisely. Indeed, there are but two choices: data can either be saved frequently, or occasionally.

The Paradox Custom Configuration Program, or CCP, is copied automatically to the Paradox3 directory of your hard disk during installation, if you followed Chapter 2, that is. So, naturally, the working directory must be Paradox3 before the CCP can be run. The easiest way to run the CCP is from within Paradox itself. To do this: press **S** to choose Scripts from the main menu; press **P** to select Play; press **<Enter>** and choose Custom. Then, press **y** or **n** to indicate whether or not a monochrome monitor is being used.

To run the CCP from Dos simply enter **paradox3 custom** in the paradox3 directory – note, to do this paradox3 must be the default directory. It is inadvisable to run the CCP by pressing **Ctrl-O** to resort to Dos as many machines with under 1 MByte of memory will cause the Insufficient memory prompt to appear.

The Autosave feature can be modified as follows:

1. Run the CCP and press **D** to select Defaults.

2. Press **<Enter>** to choose Defaults once again.

3. Press **A** to select AutoSave.

4. Press **Y** to enable frequent automatic saving to disk.

or:

Press **N** to auto save occasionally.

5. Press **R** to return to the CCP main menu.

6. Press **D** to select Do-It!.

7. Highlight Do-It!, press **<Enter>** to select it once again.

8. Press **H** to write the configuration to your hard disk.

9. Enter **Paradox3** to rerun Paradox.

5.3 Creating Table Structures

After observing the points in Section 5.1 and, possibly, some of your own, with regard to planning, the process of creating a table structure can now be addressed. The ensuing hands-on session shows how to create a table that a personnel manager might require.

5.3.1 Hands-on Session

Consider a personnel manager that has decided upon building an initial table containing the following five fields: employee name, National Insurance number, position (in company), salary and department. This table can be created as follows:

1. With the main menu on screen, press **C** to select Create.

2. Respond to the prompt, Table, by entering **employee**. The screen shown in Figure 5.1 will appear.

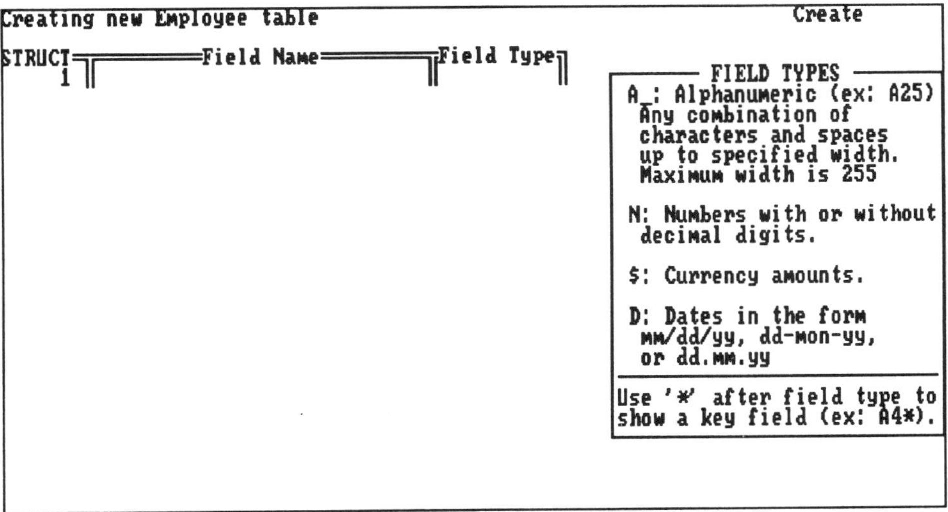

Figure 5.1: Creating a table

3. At this stage, it is simply a matter of entering field names, together with their size and type: enter: **Employee**, and as this is an alphanumeric field type **A**. Now enter: **15** to indicate that the field is 15 characters in length. Continue to create the table by following the structure shown in Figure 5.2 overleaf.

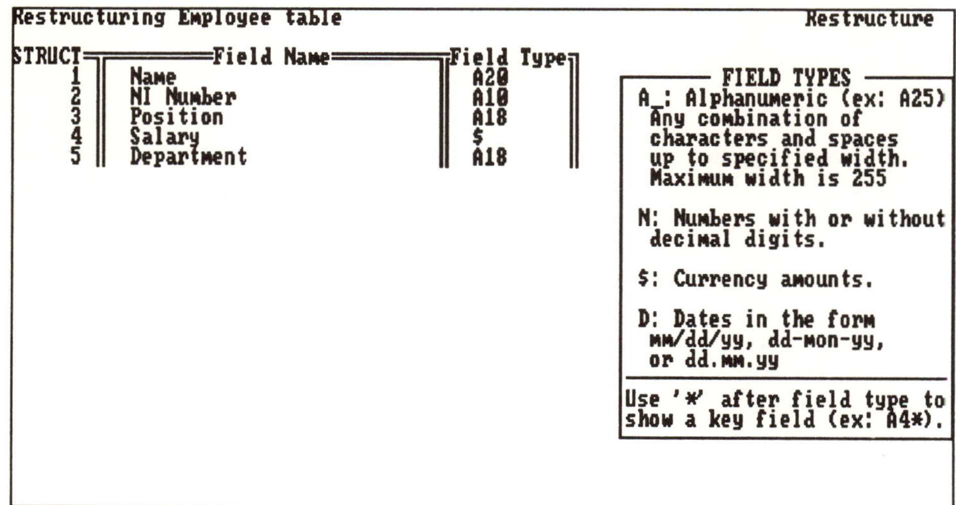

Figure 5.2: Employee table structure

4. With all field values entered, press **F10/D** to invoke Do-It! Congratulations, you have now created a table structure! (In future, it is recommended that you use the shortcut, **F2**, rather than select Do-It! from menus).

Whenever adding data to, or altering, your database, Paradox will digest changes after **F2** (Do-It!) is pressed. Pressing **F2** (Do-It!) almost always returns you to the main menu or the workspace. It is equally possible to ignore changes made by selecting Cancel from the main menu or by pressing **Ctrl-Break**.

5.4 Data Entry

Creating a table structure is, naturally, a prelude to entering data. Keying-in the relevant field values is often left to the data-entry clerk or the secretary. The more independent among you, however, will need to know how to enter and generally edit data.

Consider the Employee table shown in Figure 5.3 opposite. The following hands-on session shows how to enter such data.

5.4.1 Hands-on Session

This session shows how to enter data. If you make any mistakes, simply press **<Backspace>** to delete the offending characters. A swifter method of editing is discussed in the next subsection.

```
27.04.90                              Standard report                              Page    1


Name                   NI Number    Position               Salary             Department
--------------------   ----------   ------------------     ----------------   ------------
John Howard            DS659834E    Technical Author              15,000.00   Technical
Josh Clements          ED337294A    Technical Author              15,000.00   On-site
Ken Lethbridge         TS876554W    Technical Author              15,000.00   On-site
Peter Wilson           TD667854G    Clerk                         14,445.00   Technical
Steven Milligan        WE874599N    Clerical assistant            10.000.00   Technical
Sue Baker              IB679833E    Clerical assistant            10,000.00   Technical
```

Figure 5.3: Employee table

1. With the main menu on screen (obtainable by pressing **F10**), press **M** to select Modify.

2. Press **D** to select Data Entry.

3. In response to Table: press **<Enter>**; and select the Employee table.

4. Enter: **Peter Wilson.**

5. Enter: **TD667854G** to establish Peter Wilson's National Insurance number.

6. Continue entering the field values shown in Figure 5.3. Remember, you can use the arrow-keys on the numeric keypad to move about the table.

7. To complete the data entry session, press **F2** (Do-It!).

5.4.2 Editing Fields

Because data is entered at a brisk pace, the not so accurate keyboard operator invariably makes mistakes. In Data-Entry or Editing mode, Paradox does not work in the same fashion as a full screen editor associated with a conventional word processor – as you will have noticed during the previous hands-on session.

For example, to correct the misspelling *Wlson* requires the deletion of *lson* using **Backspace**, and typing *ilson*. Incidentally, you can delete the whole of a field by pressing **Ctrl-Backspace.**

This clumsy and time consuming method of editing is avoided by using Field View. Field View temporarily turns the field into a full-screen editor. Using Field View is straightforward: in edit mode, simply position the cursor amid the appropriate field and press **Alt-F5**, edit the field as necessary (using Backspace, left-and right-arrow-keys), then press **<Enter>** to return to normal editing mode.

5.5 Editing Shortcuts

Efficient data-entry and editing depends upon exploiting shortcuts. Bad habits such as invoking features in an awkward or time-consuming way are hard to break, so, adopt the easiest methods now. The following table shows some basic editing shortcuts.

Operation	***Key(s)***
Copy field value from previous record	Ctrl-D
Delete field	Ctrl-Backspace
Delete record	Del (on numeric keypad)
Field View	Alt-F5
Finish editing	F2
Make room for new record	Ins

Table 5.1: Editing tables

5.6 Moving About Tables

Whether editing or simply viewing tables, achieving maximum mobility in terms of cursor movement can help matters. The following short table embodies all methods of moving the cursor.

Operation	***Key(s)***
Down one screen	PgDn
First field	Ctrl-Home
First record of table	Home
Last field	Ctrl-End
Last record	End
One field left	Left arrow
One field right	Right arrow
One screen left	Ctrl-Left arrow
One screen right	Ctrl-Right arrow
Up one screen	PgUp

Table 5.2: Moving about tables

5.7 About Field Types

In Hands-on Session 5.3.1, certain field types were defined so as to store specific field values. Correctly defining field types makes life much easier. For example, entering dates into an appropriate date field as opposed to an alphanumeric field frees you from having to enter dots (or other separators) between days, months and years like so, 4.10.90. Simply pressing **<Space>** will cause the dot to be inserted.

Available field types are as follows:

A **Alphanumeric** fields are naturally used to store names, addresses and other textual-type material

N **Number** fields can store up to 15 significant digits. The width of the field plays a role in the number of digits displayed (see Section 5.11)

$ **Currency** fields are a variation of Number fields, except, of course, numbers are kept to two decimal places. Negative numbers are contained in brackets. When entering amounts it is not necessary to enter amounts in the following form, 300.00, simply enter 300

D **Date** fields can store dates from January 1, 100 to December 31, 9999. Date fields are intelligent in that leap years are recognised.

5.8 Key Fields

Occasionally, the possibility of duplicating field values has to be avoided. For example, in the simple process of creating a register, a great deal of time and effort could be wasted by duplicating records. This can be remedied by including a key field. Key fields are declared while structuring or restructuring a table, by inserting an asterisk (*) after the field type, as indicated on the screen. A key field must be the first in a table, ie the leftmost field.

Any attempt to enter an existing value within a key field will be met by a key violation. Key fields also present the user with the ability to sort records by simply pressing **F2** (Do-It!).

The main limitation of including a single key field is that different records may share certain field values. This is remedied by including a multi-field key where more than one field value (in a single record) must be duplicated in order to obtain a key violation. Multi-field keys are discussed in the next chapter where Paradox is applied to a practical situation.

5.9 Borrowing Table Structures

When creating a database, table structures can be markedly similar, or, in some instances, duplicated. For example, you may decide that information is easier to manage when stored in a number of smaller tables rather than one large one.

In such circumstances, you need only create one table structure and then borrow that structure to create other tables. For instance, suppose you wanted to create two tables each containing the very same fields and field types.

First you would create the table structure as discussed in Hands-on Session 5.3.1. Now take a look at the following Hands-on Session which shows how to borrow this existing table structure.

5.9.1 Hands-on Session

1. With the main menu on screen, press **C** to select Create.

2. Enter the name of a table, **Person1**, for instance.

3. The screen shown in Figure 5.1 will then appear.

4. Press **F10** to produce the menu.

5. Press **B** to select Borrow.

6. In response the prompt, Table:, type the name of the table from which you want to borrow, or press **<Enter>** and select the appropriate table.

It is quite practical to edit the borrowed structure to cater for additional requirements.

7. Finally, press **F2** to store the table structure.

5.10 Copying Tables

Using Borrow to copy an existing table structure is flawed where it is necessary to 'borrow' the contents also. To duplicate tables as well as data therein, the Copy feature is used. However a table can also be copied by querying. This latter method can be used to copy fields from a number of tables. You will learn more about Querying in Chapter 7.

The following Hands-on Session shows how to use the Copy feature.

5.10.1 Hands-on Session – copying tables and backing up data

Primarily, the Copy feature is intended for backing up files so as to minimise the possibility of data-loss through user-error or machine malfunction. It is extremely flexible in that it can be used to copy tables, forms reports, scripts and graphs.

To copy a table and its family:

1. Press **T** to select Tools from the main menu.

2. Choose Copy, and press **T** to select Table.

This primes the copy feature to duplicate a table and its accompanying family.

3. Press **<Enter>** and select the table you wish to copy.

4. Finally, type the name of the table to which you want to copy the table.

5.10.2 Copying Tables by Querying

In the previous chapter, a query form was used to list a group of records. This QBE (Query By Example) facet can be massaged so as to copy the entire contents of, or portions of, one or more tables. Because QBE is discussed in detail in Chapter 7, we shall look at copying data from just one table.

The following Hands-on Session shows how to copy the Employee table by querying:

5.10.3 Hands-on Session

1. Press **Alt-F8** to clear all images.

2. Press **A** to select Ask from the main menu.

3. Press **<Enter>** to list tables in the working directory, or include the name of the directory where the Employee table is stored.

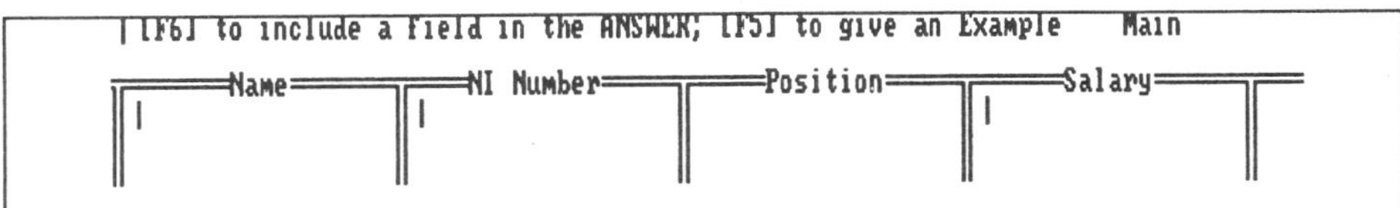

Figure 5.4: Query form

4. Select the Employee table.

5. Press **F6** (Checkmark) in each field of the query form as shown in Figure 5.4.

6. Press **F2** (Do-It!) to produce the Answer table shown in Figure 5.5.

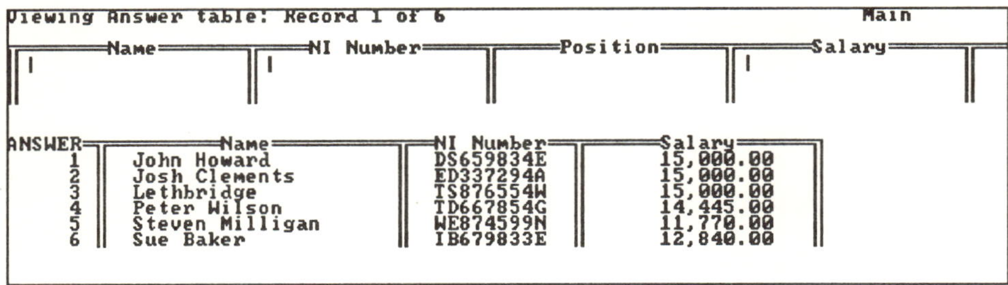

ANSWER	Name	NI Number	Salary
1	John Howard	DS659834E	15,000.00
2	Josh Clements	ED337294A	15,000.00
3	Lethbridge	TS876554W	15,000.00
4	Peter Wilson	TD667854G	14,445.00
5	Steven Milligan	WE874599N	11,770.00
6	Sue Baker	IB679833E	12,840.00

Figure 5.5: Answer table

As the Answer table is stored temporarily, it is necessary to rename it:

7. Press **F10/T** to select Tools.

8. Press **R**, or **<Enter>**, to select Rename.

9. Press **T**, or **<Enter>**, to choose Table.

10. Press **<Enter>** and select the Answer table.

11. Enter a new name such as **NI**, for instance.

If a table by the new name already exists you will be given the opportunity to cancel the action.

A pathname can be included at stage 11 to write the table to another directory; for example, you could enter **sample/NI** to write the table to the Sample directory.

5.11 Restructuring Tables

However much careful thought is given to planning, structuring tables to exact requirements can be difficult. Using Paradox, field types, number of fields and width of columns, can be altered by restructuring.

On screen, column widths can be altered by invoking the ColumnSize feature which emanates from Image on the main menu. The following Hands-on Session shows how to do this:

5.11.1 Hands-on Session – resizing columns

1. Firstly, press **V** to select View from the main menu.

2. Press **<Enter>** and select the Employee table.

Now let us look at narrowing the Name field or column.

3. Press **F10** to produce the main menu.

4. Select Image.

5. Press **C** to select ColumnSize.

6. Position the cursor amid the Name field and press **<Enter>**.

You can select other fields by simply moving the cursor.

7. Press **<right-arrow-key>** to enlarge the column, and press **<left-arrow-key>** to it.

8. When satisfied with the column size, press <Enter>.

To make the column size permanent: with Employee the current image, press **F10/I/K** to select KeepSet.

5.11.2 Hands-on Session – restructuring tables

This Hands-on Session shows how to restructure tables.

Suppose, for the sake of argument, it was necessary to restructure the Employee table created in Hands-on Session 5.3.1. It does not matter if you have not got the exact table available, you can easily apply the following techniques.

1. Select Modify from the main menu.

2. Choose Restructure, and press **<Enter>** to list tables in the working directory.

3. Select the Employee table.

You are now free to restructure the table as if creating it for the first time.

As with tables, field names can be edited using Field View (invoked by pressing **Alt-F5**), which can be switched off by pressing **<Enter>**. Field types can also be changed and edited using Field View.

To insert a new field amid the structure, press **Ins** within the appropriate field number, and then enter the field name and type. Fields can be deleted by pressing **Del** (on the numeric keypad).

And if, during restructuring, you could do with some assistance, press **F10** and select Help, or simply press **F1**.

5. Finally, press **F2** when satisfied with the table structure. Alternatively, you can ignore a newly created table structure by pressing **F10/C** to select Cancel.

5.12 Data Entry Using Forms

An alternative to Entering Data via tables is to use forms, where you simply type field values alongside appropriate field names. Adopting this method, a degree of user-friendliness is gained, as the order in which data is entered becomes more apparent. Figure 5.6 shows a standard form associated with the Employee table.

```
Viewing Employee table with form F: Record 1 of 6                Main ═▼

                                                    Employee    #    1
Name:          John Howard
NI Number:     DS659834E
Position:      Technical Author
Salary:                   15,000.00
Department:    Technical
```

Figure 5.6: Standard form associated with the Employee table

To illustrate the use of forms, try experimenting with the Employee table (created in Hands-on Session 5.3.1). Entering data via forms is carried out by first viewing the table on screen by selecting View from the main menu. Then, press **F7** (Form Toggle) to produce the form shown in Figure 5.6. Now press **F9** (Edit) to edit data using the form. To recap: it is possible to move from one record to the next by pressing **PgUp** and **PgDn**. Moving from one field to another is simply a matter of using the up- and down-arrow-keys.

Many of the key combinations used to perform various tasks in form edit mode are intuitive to the user already familiar with editing tables. For example, **Ctrl-Backspace** will delete a field, and Ins will insert a new record at the position denoted by the number shown in the top right corner. However, to give a concise guide to editing via forms, the following table shows all relevant keystrokes:

Operation	*Key(s)*
Move cursor	
Down one field	Down arrow
First field of current record	Ctrl-Home
First record of table	Home
Last field of current record	Ctrl-End
Last record of table	End
Next field	Right arrow
Previous field	Left arrow
Up one field	Up arrow
Edit form	
Copy field from previous record	Ctrl-D
Delete field	Ctrl-Backspace
Delete record	Del (on numeric keypad)
Field view	Alt-F5
Insert record	Ins
Store editing session	F2 (Do-It!)
Toggle between table and form	F7

Table 5.3: Editing/Data entry using forms

Forms for data entry are ideal where applications are not bound to be used by familiar users. For example, in a working environment, a variety of users might use an application, and for the not so competent computer user a degree of user friendliness can be introduced. (Chapter 9 addresses the use and creation of forms.)

5.13 Validity of Field Values

Each time a field value is entered or edited, its validity is checked. For instance, alphanumeric values are invalid within numeric fields. Beyond such default validity checks, it is possible to use ValCheck to specify your own criteria, perhaps to ensure that values meet a required format.

5.13.1 Default Values

ValCheck can be harnessed so as to ensure that fields left empty are automatically filled with a default value. For example, you might do this where each record contains the year.

The following steps show how to establish a default value:

1. Press **M** to select Modify from the main menu.

2. Press **E** to choose Edit.

3. Press **<Enter>** and select the appropriate table.

4. Press **F10** to call upon the Edit menu.

5. Press **V** to choose ValCheck

6. Press **D** to select Define.

7. Move the cursor to the field you wish to check, as prompted, and press **<Enter>**.

8. Press **D** to select default.

9. Enter the required value.

6

A Typical Application

To introduce some reality, and some light relief, this chapter recollects initial experiences with Paradox. Paradox, as described here, is applied to a technical writing company, a fact which is immaterial, but mentioned nevertheless. Within the company, like so many others, information stored includes: clients' names and addresses, items purchased and amounts received. The information is then used to mail merge, invoice clients and generate graphical presentations.

This database application is developed in Chapter 11, where Paradox is modelled to exact requirements with appropriate menus and screens.

Finally, it is assumed that you have read some of the Paradox documentation, or Chapters 4 and 5 of *Power of Paradox*.

6.1 The Application

The arrival of Paradox was met with one immediate reaction: "How many manuals?" Don Steele, who imparted these words, thinks that all the technical writers in the world had a hand in their creation. Convincing Don about Paradox's ease of use was difficult as he adheres to the belief that the inclusion of vast amounts of documentation confirms a program's lack of user-friendliness. It was not until he saw Paradox loaded and tinkered about with it via the menus that he conceded it was 'amicable'. In fact, he eventually admitted that: "Unlike other databases, Paradox neither caused drowsiness nor bad language". However, these symptoms may be experienced if not in possession of *Power of Paradox.*

A descriptive algorithm, which concisely describes a database application, is best left to the end-user, if you yourself are not the end-user that is. Simply ask the prospective user what is required.

As is so often the case, this database application involves information storage pertaining to clients' names and addresses, turnover, expenditure and employees. In Sal's words, he also wanted to mail merge, turn the screen inside out with snazzy graphs, and be able 'to boldly go' into the depths of his data where he had previously been unable to tread. He also demanded that it should be so easy to use, that he would not need to read a thing, and his last concern was that of data security.

To all intents and purposes, this concise list of requirements is a descriptive algorithm, which tells what is expected from the database application. It constitutes a starting point for top-down analysis (or top-down design). Top-down analysis is simply a design method where we begin by gaining an overall picture of what is required, and step by step work our way 'down' to more intricate detail such as the contents of tables, reports and so forth.

In contrast, bottom-up analysis, a more difficult approach, involves beginning with the design and creation of tables, and suchlike, and working upward to an overall database solution.

6.1.1 Design Matters

The descriptive algorithm can now be structured so as to comprise appropriate tables. Though common sense is as good a guide as any when deciding upon the type of tables to use, you might like to return to Chapter 5 for advice. Jotting down the tables and associated information in the following manner, is an obvious starting point:

Client	clients' names and addresses
Turnover	amounts received
Employees	employees' names and addresses
Work	work in progress together with who, exactly, is working on what
Outgoing	outgoings and addresses.

Decide what information should be stored in each table, and bear in mind that, though it is possible to restructure tables indefinitely, careful planning at the outset can save time in the long term.

Although difficult and sometimes impossible, try to pinpoint those tables likely to be linked or related. For example, personal experience tells that invoicing is best implemented by linking two tables. The Client table and the Turnover table are two such tables.

Such considerations are often matters of hindsight to the novice. However, the possibility of recognising them at an early stage is increased by jotting down all tables and trying to anticipate links which will eventually materialise, as shown in Figure 6.1.

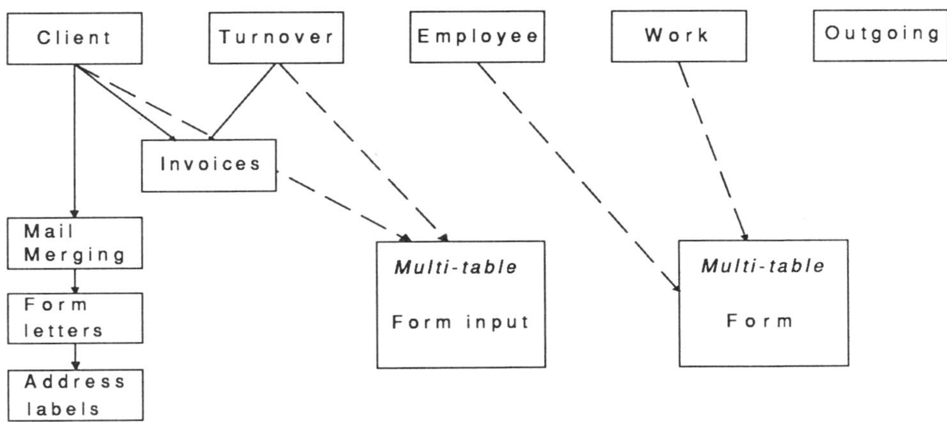

Figure 6.1: Database application

The table structure spells out the already mentioned link between the Client and Turnover table. Therefore, at this early stage it is understood that the mentioned pair of tables must share a common field.

Next, tables should be reduced to their respective fields, paying particular attention to field types and how they should be arranged. Beginning with Client and Turnover tables, these will contain the fields shown in Figure 6.2, where those marked with an asterisk are key fields.

Client:		Turnover:	
Company	A*	Company	A*
ID	N	Date	D*
Name	A	Amount due	$
Street	A	ID	N
City	A	Amount received	$
Postcode	A	Date received	D
Tel	A		

Figure 6.2: Fields of Client and Turnover tables

The Client table is fairly straightforward, all the fields are alphanumeric except ID, which is numeric. Note, each letter suffix reflects the field type according to Paradox.

Equally simple, the Turnover table comprises two date fields, two currency fields, a numeric field and an alphanumeric field.

The Company field, a key field, will be used to link the tables to produce an invoice in the form of a multi-table report. As such, this must be the leftmost field in the table. The key field in the Client table serves to detect duplication of data entries, where any attempt to enter an existing company name will be regarded as a data violation and unacceptable. This naturally ensures that each company record is entered only once. Furthermore, after pressing **F2** (Do-It!), all entries will be arranged in ascending order.

Unlike the Client table, the Turnover table comprises a multi-field (or concatenated) key because Clients will appear more than once. Using multi-field keys an invalid data entry is one in which all key fields are duplicated, which is unlikely in most instances. As such, by designating the Company field and the Date field a multi-field key, company names can be duplicated.

There is little choice in regard to placing multi-field keys, they must be the leftmost fields. Incidentally, the leftmost field of a multi-field key is termed the primary key field, according to which records are sorted following 'Do-It!'. Where two primary key fields are the same, records are sorted according to the other key fields.

6.1.2 Creating Directories

Where Paradox is used for a number of applications, it is preferable to confine each to its own directory. This assists in generally selecting tables (as there will be fewer to choose from).

The ensuing stages show how to create a directory and to store all tables and respective families, thus keeping clear the main default directory (Paradox3) as well as the Sample directory:

1. Press **T** to select Tools from the main menu.

2. Press **M** to choose More.

3. Press **T** to select ToDos

4. Enter: **md\paradox3\access**, creating a new directory called Access.

5. Enter: **exit** to return to Paradox.

(In future, you might like to resort to Dos by using the shortcuts, **Ctrl-O** or **Alt-O**.)

6.1.3 Changing Working Directories

Under normal circumstances, viewing, editing, creating or manipulating tables require that you go into the Access directory. For example, to view tables in the newly created directory, it is necessary to enter **access**.

The Access directory becomes freely available when made the working directory. To do this, press **F10/T/M/D** to select Directory, and then enter: **access**. (It is, needless to say, important to know how to change working directories in this manner.)

6.1.4 Declaring a Default Working Directory

Working directories declared using Tools exist until Paradox is unloaded. A default working directory, active each time Paradox is loaded, can be achieved using the Paradox Custom Configuration Program (or CCP).

A default directory can be created as follows:

The Paradox Custom Configuration Program, or CCP, is automatically copied to the Paradox3 directory of your hard disk during installation. So, naturally, the working directory must be Paradox3 before the CCP can be run.

The easiest way to run the CCP is from within Paradox itself; press **S** to choose Scripts from the main menu; press **P** to select Play; press **<Enter>** and choose Custom. Press **Y** or **N** to indicate whether or not a monochrome monitor is being used.

To run the CCP from Dos simply enter: **paradox3 custom** in the Paradox3 directory. It is inadvisable to run the CCP by pressing **Ctrl-O** to resort to Dos as many machines with under 1 MByte of memory will cause the Insufficient memory prompt to appear.

To make Access the default directory:

1. Press **D** to select defaults.

2. Press **<Enter>** to choose Defaults once again.

3. Press **S** to select SetDirectory.

4. Enter: **access**, giving the Dos path, c:\paradox3\access

5. Press **R** to return to the main menu.

6. Press **D** to select Do-It!

7. Highlight Do-It! and press **<Enter>**.

8. Press **H** to write the configuration to your hard disk.

9. Return to Paradox by entering: **paradox3**

6.2 Creating Tables

Creating the Client table structure is quite straightforward; it is simply a matter of selecting Create from the main menu, entering an appropriate table name, and then structuring the table. Creating a table structure was addressed in Hands-on Session 5.3.1. Figure 6.3 shows the structure adopted for the Client table, where the key field is designated a single asterisk, as shown.

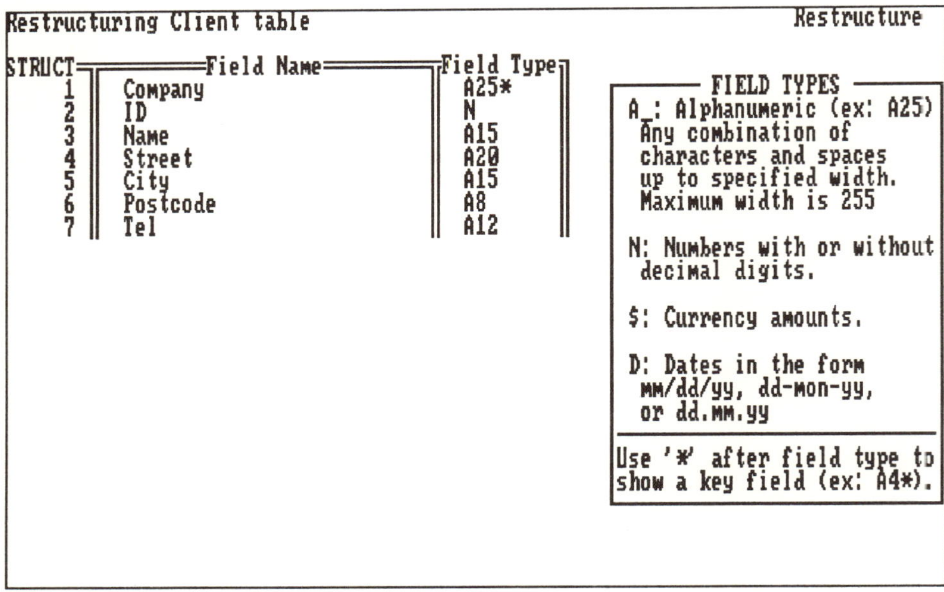

Figure 6.3: Client table structure

6.3 Data Entry

Entering data for the first time can be a painstaking affair, particularly where the company or individual is disorganised and information has to be reaped from literally hundreds of sources, such as files, accounts, invoices and sometimes scraps of paper.

Occasionally, however, you might be lucky and find that use has been made of another database or spreadsheet, in which case data can be imported. By selecting Tools and then Import, files can be read from Quattro, Quattro Pro, Lotus 1-2-3, Symphony, dBase, IBM Filing Assistant, Reflex and Visicalc. Where none of these standard packages has been used, it is probably best to convert the data into Ascii format and then proceed to import it.

In this particular instance all data had to be keyed in from invoices, business cards, pages of a diary and scraps of paper – an arduous process which took a whole day. The beginnings of the Client table are shown in Figure 6.4.

Company	ID	Name	Street	City	Postcode	Tel
AST Ltd	107	John Farr	20 Tobby Street	Manchester	MA5 2ER	0625 652398
Brett Ltd	106	John Sawyer	7 Virginia Road	Bristol	BS1 3CH	0272 865612
DG Computers Ltd	109	Dave Trent	2 Morris Street	Bristol	BS1 3CH	0272 561238
Morris Technology Ltd	105	Dave Arnfield	12 Grand Oak Street	Manchester	MA3 3TY	0625 878881
Mount Clove Ltd	101	Sue Phelps	Gordons Park	Birmingham	TWN 3KY	0876 678446
SouthGate Ltd	102	John White	10 Walters Road	London	SW6	0194 284653
TriTech Ltd	103	J Wallace	14 Wimpole Street	London	W1 6QT	0194 675412
Wilkins Technology Ltd	104	Chris Wilkins	Gordons Park	Birmingham	TWN 3KY	0876 678423

Figure 6.4: The Client table

Remembering, or referring to, the editing techniques discussed in the previous chapter, you might like to enter the information shown.

6.4 Turnover

The Turnover table basically contains all amounts due and received, together with dates and company names. This table is useful in a number of respects: it can be used to quickly generate a list of debtors; to produce a graph of amounts received or amounts owed; and it can also be used to check on verbal contracts – what a client agrees to pay can be quite different from what is actually paid, particularly where an invoice has not been sent to the client.

Try and create the Turnover table structure shown in Figure 6.5 overleaf.

(The Turnover table can be created by first querying the Client table so as to produce a list of company names and ID numbers only. Then, the resultant Answer table can be renamed using Tools from the main menu. Finally, use can be made of the restructure feature to add the four fields previously discussed. Then make the Company and Date fields into a multi-field key.)

For the purposes of experimentation, enter the data shown in Figure 6.6 overleaf.

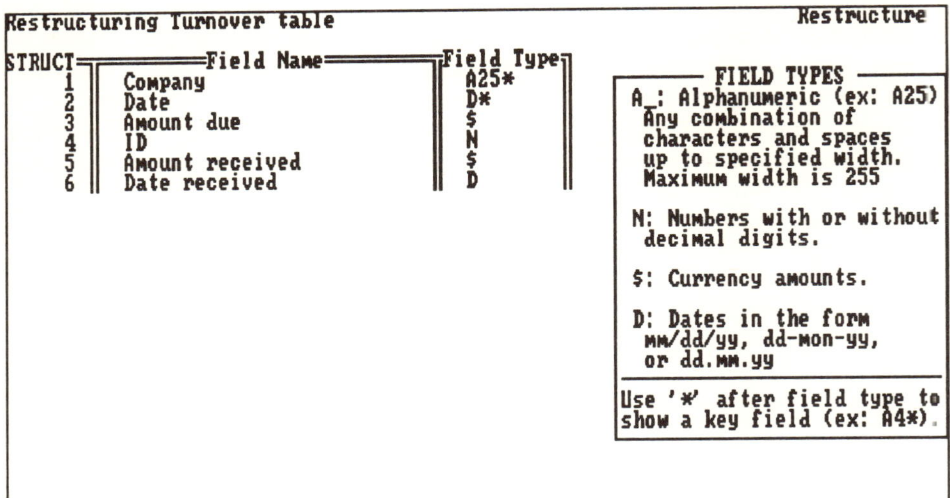

Figure 6.5: Turnover table structure

Company	Date	Amount due	ID	Amount received	Date received
AST Ltd	17.04.89	8,000.00	107	8,000.00	20.06.89
Brett Ltd	9.07.89	5,500.00	106	5,500.00	29.08.89
DG Computers Ltd	25.05.89	8,000.00	109	8,000.00	27.07.89
Morris Technology Ltd	6.03.90	6,000.00	105		
Mount Clove Ltd	4.05.89	10,500.00	101	10,500.00	6.07.89
Mount Clove Ltd	9.06.89	17,500.00	101	17,500.00	4.08.89
SouthGate Ltd	5.01.90	9,000.00	102		
TriTech Ltd	25.05.89	5,000.00	103	5,000.00	28.07.89
TriTech Ltd	27.02.90	6,500.00	103		
Wilkins Technology Ltd	13.04.89	14,000.00	104	14,000.00	15.06.89
Wilkins Technology Ltd	18.01.90	5,000.00	104		

Figure 6.6: Turnover table

6.5 Invoices

Invoicing clients should now be easy, it will just be a matter of designing an appropriate report and outputting it to the printer. This whole operation is covered in due course. Before then, however, we look at a technique which can be used to see whether or not a client has actually been invoiced, as you can easily forget! To accommodate this aspect, another field is required. The field needed is of the Boolean variety, which means it can have one of two values, ie Yes or No. A numeric field can be used, where 0 indicates that an invoice has not been sent, and 1 shows that one has. As it is a numeric field, the matter can be taken further where the number of invoices sent can be recorded and shown – some clients might need a little more encouragement than others! Invoke Restructure, and add the numeric field shown in Figure 6.7.

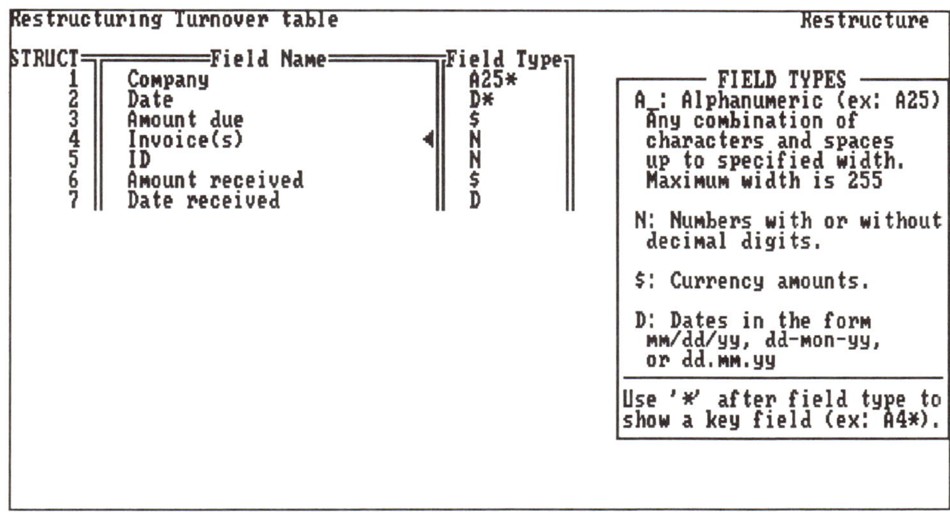

Figure 6.7: Turnover table with added Invoice (Boolean) field

Invoicing a client is carried out by designing a report; achieving a hard copy of information always requires a report. Reports are easy to design, and you can attach as many as 14 to any one table. Figure 6.8 shows the invoice required.

```
****************************************************************************
*                              I N V O I C E                               *
****************************************************************************
ABC Technical Services, 3 Bowers Street, London WE7.  Tel 01 542 675412

Company: Brett Ltd
         John Sawyer
         7 Virginia Road
         Bristol

Amount: 5,500.00

Date: 9.07.89

****************************************************************************
```

Figure 6.8: The invoice required by the application

Because the required fields exist in both Client and Turnover tables, it is necessary to call upon Paradox's relational aspect.

(The alternative of creating another table containing all the fields necessary to create the shown invoice is possible, but it is not good practice, for three reasons: first, it will lead to a great deal of wasted disk space; secondly, tables can become too large; and thirdly, such an approach is contrary to the whole relational database concept.)

Because the invoice will link two tables, the report can be accommodated within the families of either one. For the sake of logic, however, and to make the application slightly more intuitive – an important aim – the report becomes an object of the Turnover table.

The report shown in Figure 6.8 can be designed as follows:

1. Select Report from the main menu.

2. Press **D** to select Design.

3. Press **<Enter>** and select the Turnover table.

4. Press **<right-arrow-key>** so as to highlight report 1.

5. Press **<Enter>** to select report 1.

6. Enter **Invoice**.

7. Press **F** to select Free-Form to lead to a screen of the sort shown in Figure 6.9.

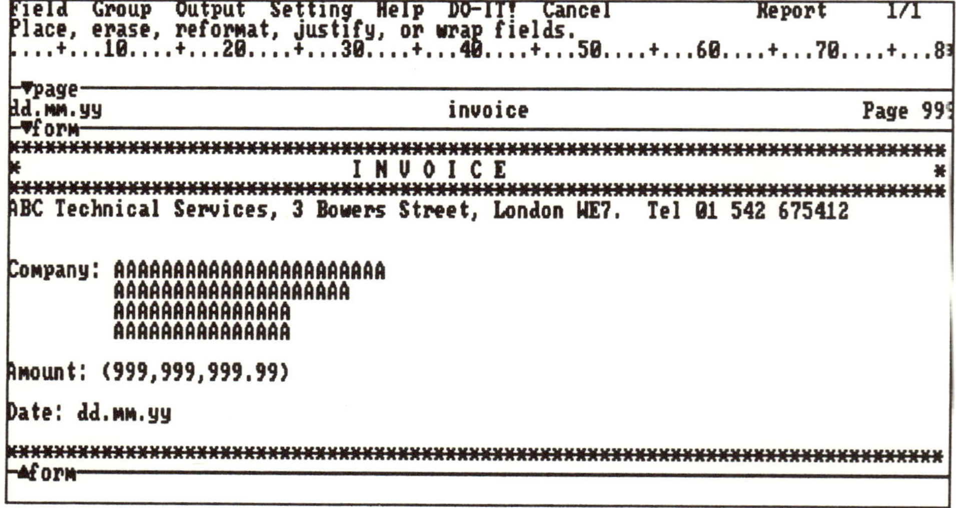

Figure 6.9: The Invoice on screen

8. Press **F10** to call up the menu.

9. Press **F/L** to choose Lookup.

Now, the Turnover table has to be linked to the Client table, for reasons previously discussed:

10. Press **L** to select Link; press **<Enter>** and select the Client table.

11. The prompt, *Select TURNOVER field to match Company in Client,* indicates that the common key field is Company, so, press **<Enter>** to choose the Company field.

Having successfully linked the Turnover and Client tables, fields from either table can be placed in the report (invoice).

12. Press **Ins** to place the screen in insert-mode – this is confirmed by Ins in the top right of the screen. Now establish the asterisks, company name and address as shown in Figure 6.9. The design chosen is arbitrary but it must exist within the actual form, somewhere.

13. Delete the Amount received field: press **F10/F/E**, and position the block cursor amid the nines which represent the field, then press **<Enter>**.

14. With Ins shown in the top right corner of the screen – achieved by pressing Ins – delete Amount received using the delete keys.

15. Repeat steps 13 and 14 to erase ID and Date received fields (and text). If you added the Invoice (Boolean) field, delete this also.

16. Again with Ins shown in the top right corner of the screen, position the cursor immediately following the Company field and press **<Enter>** three times so as to make space for the additional fields.

17. Press **F10/F/P/R** to place a regular field.

18. Highlight the linked table [<Client>], and press **<Enter>** to produce a list of fields in the Client table – you are now free to place any of them.

19. Highlight Street and press **<Enter>**.

20. Position the cursor beneath the Company field and press **<Enter>** to place the Street field. Resize the field as required using the arrow keys and press **<Enter>**. If necessary, you can line the field up as you would with any word processor, provided you are in insert-mode.

22. Repeat stages 17 to 20 placing the fields City and Postcode as in Figure 6.9.

Note: To delete the default header appropriately position the cursor and press **Ctrl-Y**.

23. Finally, press **F2** (Do-It!) to record the report

If the design of a report has to be abandoned midway, press **F2,** return to it by pressing **F10/R/C** to select Change, and then retrace the main steps by pressing **<Enter>** at the appropriate points.

6.5.1 Printing Invoices

Printing invoices so as to confine each to a single page is naturally important. Though trying to print on single sheets can be a process of trial and error, a technique can be refined using Setting on the Report menu. However, before then, with a printer on-line print invoices as follows:

1. Press **F10/R/O** to select Output.

2. Press **<Enter>** and choose the Turnover table.

3. Press **1** to select the invoice.

4. Press **P** to print invoices.

Invoices will be printed in one continuous stream where, no doubt, they will have spilled over from one page to another.

To demonstrate how a page size can be set, change the Invoice, by typing **F10/R/C**; press **<Enter>** and select the Turnover table; enter **1**; press **<Enter>**. Press **Ctrl-V** to give a vertical ruler, so as to indicate the length of the report.

By first pressing **Ins,** it is possible to introduce space between the form band and the top and bottom of the page. By carefully matching the number of lines on each page to those printed, it is possible to print reports exactly as required. In the case of pre-printed stationary, further attention must be paid to distances between fields and so forth.

In this instance, the requirement was to print a single invoice after which Paradox should pause. Also, the listing paper used, according to printer settings was 45 lines deep. Both requirements are implemented by changing the report design.

Setting the page length to 45 lines is achieved by pressing **F10/S/P/L** and entering **45**. The pause between pages can be achieved by pressing **F10/S/W/Y**. With the vertical ruler on screen, ensure that the report is 45 lines deep. Press **F2** to record the changes made.

To print invoices:

1. Press **F10/R** to select Report.

2. Press **O** to select Output.

3. Press **<Enter>** and choose the Turnover table.

4. Press **1** to select the invoice report.

5. Press **P** to send the report (invoices) to the printer.

6.5.2 Printing a Single Invoice

Depending upon the size of business, the procedure of printing invoices for the whole of a table is not a common occurrence. Indeed it is more common to print a single invoice.

For one moment, consider viewing the turnover table and realising that Southgate Ltd (record number 7) should be invoiced. This invoice can be printed as follows (before beginning, ensure that each invoice is printed on a single page – see previous subsection):

1. View the Turnover table on screen.

2. Press **F10** to produce the main menu.

3. Press **R/R** to select RangeOutput.

4. Press **<Enter>** twice to select the Turnover table. Note, if you have switched off your computer after changing to the Access directory, you will have to make Access your working directory once again by following the steps outlined in Section 6.2.

5. Press **1** to select the invoice.

6. Press **P** to send the report to the printer. Of course, for the purposes of experimentation it is quite practical to select Screen.

7. As record number 7 is required – which will be printed on page 7, press **Backspace** and enter **7** in response to the prompt, *Beginning page number:*

8. Enter **4** in response to, *Ending page number:*

9. Because a pause exists between pages, it is necessary to press any key four times before the actual invoice is printed – this will not be the case where the report is output to the screen.

The inconvenience of having to press any key a number of times to correspond with the record number is eliminated by placing the report in a continuous printing mode. If uncertain as to how this is achieved, the following steps will help:

1. Press **R** to select Report from the main menu.

2. Enter **C** and select the Turnover table.

3. Enter **1**, press **<Enter>** again, then press **F10/S** to select Setting.

4. Press **W/N/F2**.

6.6 Mail Merging

Receiving personalised mail which offers congratulations on being ''chosen from the entire population of the world to take part in a competition'', or something similar, is quite frequent nowadays. Such mail is produced on a computer using a mail merge facility. The senders have merely listed target-addresses, yours included, and inserted them into a standard form letter. Of course, these manifest themselves in a number of guises, with today's evermore imaginative advertising and marketing techniques.

Besides a constant source of irritation to many recipients, mail merging is a useful technique for the business user. 'Mail shots' where maybe 100s or 1,000s of letters are sent out using a single form letter, represents one method of marketing, advertising or selling.

(A number of packages can be harnessed for mail merging purposes. Professional word processors, WordStar 5.0, WordStar 5.5 and WordStar 2000 each have the program MailMerge. WordPerfect 5.0 and Borland's very own Sprint can also be used, but with a little more difficulty. Using Sprint and Wordperfect 5.0 for mail merging is covered in *Mastering Sprint* (Sigma Press) and *Moving Up To WordPerfect 5.0* (Sigma Press).)

Initially, for this particular application, it was necessary to send a standard form letter advertising new services to all clients. The form letter for such an undertaking is shown Figure 6.10 opposite.

Clearly this is, once again, a matter of designing an appropriate report containing both fields and the main body of the letter.

6.6.1 Creating a Form Letter

Form letters may include fields within the text itself. This helps personalise the letter, by including the addressee's name where necessary. Observing many of the points experienced during the creation of an invoice, you should be able to produce a form letter. If in doubt, however, the following steps illustrate the creation of the form letter/report shown in Figure 6.10.

A.B.C

Technical Services Ltd

May 2, 1990

John Farr
AST Ltd
20 Tobby Street
Manchester
MA5 2ER

Dear John Farr,

You may like to know that, ABC Technical Services now offers complete 'manual solutions', from writing, illustration, through to printing and binding.

If you would like to know more about this new service, contact us today.

Yours sincerely,

Desmond Hart

Figure 6.10: A typical form letter

1. Press **R** to select Report from the main menu.

2. Press **D** to select Design.

3. Press **<Enter>** and select the Client table.

4. Press **<right-arrow-key>** so as to highlight report 1.

5. Press **<Enter>** to select report 1.

6. Enter **advert**.

7. Press **F** to select Free-Form, to lead to the sort of screen shown in Figure 6.11.

8. Press **F10** to call up the menu.

9. Delete the Tel field: press **F/E**, move the block cursor to the field and press **<Enter>**. Press **Ins** and delete the field name, Tel:

10. Using this same approach, delete the Company field and the ID field. Also, delete

the header using Erase and the delete keys, or, simply press **Ctrl-Y**.

```
Changing report R10 for Client table                             Report     1/1
Form Band, Field Squeeze
....+...10....+...20....+...30....+...40....+...50....+...60....+...70....+...8
▼form
                                                         M o n t h dd, yyyy


AAAAAAAAAAAAAAA
AAAAAAAAAAAAAAAAAAAAAAAAA
AAAAAAAAAAAAAAAAAAAA
AAAAAAAAAAAAAAA
AAAAAAAA

Dear AAAAAAAAAAAAAAA,

You may like to know that, ABC Technical Services now offers complete 'manual
solutions', from writing, illustration, through to printing and binding.

If you would like to know more about this new service, contact us today.


Yours sincerely,
```

Figure 6.11: Form letter (report)

11. Align all address fields to the left using the Backspace key.

12. Move the cursor to the beginning of the Street field and press **<Enter>**.

13. Press **F10/F/P/R** and select the Company field.

14. Position the cursor directly beneath the Name field and press **<Enter>** twice.

15. With Ins shown in the top right of the screen, position the cursor beneath the address and type **Dear.**

16. Place the Name field directly after Dear: press **F10/F/P/R** and select the name field. Move the cursor to the appropriate point and press **<Enter>** twice.

17. Type the form letter shown, and include an address if not using headed note paper.

18. Include a date: press **F10/F/P/D**; select the date format required and place it as you would a regular field.

19. After completing the text, press **F2.**

Set the page length as discussed in subsection 6.5.1, and try outputting the form letters to the screen according to guidance provided in subsections 6.5.1 and 6.5.2.

When output, the Name field is accompanied by leading and trailing blanks. Such horizontal space is eliminated by using FieldSqueeze, in the following manner:

1. Press **R** to select Report from the main menu.

2. Press **C** to select Change.

3. Press **<Enter>** and select the Client table.

Remember, to select the Client table in this manner, Access must be the default directory, as previously discussed.

4. Highlight 1 and press **<Enter>**.

5. Press **<Enter>** to leave the report description unchanged.

6. Press **F10/S** to select Setting.

7. Press **R** to choose RemoveBlanks.

8. Press **F/Y** to remove all field blanks in the form band.

9. As always, press **F2** to complete the operation.

Though Paradox is particularly flexible when it comes to restructuring tables and so forth, modified fields following restructure are erased from accompanying forms and reports.

For instance, if the Company field in the Client table were now altered using Restructure, it would disappear from the address, in which case it must be reinserted. The message here is, don't go designing reports and forms before being absolutely satisfied with tables.

6.6.2 Address Labels

Though form letters are often mailed using envelopes with transparent windows, address labels are frequently required. Printing address labels involves creating a report which contains address fields only. Take a look at the report shown in Figure 6.12 overleaf.

The address label report shown was not created from scratch, but is a modified version of the Form letter. First, the form letter was copied to report 2 of the Client table and then appropriately changed. Copying reports, graphs, and other objects is an important aspect of using Paradox, as it saves a considerable amount of time. The following stages illustrate how to create the report shown:

```
Field  Group  Output  Setting  Help  DO-IT!  Cancel               Report Ins 1/1
Place, erase, reformat, justify, or wrap fields.
....+...10....+...20....+...30....+...40....+...50....+...60....+...70....+...8
▼page
▼form
          AAAAAAAAAAAAAAA
          AAAAAAAAAAAAAAAAAAAAAAAAA
          AAAAAAAAAAAAAAAAAAAA
          AAAAAAAAAAAAAAA
          AAAAAAAA
▲form
▲page
```

Figure 6.12: Report for address label

1. Press **T** to select tools from the main menu.

2. Press **C** to choose Copy.

3. Press **R** to select Report.

4. Press **S** to choose SameTable.

5. Press **<Enter>** and select the Client table. (Once again, Access must be the working directory for the Client table to be selected in this manner.)

6. Press **1** to indicate that this report is to be copied.

7. Press **2** to copy report 1 to report 2.

If the report is in use, you will be asked if you want to replace it or not. Report 1 will then be copied to report 2

Changing the form letter into an address label simply involves deleting two fields and erasing the main body of the letter. The ensuing steps show how to change the invoice (report 1) into a mail label (report 2):

1. Press **R** to select Report from the main menu.

2. Press **C** to select Change.

3. Press **<Enter>** and select the Client table.

4. Press **2** to choose report 2.

5. Press **Ctrl-Backspace**, and enter **Label.**

6. Press **F10/S/L/Y** to print the report in a label format.

7. Delete fields detached from the address; press **F10/F/E**, position the block cursor and press **<Enter>**.

8. Press **Ins** and delete the form letter. Note, you can delete lines of text by pressing **Ctrl-Y**. This can also be used to delete fields.

9. Close up the page as shown in Figure 6.12.

10. Press **F10/S/P/L**, delete page length, and enter **C** to print labels in a continuous stream.

11. Press **F2** to record changes.

The labels can be printed as follows:

1. Press **F10/R/O** and **<Enter>**.

2. Select the Client table.

3. Press **2** to select report 2.

4. Press **P** to begin printing.

Addresses can be printed away from the extreme left of labels, by editing with Ins shown in top left of the screen, or, by using Margin from the Setting menu.

6.7 Forms

For some users, data-entry via tables can become confusing where field names wander off screen. For this reason, forms, which specifically show where each field value should be entered, are sometimes preferred. Many database programmers resort to forms for data entry purely because they are easy to use and make the application slightly friendlier. Forms also provide a means of viewing data.

Designing a form is markedly similar to designing a report, but, of course, unlike reports forms are never committed to paper.

The form shown in Figure 6.13 overleaf lends itself to data-entry using the Client table.

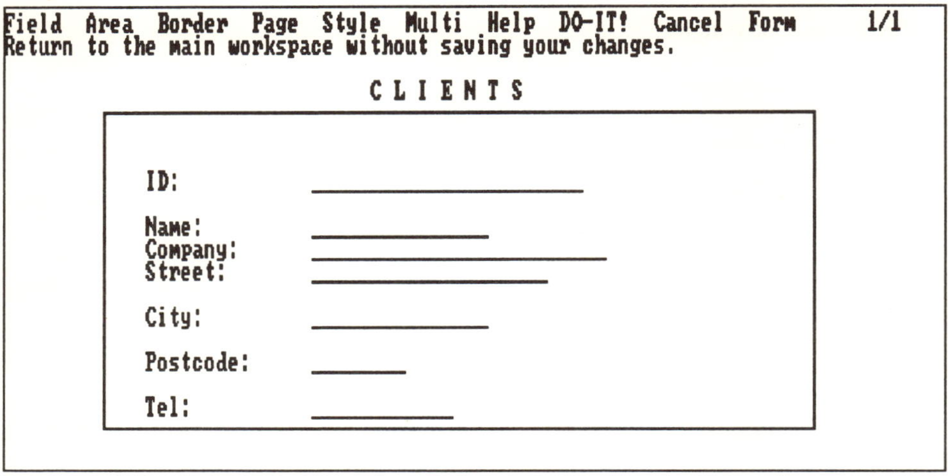

```
Field  Area  Border  Page  Style  Multi  Help  DO-IT!  Cancel  Form       1/1
Return to the main workspace without saving your changes.
                              C L I E N T S

        ID:          ____________________

        Name:        _____________
        Company:     ______________________
        Street:      _________________

        City:        _____________

        Postcode:    _______

        Tel:         __________
```

Figure 6.13: Form for the Client table

The design of forms is a matter of preference. But if advice could be offered, forms should be uncluttered by yet comprise adequate textual help, particularly where field names are concerned. In regard to borders, and there are several types available, which are often useful for creating the illusion of a pre-printed paper form.

Though the process of designing forms is intuitive, the following steps show how to create the one shown in Figure 6.13:.

1. Press **F10/F** to select Form.

2. Press **D** to choose Design.

3. Press **<Enter>** and select the Client table.

4. Press **1** to select form 1.

5. Enter **DataIn** in response to, Form Description:

6. Press **F10/F/P/R** to place a regular field.

7. Select the Name field.

8. Move the cursor to approximately the location shown in Figure 6.13. Press **<Enter>** twice.

9. Repeat stages 6 , 7 and 8 and place the remaining fields as shown. (Note: Fields can be erased by pressing **F10/F/E** and then replaced.)

10. Press **Ins**, and type the field names shown. Close up gaps that appear between the field names and fields by pressing **Backspace** as you would with a word processor.

(By positioning the cursor amid a field, the field name is shown in the top right of the screen. Fields can be erased from the Field menu and relocated. Also, if a field is placed incorrectly, press F10 before <Enter> is pressed for the second time.)

11. Press **F10/B/P** to begin placing a Border.

12. The border style is a matter of preference. For this example, however, press **S** to choose Single-line.

13. Position the cursor in the top left corner of the border and press **<Enter>**.

14. Move the cursor to the bottom right of the border and press **<Enter>**.

(Borders cannot intersect a field. They can be erased by pressing **F10/B/E**.)

15. Type an appropriate title for the form, like that shown.

16. Press **F2** to record the form.

To use the form for data entry, simply View the Client table and press **F10/I/P**, and then select the appropriate form. (See Chapter 5 for information about using forms for data entry.) This custom form can now be invoked by pressing **F7** (Form Toggle).

6.7.1 Multi-table Forms

Forms dedicated to a single table, of the type just illustrated, are limited in many applications. For example, consider using a form to enter data into the Turnover table: updating the Client table to include new clients would be difficult. What is needed is a form which can link the Client table to the Turnover table. This would make data entry considerably easier – as Company names are entered into the Turnover table, new clients will be spotted immediately, as they will not be shown on the form. Confusing? all will soon become clear.

Such multi-table forms make life easier. Take a look at the one shown in Figure 6.14. This provides the link necessary to make the process of data-entry less haphazard. (Using Paradox, multi-table forms are essential for almost all applications.)

The following stages show how to create the multi-table form shown in Figure 6.14.

1. Here, the form created previously (shown in Figure 6.13) will be embedded into a master form which resides in the family of the Turnover table. That is to say, it will be inserted completely into the form created here. However, before it can be embedded, the Company field, the link field which relates it to the Turnover table,

must be erased. Yes, this is a peculiar, but essential requirement for the creation of a multi-table form.

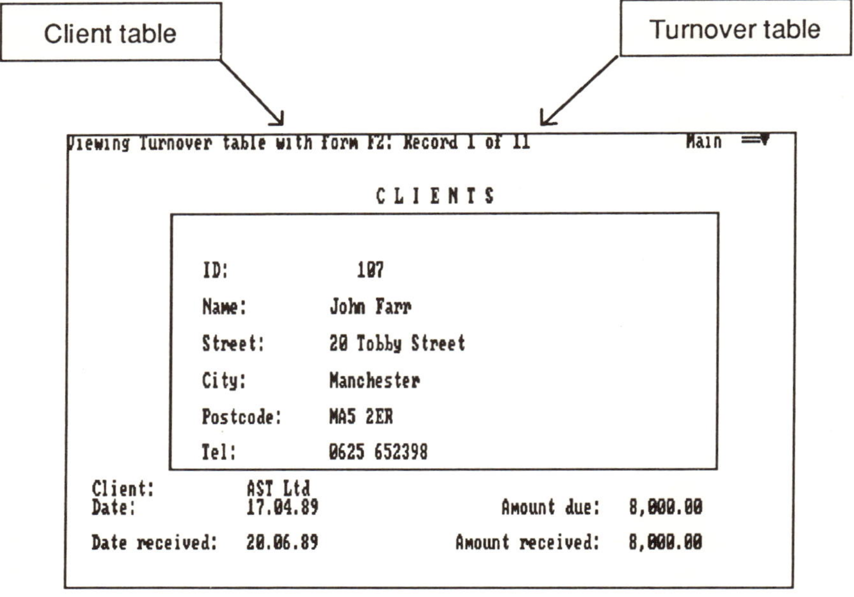

Figure 6.14: A Multi-table form

The Company field can be erased as follows:

2. Press **F10/F/C** to select Change.

3. Press **<Enter>** and select the Client table.

4. Press **1**, or whichever unused form you chose for DataIn.

5. Press **<Enter>** to leave the form description unchanged.

6. Press **F10/F/E** to choose Erase.

7. Position the cursor amid the Company field and press **<Enter>**.

8. Press **Ins** and delete the field name, Company.

9. Press **F2** to record changes made.

Now to design the master form:

10. Press **F10/F/D** to select Design.

11. Press **<Enter>** and select the Turnover table.

12. Press **1**, or select an alternative unused form.

13. Arbitrary, of course, enter **Input** in response to the prompt, *Form description:*

14. Press **F10** to invoke the Design menu.

15. Press **M/T** to begin embedding the DataIn form previously created using the Client table.

16. Press **P/L** to Link the Client table.

17. Press **<Enter>** and appropriately select the Client table.

18. Press **1** or whichever number corresponds to the form you used.

19. In response to, *Select TURNOVER field to match Company in CLIENT*, simply choose Company, the common key field.

20. Presented with a large block, which represents the DataIn form, position it in the upper half of the screen, and press **<Enter>.** Left on the screen will be shaded area indicating where, exactly, the form will be embedded.

21. As with the design of the previous form, fields from the Turnover table can be included in the normal manner. Try placing the fields such as those shown in Figure 6.14. (Remember to reduce the width of the currency fields).

22. Type an appropriate name for the form.

23. Finally, press **F2** to record the multitable form.

To actually use the form for editing or viewing data, make the Turnover table the current image, press **F10/I/P** and select the Input form.

A slight disadvantage of using this particular multitable form, must be the need to press **F3** and **F4** (Up Image and Down Image) to move between fields from different tables.

This drawback, however, is outweighed by obvious advantages: records from both the Client and Turnover tables can be viewed or edited simultaneously. For example, all the related data pertaining to one client can be entered in a more logical manner. The most important advantage, however, is the way in which the Client table can be updated.

To illustrate this last advantage and the way in which the form marries the Client and Turnover tables: using the Input form, try entering a company name which is not in the Client table, and then press **F3** (Up Image) or **Ctrl-L**. Such an entry is immediately met with blank fields, indicating that it is a new client and, therefore, appropriate information must be entered. As such, the possibility of duplicate records being entered into the Client table is greatly reduced.

6.8 Creating More Tables

The database is now beginning to take shape. Mail merging, invoicing and an efficient method of data entry using a multitable form, have been included. Now we look at methods of monitoring work in progress, and work undertaken or being completed by employees.

Incorporating this facet involves creating another two tables: Employee and Work tables.

Shown below are the Work table fields:

Work:

    Name   *
    Start date *
    Deadline
    Client
    Project
    Amount due
    Comment

The Work table has to be keyed for the creation of a (linked) multitable form. As employee names will recur in the Work table, it is necessary to include a multifield key. Observing rules which govern such keys, Name and Start date are used as key fields.

Moving on to the Employee table, which must also be keyed:

Employee:

    Name   *
    NI Number
    Position
    Salary
    Department

The Employee table was created in Chapter 5, so, restructure it to key the Name field.

Create the Work table structure according to that shown in Figure 6.15.

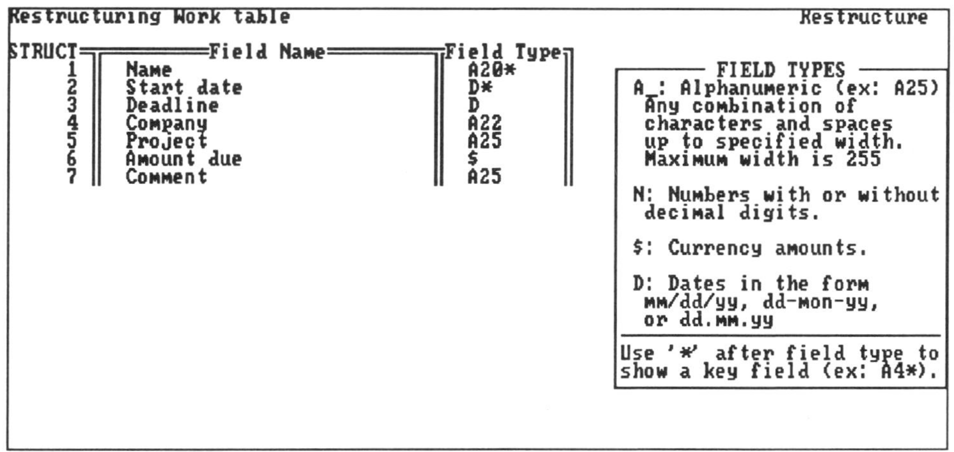

Figure 6.15: Work table structure

6.9 Linking Employee and Work Tables

Consider a multi-table form that could be used to view and edit records from both the Employee and Work tables, of the sort created in Subsection 6.7.1. The first step in creating such a form (shown in Figure 6.17) is to create the Master form shown in Figure 6.16, which emanates from the Work table.

```
Field  Area  Border  Page  Style  Multi  Help  DO-IT!  Cancel  Form  Ins 1/1
Place, erase, reformat, recalculate, or wrap a field.
                           W  o  r  k

          Name:         ____________________
          Start date:   ___________
          Deadline:     ___________
          Company:      ______________________
          Project:      _________________________
          Amount due:   _______________________
          Comment:      _________________________
```

Figure 6.16: Master form (using Work table)

Establishing such a form is covered in detail in Section 6.7. However, try to confine the form to the lower half of the screen.

Here are some reminders about designing forms:

- ❑ Erase field: press **F10/F/E** to choose Erase. Position the cursor amid the company field and press **<Enter>**
- ❑ Place field: press **F10/F/P/R** to place a regular field. Move the cursor to the approximate locations shown in Figure 6.16. Press **<Enter>** twice
- ❑ Type field names: press **Ins** to convert the screen into a text editor
- ❑ A detail form must be created using the Employee table. Note, the Name field must be omitted because it is the link field. Finally, the detail form must be embedded into the master form, as shown in Figure 6.17. (Embedding a form is covered in Subsection 6.7.1.) Note: When creating the detail form position it in the upper part of the design screen.

Try creating this form for yourself by observing the format shown in Figure 6.17.

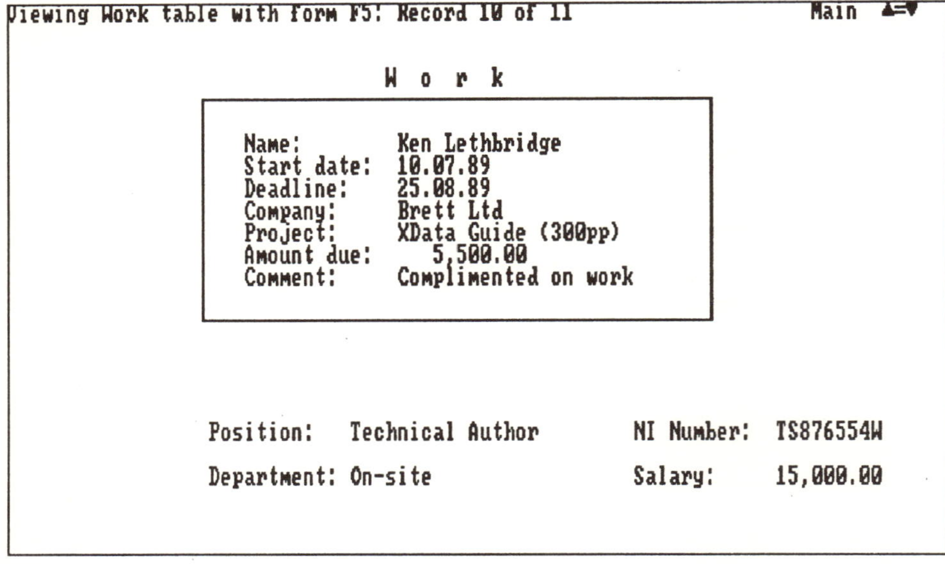
Viewing Work table with form F5: Record 10 of 11 Main

W o r k

Name: Ken Lethbridge
Start date: 10.07.89
Deadline: 25.08.89
Company: Brett Ltd
Project: XData Guide (300pp)
Amount due: 5,500.00
Comment: Complimented on work

Position: Technical Author NI Number: TS876554W

Department: On-site Salary: 15,000.00

Figure 6.17: Multi-table form linking Employee and Work tables

This multitable form can now be used to enter data into either table. As with the Input form, it is necessary to use **F3** (Up Image) and **F4** (Down Image) to edit both tables. **Ctrl-L** can be used to resynchronise records.

Optional, of course, but for practice, enter the records shown in Figure 6.18 into the Work table - the fields can be entered using the multitable form.

Name	Start date	Deadline	Company	Project	Amount due	Comment
John Howard	4.05.89	7.06.89	Mount Clove Ltd	Work practice manual	10,500.00	Completed on time
John Howard	9.06.89	3.07.89	Mount Clove Ltd	In-house safety manual	17,500.00	Completed on time
John Howard	27.02.90	5.06.90	TriTech Ltd	Overview - SparkWord	5,000.00	
Josh Clements	17.04.89	5.05.89	AST Ltd	BSI Guide	8,000.00	2 days over deadline
Josh Clements	25.05.89	24.07.89	DG Computers Ltd	User's Guide	8,000.00	Completed on time
Josh Clements	5.01.90	2.03.90	SouthGate Ltd	IceTec Manual	9,000.00	
Josh Clements	5.03.90	4.05.90	Morris Technology Ltd	Work instructions	6,000.00	
Ken Lethbridge	13.04.89	19.05.89	Wilkins Technology Ltd	Manual - ZTec (part 1)	14,000.00	Dissatisfaction - styl
Ken Lethbridge	25.05.89	7.07.89	TriTech Ltd	Comms manual - T23	6,500.00	Confusion over length
Ken Lethbridge	10.07.89	25.08.89	Brett Ltd	XData Guide (300pp)	5,500.00	Complimented on work
Ken Lethbridge	18.01.90	10.04.90	Wilkins Technology Ltd	Manual - ZTec (part 2)	5,000.00	

Figure 6.18: The Work table

6.10 Graphs

The Turnover table is useful to keep track of overall income using a graph. Graphs can be produced by selecting Image from the main menu, or, by opting for the less keyboard intensive alternative of pressing **Ctrl-F7**.

The following stages show how to generate a graph from the Turnover table:

1. With the Turnover table on screen, position the cursor in the Amount received field.

2. Press **Ctrl-F7** to produce the graph shown in Figure 6.19.

(No doubt the titles will have clashed on your graph - see Chapter 8.)

You have probably noticed something strange about the graph produced. The X-axis, instead of showing values from the first non-numeric field (ie the Company field), as is normally the case, shows Date field values.

This is because the Company and Date fields combine to form a multifield key, and in such cases, the X-axis always shows values from the rightmost field making up the multifield key.

Remember, key fields have an asterisk (*) suffix, when the table structure is viewed. To view a table structure, press **F10/T/I/S** to select Structure.

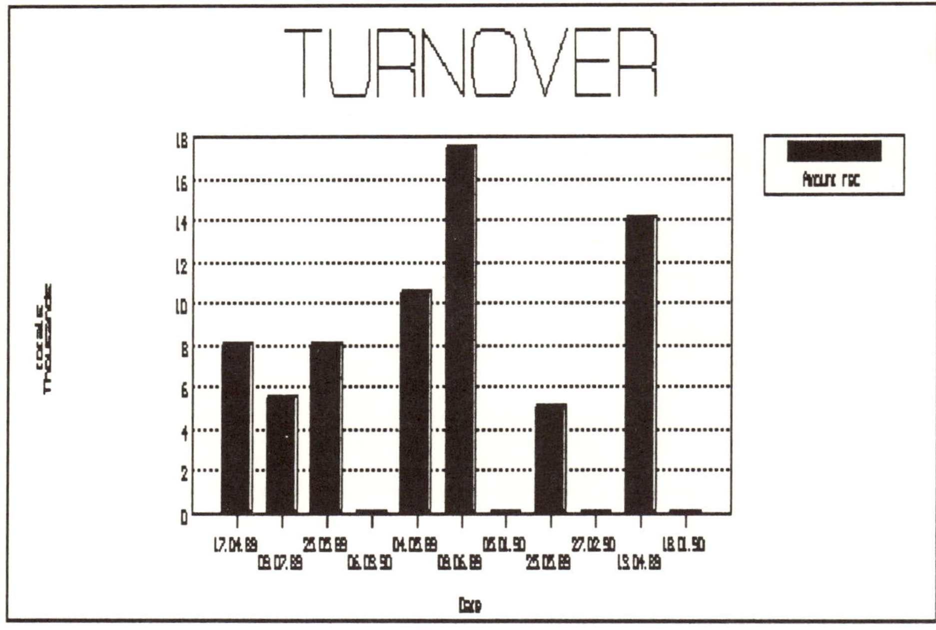

Figure 6.19: Bar graph

6.10.1 Producing Graphs by Querying

In Chapter 8, you will discover all sorts of ways in which graphs can be used. Until then, to give one example, suppose it were necessary to produce a graph where company names are listed as X-axis categories.

Bearing in mind the problem of keyed tables to produce graphs, it would not be unreasonable to assume that the table must be restructured (using Modify) in order to change what appears on the X-axis.

Unfortunately, restructuring at this stage may corrupt our report (ie invoice) – restructuring sometimes causes the elimination of modified fields from forms and reports.

In view of this, it is better to query the table, and then generate a graph from the Answer table – querying, you will soon discover, is a frequent prelude to generating a graph.

For example, by querying the Turnover table shown in Figure 6.20, the resultant Answer table can be used to produce the graph illustrated in Figure 6.21, where Companies form X-axis categories.

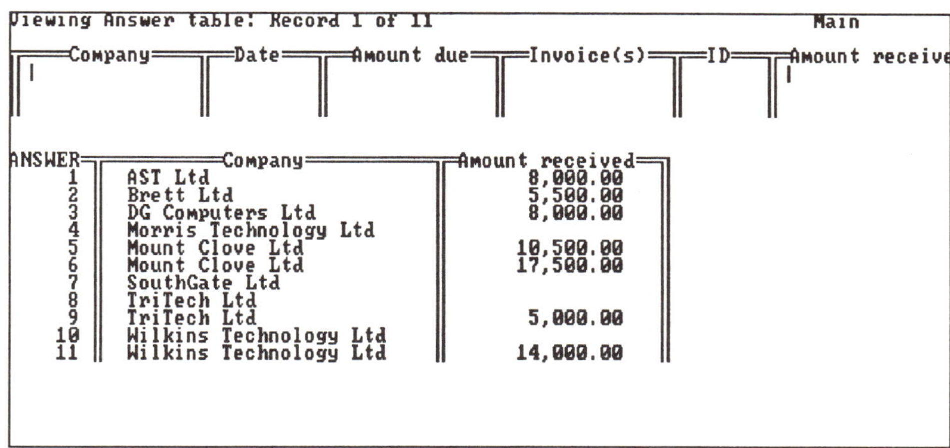

Viewing Answer table: Record 1 of 11 Main

Company	Date	Amount due	Invoice(s)	ID	Amount receive

ANSWER	Company	Amount received
1	AST Ltd	8,000.00
2	Brett Ltd	5,500.00
3	DG Computers Ltd	8,000.00
4	Morris Technology Ltd	
5	Mount Clove Ltd	10,500.00
6	Mount Clove Ltd	17,500.00
7	SouthGate Ltd	
8	TriTech Ltd	
9	TriTech Ltd	5,000.00
10	Wilkins Technology Ltd	
11	Wilkins Technology Ltd	14,000.00

Figure 6.20: Query to produce Company and Amount received fields

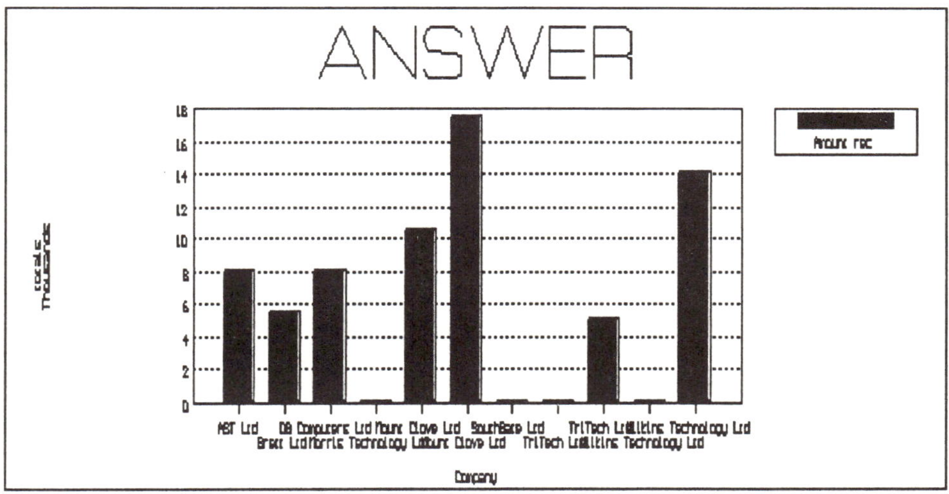

Figure 6.21: Bar graph generated from resultant Answer table

Notice that, by default, the Table name is used for the graph title. No doubt your labels clashed with each other. See Chapter 8 for ways of remedying this.

6.10.2 Customising Graph Settings

Among the many graph types available, which are fully discussed in Chapter 8, the bar graph is the simplest. To whet your appetite, however, Figure 6.22 shows a rotated bar graph.

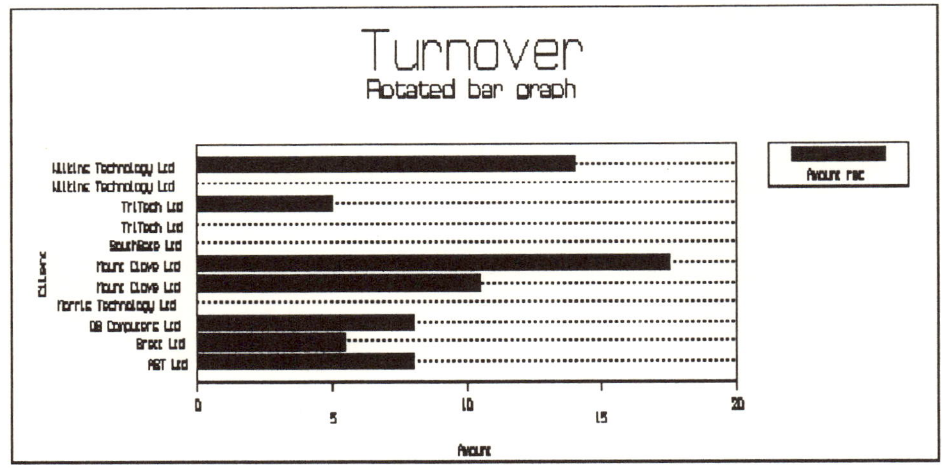

Figure 6.22: Rotated bar graph

The following stages show how to generate this graph from the Turnover table:

1. Press **F10/I/G** to select Graph.

2. Press **M** to choose Modify, giving the screen shown in Figure 6.23.

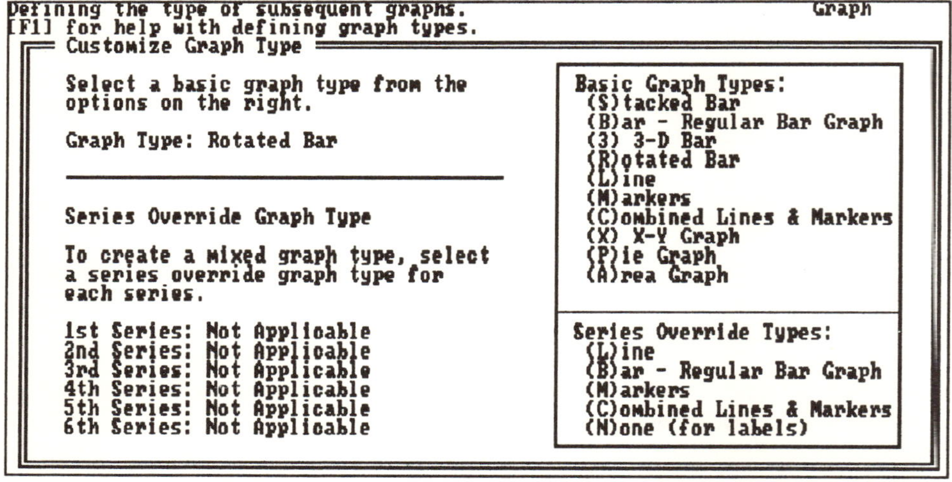

Figure 6.23: Creating a graph type

3. Press **R** to change the graph type to Rotated Bar.

4. Now labels for X and Y axes must be swapped: press **F10/O** to select Overall; press **T** to choose Titles.

5. Complete the screen as shown in Figure 6.24.

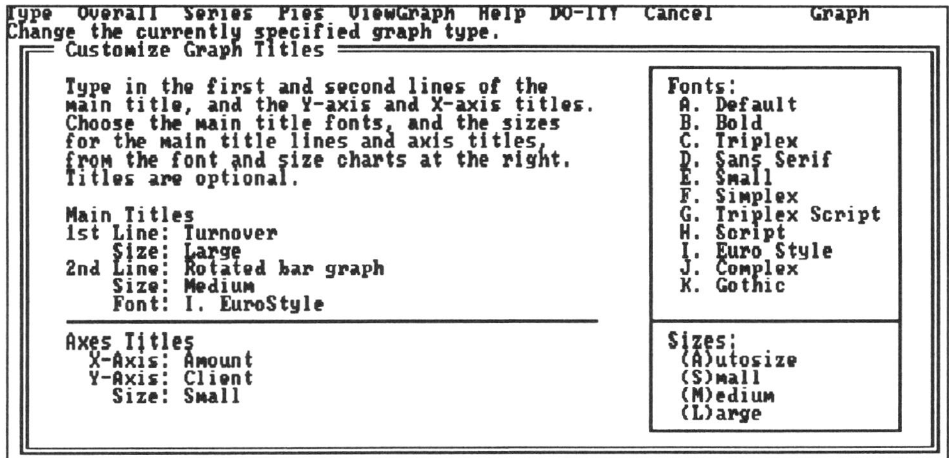

Figure 6.24: Graph titles

6. Press **F2** to record the settings.

Query the Turnover table as shown in Figure 6.20 (if you have cleared the Answer table that is), and with the cursor amid the Amount received field of the resultant Answer table, try invoking the rotated bar graph by pressing Ctrl-F7, giving the graph shown in Figure 6.22.

6.11 Scripts

Some of the standard Paradox tasks may have struck you as rather keyboard intensive. To combat this, keyboard operations can be recorded as scripts, and played back when required.

To offer an example script: it is not unusual to find yourself, at some stage, placing all tables in the workspace. As such, it might be a good idea to create a script which will do this automatically.

Such a script can be achieved as follows:

1. Press **S** to select Scripts from the main menu.

2. Press **B** to choose BeginRecord.

3. Enter **view** in response to Script:

Every key you press from here on will be recorded in the script.

4. Press **F10/V** followed by **<Enter>**, and select the Employee table.

5. Press **F10/V** followed by **<Enter>** once again, and select the Turnover table.

6. Repeat step **5**, selecting all tables in turn.

7. Finally, press **F10/S/E** to choose End-Record.

To play the script:

8. Press **F10/S/P** to select Play.

9. Press **<Enter>** and select View.

As this script is executed each time Paradox is loaded, it is advantageous to play it while loading Paradox. This can be achieved by entering **paradox3 view** from Dos. You can run any script from startup by simply including it as a suffix.

6.11.1 Query Scripts

Query scripts are similar in operation to ordinary scripts; they can be used to record and play queries. They are recorded using QuerySave, which simply saves all query forms in the workspace.

The following stages illustrate how to use QuerySave:

1. Establish the query shown in Figure 6.20.

2. Press **F10/S/Q** to select QuerySave.

3. Enter **graph** in response to, Query script name:

4. The graph query script can be played in the normal manner, see Section 6.11.

When a query script is played, query forms are merely written to the workspace - you have to press **F2** to carry out the query.

6.11.2 Queries in Normal Scripts

Queries and other keyboard operations can be combined using ScriptRecord in the normal manner. This is essential for situations such as that discussed in Subsection 6.10.1. For example, to automate the process of producing such a graph, the following keyboard and query operations must be combined:

- Query the Turnover table to produce an answer table containing the Company and Amounts received fields
- Rename the answer table Income
- Produce a graph using the Income table.

Focusing on this method of automatically generating a graph, the following steps show how to create such a script:

1. Because this script will mean constantly overwriting a table, it is necessary to create the table which will be overwritten. So, press **F10/C** and enter **income**, create one dummy field and press **F2**.

2. Press **S/B** to select BeginRecord.

3. Enter **income** in response to Script:

4. Enter **A** and select the Turnover table.

5. Press **F6** in both the Company field and the Amount received field. Then press **F2** to implement the query.

6. Press **F10/T/R** to select Rename. Press **T** to indicate you want to rename a table.

7. Press **<Enter>** and select the Answer table.

8. Enter **income** to rename the Answer table.

9. Press **R** to replace the existing income table.

10. Position the cursor in the Amount received field and press **Ctrl-F7**.

11. Finally, to end the script recording, press **Esc/F10/S/E** to select End-Record.

6.11.3 Instant Script Recordings

A simpler and less permanent method of playing back sequences of keystrokes is Instant Script Record. An instant script is begun and terminated by pressing **Alt-F3**. The script can then be played by pressing **Alt-F4**.

By default, instant scripts are called Instant – no prizes for guessing that! As just one instant script can be recorded, it is worth reserving for your most frequently used series of keystrokes.

An interesting application of instant script is for the selection of named scripts. For example, the following simple steps show how to create this prelude:

1. Press **Alt-F3** to begin the recording.

2. Press **F10/S/P** and press **<Enter>**.

3. Press **Alt-F3**, once again, to complete the instant script recording.

6.12 Data Security and LANs

LANs (or Local Area Networks), which provide a mutli-user environment so as to allow a number of users access to applications, are nowadays common. Not only has the proliferation of LANs been driven by their obvious advantages but also by diminishing costs.

LANs can lead to considerable savings in hardware costs. Only the host computer need be fast and comprise an appropriate amount of storage space. Users sharing the system can use simpler machines, often without hard disks, in the form of workstations. Workstations have now come to mean an almost stripped desktop computer, which might not have any magnetic storage capability at all.

It is not all good news, however, as LANs can sometimes make a computer system a little too open, with users able to access virtually any information – few systems analysts/designers take adequate security precautions. I would go so far as to say that, currently, industry and commerce, the civil service and local authorities are in an absolute mess when it comes to maintaining confidentiality of information.

Of course, such problems are not confined to LANs. Protecting information on a standalone PC used by a number of users is equally important.

Beginning with a simple method of protecting tables using Paradox, suppose you wanted to protect the Employee table by assigning a password to it. This can be achieved as follows:

1. Press **F10/T/M/P** to select Protect.

2. Press **P** to choose Password.

3. Press **T** to select Table.

4. Press **<Enter>** and select the Employee table.

5. Enter a password twice. Press **F2** to record the password.

Don't forget to jot down your passwords and keep them in a safe place.

Now, each time you want to view or edit the Employee table it will be necessary to enter the chosen password. Password protected tables are encrypted to an extent that they cannot be viewed from Dos. To remove a password from a table, follow the above steps, but type the password at stage 5 and press **<Enter>** twice.

Incidentally, you can assign a password to a script merely by pressing **S** at stage 3.

6.12.1 Auxiliary Passwords

Before pressing **F2** in stage 5 of the previous section, you will have noticed the screen shown in Figure 6.25. This permits the creation of auxiliary passwords.

```
Defining auxiliary password 1 of Turnbool table                    Password
[F1] for help with setting password options.  [F7] for table view

Auxiliary password:  alpha                                             Page 1

 Table Rights  ReadOnly                    Family Rights  FVRS◄

 Enter one  | Rights conferred             Enter all that apply, ◄┘ for none

 All        | all operations               (F)orm      | change forms
 InsDel     | change contents              (V)alCheck  | change validity checks
 Entry      | data entry and updates       (R)eport    | change reports
 Update     | update nonkey fields         (S)ettings  | change image settings
 ReadOnly   | no modifications

 Field Rights Enter ReadOnly or None for each field or leave blank for All.

Company
Amount due
Date
Amount received
Date received
Invoices sent
```

Figure 6.25: Auxiliary passwords

These provide a means of grading a user's access to information. For example, it is possible to limit users to viewing information only.

To create an auxiliary password which provides this limited access, first repeat the stages in Section 6.12 until the screen shown in Figure 6.25 is encountered – do not press **F2**, however. Complete the form as shown in Figure 6.25. Finally press **F2**.

Here on, the auxiliary password, alpha, will permit users merely to view information. It should be added that, there is no need to constantly enter passwords, they only need to be entered once during a Paradox session.

7

Asking Questions – Query By Example

This chapter escorts you through the various ways in which Query by Example (QBE) can help with interrogating and manipulating data. Here, you will find that QBE is the mainstay of information management using Paradox. You will discover how QBE can help in objective decision making, rather than that made based upon 'gut feelings' (which some decision makers refuse to give up).

You have already seen how QBE can help when building tables (in Chapter 5) and how it can be used to graph selected fields (in Chapter 6). By first recapping many of the previously discussed points, you will then move onto multi-table queries, sets, groups and calculations.

Paradox is reasonably intelligent when it comes to querying. It doesn't need to be given a series of instructions; you fill in a query form, or number of query forms, and Paradox does the rest.

Concise information about QBE can be found in Table 7.2 and the Appendix.

7.1 Decision Making

The assumtion that information management is simply a matter of data storage and retrieval becomes conspicuously false when trying to interpret information. Often, underlying trends are not manifestly obvious. It is a bit like climatic changes in the weather, records and your senses tell you that it is changing, but you do not know why. Scientists and erudite individuals will theorise, and people will believe whatever is on offer, as people do. But until solid scientific research is carried out, based upon scientific and empirical data, little is achieved; relating, analysing and querying scientific/empirical data is the only sure method of achieving an explanation about any such phenomenon – not that global warming is being denied!

Just as scientists, futurologists, and the unashamed sensationalists, of which there is an inexhaustible supply, sometimes chance their arms on one theory or another, decision makers often rely on 'gut feelings'. I know that some, dare I say, older business men pride themselves on their ability to make such subjective decisions. Perhaps there is a pioneering spirit which refuses to lie down and die; speculators dug for gold and drilled for oil where that indefinable sense told them to; and discoverers simply sailed into unchartered waters.

Borne out by the failure of the Sinclair C5, subjective decision making remains an inescapable fact of life. In the City, speculators subjectively decide to buy or sell stocks and shares based upon little or no information. Many regard this behaviour both frightening and irresponsible. Frightening, in that the money markets are as unpredictable as a wild horse and, irresponsible, in that the future of plcs and British industry in general is governed by such speculation.

If subjective decision making has a place, the most legitimate example stems from market research. What do you do when researching a market? You basically pinpoint potential customers that are likely to buy a forthcoming product. All right so far. Now for the ubiquitous question, would you the customer want to buy such an item at such a price?

When it comes to a particularly innovative product, problems are encountered in that people genuinely do not know what they want. Take the music industry, for instance, hit records are so outlandish, often, they are initially considered silly. The film industry is equally unpredictable. Few would answer yes to: would you like to see a film about a creature from another planet, which is a cross between a reptile and a teddy bear, come to earth and befriend some children? Yet such a film, ET, broke all box office records.

Seemingly, market research is often plagued by the ultimate imponderable: is it viable to fill that hole in the market?

Moving away from such abstraction, Paradox cannot make objective decisions for you, but using QBE it is possible to ask pertinent questions which will certainly help. Furthermore, the 'What-if' concept of altering a few data items to see what results has to be encouraged.

7.2 What-if with QBE

There are so many areas in which QBE can help, it is difficult to know where to begin when cataloguing its uses. One use was illustrated in Chapter 6 where is was necessary to generate a graph using selected fields. There are, of course, many instances where it is necessary to pluck data from tables using QBE. Sometimes, it is even necessary to query Answer tables. Such iterative querying as it were, finds application in many What-if scenarios.

Playing What-if need not be confined to using spreadsheets such as Lotus 1-2-3, Quattro Pro, and the many others. It is just as at home using Paradox.

To illustrate one hypothetical What-if situation, suppose there were a fixed budget to send (a limited number of) letters to clients. Sensibly, the letter would be sent to those clients that have made the highest purchases. To do this, you might query data so as to list only those clients with orders greater than £1,000. From the number of records in the Answer table, it would then be possible to see whether not the budget is overspent.

Assuming the budget does not cover it, the Answer table can be queried to list clients that have made orders of at least £1,500. Increasing the order value in gradual increments would help optimise the budget.

7.3 How to Query Information

To a great extent, using QBE is an intuitive process, guiding the user through the intricacies of what usually requires a computer language. The whole QBE concept is based upon the user filling in query forms which reflect what is required.

The following hands-on session shows how to query a table.

7.3.1 Hands-on Session

1. With Access the working directory, press **F10/A** to select Ask.

2. Press **<Enter>** and choose the Work table.

3. The query form, which mirrors the structure of the Work table, shown in Figure 7.1 will appear.

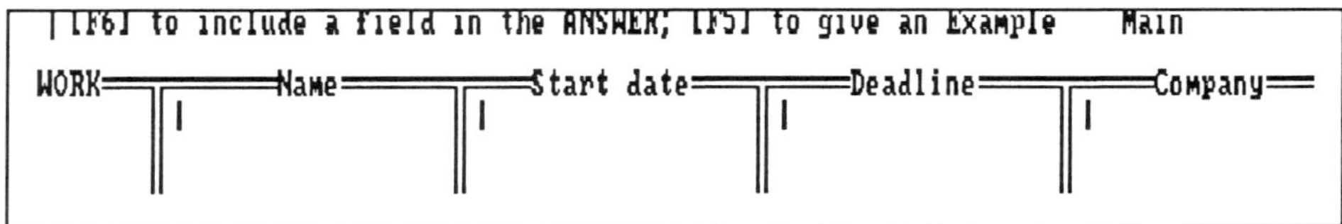

Figure 7.1: Query form (Work table)

4. Next, it is necessary to fill in the form so as to tell Paradox which fields should be included in the Answer table. Type the query expression shown, by pressing **F6** (check mark) in the appropriate columns.

5. Press **F2** to perform the query.

7.4 Commonly Used Operators

After some practice, querying can be refined so as to ask literally anything about your data, ranging from listing field values, to performing calculations. However, before then it is necessary to run through some commonly used query statements.

7.4.1 Listing Fields

Fields can be listed by inserting check marks in appropriate columns of a query form. Check marks, established by pressing **F6**, list field values in ascending order. Even date fields will be arranged so that older entries are listed first.

To illustrate querying to list fields, press **F10/A** to select Ask, press **<Enter>** and select the Employee table; press **F6** in both the NI Number field and the Department field; then press **F2** to produce the Answer table shown in Figure 7.2.

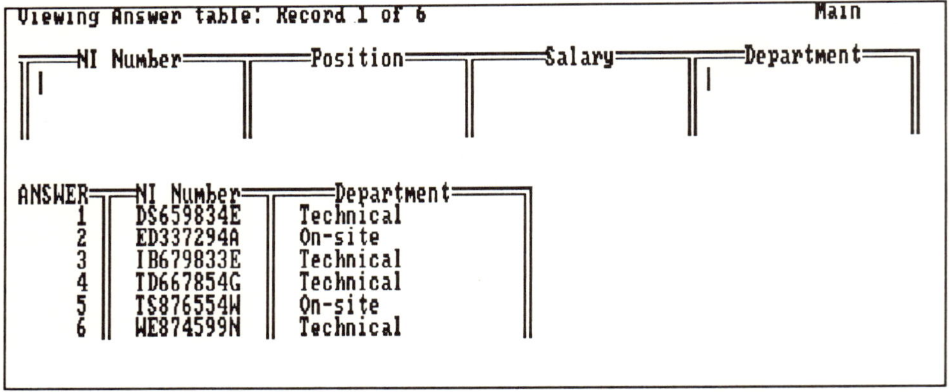

Figure 7.2: Answer table

As you will know by now, Answer tables are temporary. To store an Answer table, it must be renamed using Tools, as discussed in Chapter 5.

7.4.2 Sorting Fields in the Answer Table

By default, the order in which fields appear in the Answer table depends upon the order in which columns are arranged in the query form. However, if you press **Ctrl-R** to rotate columns and generally rearrange the sequence of fields in the query form, the Answer table will be unaffected.

Making the field order of the Answer table consistent with that of the query form, means running the Paradox Custom Configuration Program and selecting **D**efaults/**Q**ueryOrder/**I**mageOrder, as follows:

1. The Paradox Custom Configuration Program, or CCP, is automatically copied to the Paradox3 directory of your hard disk during installation. So, naturally, the working directory must be Paradox3 before the CCP can be run. The easiest way to run the CCP is from within Paradox itself; press **S** to choose Scripts from the main menu; press **P** to select Play; press **<Enter>** and choose Custom. Press **y** or **n** to indicate whether or not a monochrome monitor is being used.

To run the CCP from Dos simply type paradox3 custom in the paradox3 directory.

2. Press **D** to select Defaults.

3. Press **<Enter>** to select Defaults once again.

4. Press **Q** to choose QueryOrder.

5. Press **I** to select ImageOrder.

6. Press **R** to return to the main menu.

7. Press **D** to invoke Do-It!

8. Invoke Do-It! once again, by highlighting it and pressing **<Enter>**.

9. Press **H** to write the configuration file to your hard disk, if you are not using a network that is.

Configuring Paradox so as to make Answer tables compatible with query forms, gives control over the resultant sort order of a query. Columns in the Query form can be rotated and arranged so as to produce the sort order required.

7.4.3 Listing All Field Values

Including a check mark, by pressing **F6** in the appropriate field, results in a list of field values ignoring duplications. To list all field values use is made of Check Plus (**Alt-F6**). Try using this with the Turnover table. It will be noticed that Check Plus does not cause field values to be sorted in the Answer table.

7.4.4 Changing Field Names

Check Plus (**Alt-F6**) can also be used to change field names. Using it in this capacity requires the accompaniment of the Special Operator As, which indicates that a new name for the field follows.

The following steps illustrate the process of changing field names:

(Note that, here, the Access directory is used.)

1. Press **A** to select Ask from the main menu.

2. Press **<Enter>** and select the Employee table.

3. In the Name field, press **Alt-F6** to include a Check Plus.

4. Press **<Space>** and type **as**, the Special Operator.

5. Press **<Space>** once again, and type a new field name, such as Employee, for example.

6. Press **F2** to produce the answer table shown in Figure 7.3.

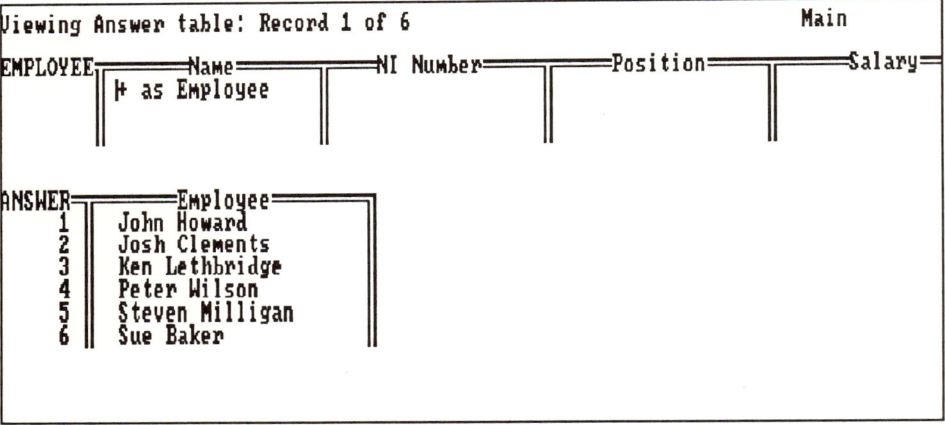

Figure 7.3: Using the As operator

7.4.5 Sorting Field Values

Records in an Answer table are sorted according to field values from left to right (see Subsection 7.4.2). For example, if more than one check mark was included, records in the Answer table would be sorted according to the leftmost fields in the query statement.

7.5 Pinpointing Records by Querying

You have already discovered how the Zoom feature is used to find particular field values. Querying can be used in a similar capacity to locate and extract certain field values. This can help when creating graphs and generally manipulating data.

The simplest method of selecting records is to simply include the field value you require directly after the check mark. For example, to list the name John Howard, simply include it in the query statement as shown in Figure 7.4:

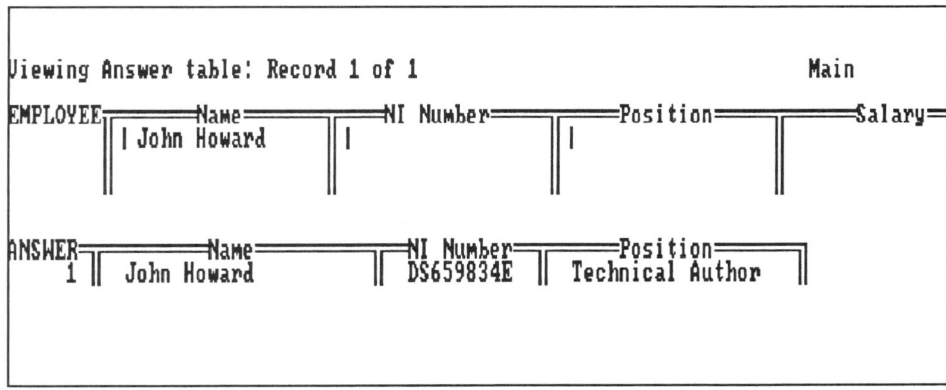

Figure 7.4: Query form (to locate John Howard value)

If the check mark is not inserted prior to the selection criteria, that field will not be listed. It will, nevertheless, remain active in influencing the overall query statement.

In many instances, the user is uncertain as to which field value should be listed in an Answer table. In such circumstances, a more general approach is required, which loosely relates the stated selection criteria to field values. There are two methods by which this approach can be achieved.

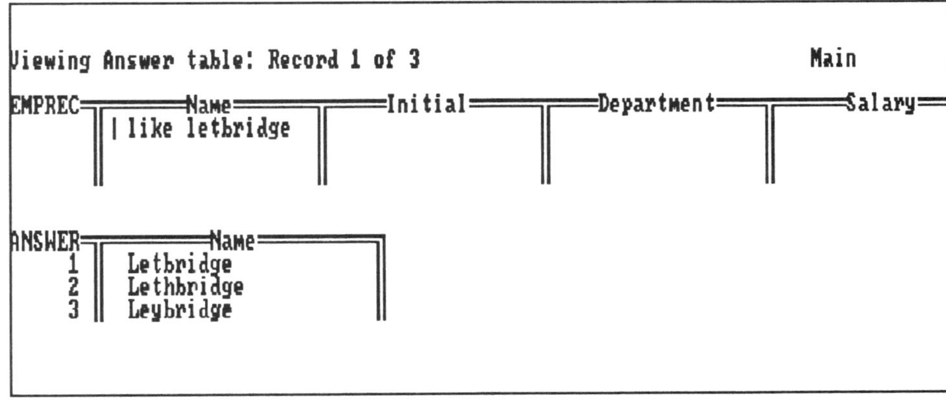

Figure 7.5: The Like operator

The first and most obvious of these involves using the Like operator. For example, supposing you are looking for the name, Lethbridge, but you are uncertain of its spelling or indeed the name: was it Leybridge, Letbridge, or something similar? By including the like operator, as shown in Figure 7.5, all approximations of that name will be listed.

The Like operator performs a similar duty to wild cards. These can be included in criteria, to masquerade as single characters or a series of characters. The @ wild card operator can be substituted for a single character, while .. can be substituted for any stream of characters, including spaces.

Suppose it were necessary to list all names beginning with H and ending with S. This could be achieved by including the condition, H..S, as shown Figure 7.6. Notice that this results in all names beginning with H and ending in S, irrespective of their length.

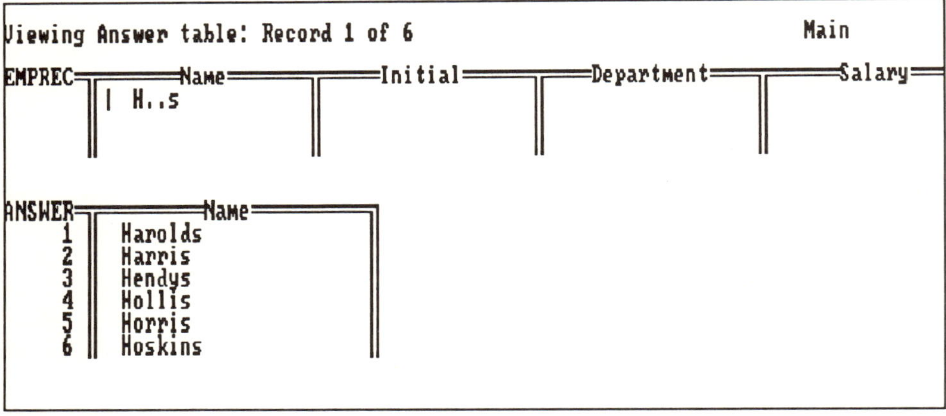

Figure 7.6: Wild cards

Wild cards can dictate various other conditions. For example, D@@@@@s will list names of seven characters in length, beginning with D and ending with s. Try using various combinations of wild cards.

7.5.1 The Not Operator

Just as listed field values must conform to a condition, field values can be listed that do not conform to a condition. The Not operator naturally performs such a function. To illustrate its use, consider the Client table in the previous chapter, and in particular the ID Number field. Figure 7.8 shows a situation where all except the client with the ID Number, 103, are included in the Answer table.

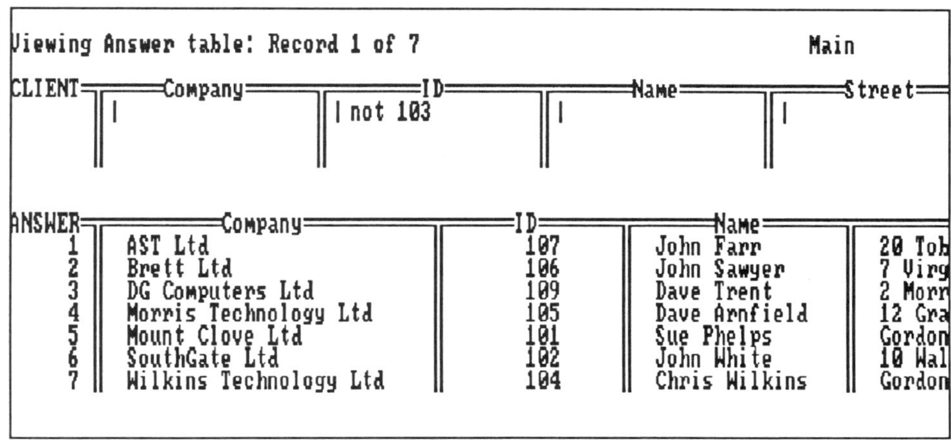

Viewing Answer table: Record 1 of 7 Main

CLIENT | Company | ID: not 103 | Name | Street

ANSWER	Company	ID	Name	Street
1	AST Ltd	107	John Farr	20 Tob
2	Brett Ltd	106	John Sawyer	7 Virg
3	DG Computers Ltd	109	Dave Trent	2 Morr
4	Morris Technology Ltd	105	Dave Arnfield	12 Gra
5	Mount Clove Ltd	101	Sue Phelps	Gordon
6	SouthGate Ltd	102	John White	10 Wal
7	Wilkins Technology Ltd	104	Chris Wilkins	Gordon

Figure 7.7: The Not operator

The Not operator can be coupled with others, to form more complex conditions. For instance, Not can be used in conjunction with like, to form statements such as, not like Leybridge.

Not can also be used with wild card patterns. For example, not H@@@@@s. There are, of course, all sorts of other variations, some of which you might like to acquaint yourself with.

7.5.2 Blank Fields

In some instances, and for whatever reason, it might be necessary to blank out a certain field. Confidentiality is one reason for doing this; perhaps a report is required, but it is desirable to omit telephone numbers. Blank is a special operator which can be used to omit field values from the Answer table. There is no real need to illustrate this, suffice it to say that you simply include the word Blank in the field where corresponding field values are to be ignored in the Answer table.

7.5.3 The Or Operator

The Or operator is used to make either-or selections where values listed must comply with either one of two conditions. Multiple either-or conditions can also be accommodated where values must meet one of a number conditions, making possible statements such as, Thomas or Evans or James.

7.5.4 Two Conditions in the same Field

Producing an Answer table where field values are selected according to two conditions is a practical requirement. For instance, if it were necessary to list records between certain dates, two conditions have to be established. Think back to the Turnover table in the previous chapter, and just suppose that you wanted to know what the turnover was between 22.05.89 and the 5.07.89. The search condition for this particular question is written, >=22.05.89, <=5.07.89, which translated into English means:

If the date is greater-than or equal-to 22.05.89 and less-than or equal-to 5.07.89, then it should be included in the Answer table. Figure 7.8 shows this particular query.

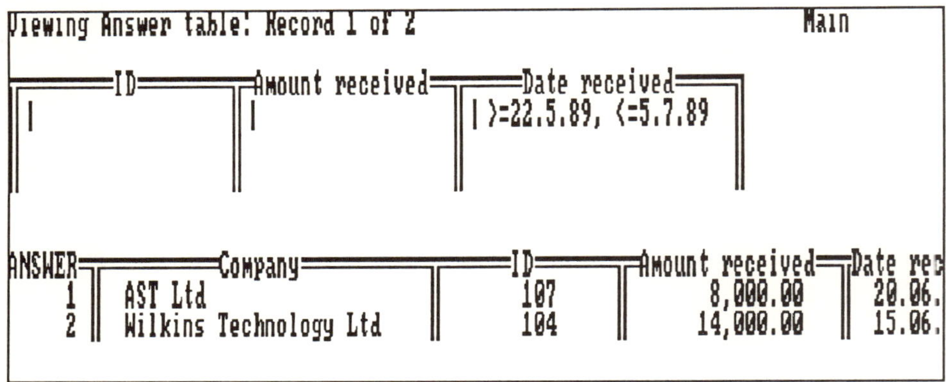

Figure 7.8: Two conditions in same field

Note, the comma acts as a logical And operator.

7.5.5 Today's Date

The Today operator is naturally used where conditions include today's date. In its simplest form it can be used to select records containing a current date. More useful, it can be harnessed to select records from a previous date to the current date with a little help from the And operator.

Here are a few simple examples:

<=Today	select records up until the present date
>=03.06.90, <=Today	select records from 3.6.90 to present date
Today	select records containing current date.

7.6 Notes on Punctuation and Syntax

Though unusual, field values may include punctuation, in which case the condition must be enclosed using double quotation marks. Selecting field values which match *Gordon, Pine,* means including a condition of the form, "*Gordon, Pine*".

Just as punctuation has to be catered for, date formats also have to be observed. Where the date format is shown as, 04.10.90, so should search conditions follow the same format. There is no need to include preceding zeros when entering dates; 2.5.89 is as acceptable as 02.05.89.

Incidentally, on screen, date formats can be changed by first viewing the appropriate table and then pressing **F10/I/F** to select Format; move the cursor to the appropriate date column and press **<Enter>**; then choose the format required. To make such screen settings permanent, press **F10/I/K** to choose KeepSet – column sizes can also be retained using KeepSet.

To create a default date format, ie one which will appear each time Paradox is loaded and include all tables, use is made of the Paradox Custom Configuration Program. The following stages show how the CCP can be used to set a date format.

1. Run the CCP as described in Subsection 7.4.2.

2. Press **S** to select Scripts from the main menu.

3. Press **P** to select Play.

4. Press **<Enter>** to list Scripts in the working directory.

5. Press **C** to run the Custom script (or CCP).

6. Press **y** or **n** to indicate whether or not you are using a monochrome monitor.

7. Press **I** to choose Int'l.

8. Press **D** to select DateFormat.

9. Choose date format required.

10. Press **R** to return to the main CCP menu.

11. Press **D** to invoke Do-It!

12. Highlight Do-It! and press **<Enter>**.

13. Press **H** to select Hard disk, if you are not using a network, that is.

Reload Paradox by entering **paradox3**.

7.7 Combining Fields

Uniting a number of fields can be helpful when creating reports, or, even to provide a more succinct representation of a table. Address fields are often singled out for this treatment. Figure 7.9 shows how to combine or concatenate fields using the Client table.

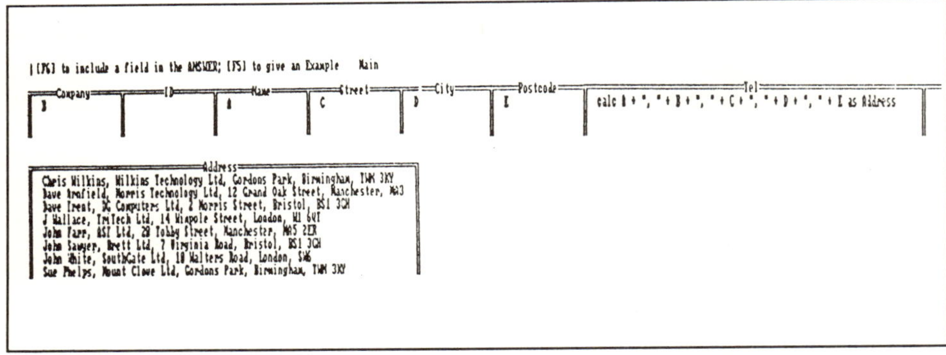

Figure 7.9: Concatenating or combining fields

7.8 Changing Field Values

QBE can be harnessed so as to emulate the search-and-replace feature commonly associated with word processors. The changeto operator affects queried tables directly, and should, therefore, be used with care – don't be silly and use this as an excuse not to use it!

There is a safety net, however, by way of a table called Changed which stores the original unaltered records. Therefore, if necessary, changed records in the table can be deleted and replaced by their former selves by adding the records of the Changed table to the table originally queried. The contents of one table can be added to another by pressing **F10/T/M/A** to select Add.

Consider for a moment, a situation where it was found that the name John Howells in a table should actually be John Howard. By first producing a query form for the table in question, you would enter, in the appropriate column, the following expression:

John Howells, changeto John Howard

Figure 7.10 shows how to use the changeto operator to replace the name John Howells with John Howard.

[F6] to include a field in the ANSWER; [F5] to give an Example Main ▼

WORK	Name	Start date	Deadline
	John Howells, changeto John Howard		

WORK	Name	Start date	Deadline	Company
1	John Howard	4.05.89	7.06.89	Mount Clove Ltd
2	John Howard	9.06.89	3.07.89	Mount Clove Ltd
3	John Howard	27.02.90	5.06.90	TriTech Ltd
4	Josh Clements	17.04.89	5.05.89	AST Ltd
5	Josh Clements	25.05.89	24.07.89	DG Computers Ltd
6	Josh Clements	5.01.90	2.03.90	SouthGate Ltd
7	Josh Clements	5.03.90	4.05.90	Morris Technolog
8	Ken Lethbridge	13.04.89	19.05.89	Wilkins Technolo
9	Ken Lethbridge	25.05.89	7.07.89	TriTech Ltd
10	Ken Lethbridge	10.07.89	25.08.89	Brett Ltd
11	Ken Lethbridge	18.01.90	10.04.90	Wilkins Technolo

CHANGED	Name	Start date	Deadline	Company
1	John Howells	4.05.89	7.06.89	Mount Clove Ltd
2	John Howells	9.06.89	3.07.89	Mount Clove Ltd

Figure 7.10: Changing field values

Note, you cannot use check marks in query statement that includes changeto(s).

Changeto can be stretched far beyond the simple search-and-replace concept. It can also be used in arithmetic operations to alter currency fields in a particularly precise manner. Speaking hypothetically, once again, consider the Employee table created in Chapter 6, where salaries have been increased by 9%. Consequently, it would be necessary to update the table so as to illustrate this increase.

To achieve this change, the Salary field must include the statement: **salary , changeto salary * 1.09** where *salary* is simply a variable to which all field values will be assigned consecutively. Also, it must be entered after pressing **F5** (Example), indicated by the fact that it is highlighted on screen. Additionally, you must include a space between examples and other elements.

Figure 7.11 overleaf shows this statement applied to the Employee table.

To return the table to its former condition, all we have to do is rename the Changed table, because in this instance all records were altered. So, press **F10/T/R** to select Rename; press **<Enter>** twice and select the Changed table; then, enter **employee** and press **R** to replace the old Employee table.

Changeto can be taken to quite extraordinary limits. For example, it is possible to include query statements that can be spread over more than one line of the query form. This, you will understand, makes them easier to enter, and also read.

```
Viewing Changed table: Record 1 of 6                                  Main

  Position          Salary                                 Department
                    salary, changeto salary * 1.09

  Name                 NI Number    Position                   Salary
  John Howard          DS659834E    Technical Author        16,350.00
  Josh Clements        ED337294A    Technical Author        16,350.00
  Ken Lethbridge       TS876554W    Technical Author        16,350.00
  Peter Wilson         TD667854G    Clerk                   13,080.00
  Steven Milligan      WE874599N    Clerical assistant      11,445.00
  Sue Baker            IB679833E    Clerical assistant      10,900.00

  Name                 NI Number    Position                   Salary
  John Howard          DS659834E    Technical Author        17,821.50
  Josh Clements        ED337294A    Technical Author        17,821.50
  Ken Lethbridge       TS876554W    Technical Author        17,821.50
  Peter Wilson         TD667854G    Clerk                   14,257.20
  Steven Milligan      WE874599N    Clerical assistant      12,475.05
  Sue Baker            IB679833E    Clerical assistant      11,881.00
```

Figure 7.11: Increasing Salaries by 9% (using changeto)

For example, suppose increases in Salary were varied. Employees on less than £14,000 receive an increase of 7% while employees earning more than that are granted an increase of 10% – sounds a bit unfair, doesn't it!

```
Viewing Changed table: Record 1 of 6                                  Main

  Position          Salary                                   Department
                    <14000, wages, changeto wages * 1.07
                    >14000, salary, changeto salary * 1.1

  NI Number    Position                  Salary        Department
  DS659834E    Technical Author       16,500.00        Technical
  ED337294A    Technical Author       16,500.00        On-site
  TS876554W    Technical Author       16,500.00        On-site
  TD667854G    Clerk                  15,889.50        Technical
  WE874599N    Clerical assistant     10,700.00        Technical
  IB679833E    Clerical assistant     10,700.00        Technical

CHANGED  Name               NI Number    Position                Salary
   1     John Howard        DS659834E    Technical Author        *********
   2     Josh Clements      ED337294A    Technical Author        *********
   3     Ken Lethbridge     TS876554W    Technical Author        *********
   4     Peter Wilson       TD667854G    Clerk                   *********
   5     Steven Milligan    WE874599N    Clerical assistant      *********
   6     Sue Baker          IB679833E    Clerical assistant      *********
```

Figure 7.12: Increasing salaries by varying amounts (using changeto)

The following expressions illustrate how this is achieved:

<14000, wages , changeto wages * 1.07

>14000, salary , changeto salary * 1.1

Figure 7.12 shows how these expressions are combined to perform the query.

Once again, as all records are altered, restoring these to their original values is simply a matter of renaming the Changed table.

7.9 Deleting Values

Deleting values is more commonly associated with editing. For example, backspace, Ctrl-Backspace and Del, are perfectly adequate when used in moderation. However, where a certain type of record becomes defunct and all such occurrences must be erased, deleting each one would take a considerable amount of time. The solution to this lies in using QBE to select and erase all records from a table.

Circumstances where a number of records must be deleted are, perhaps, more frequent than initially thought. To give one example, consider a table showing income, such as the Turnover table, where it is necessary to isolate records making up a new financial year. Naturally, to construct a table which contained only those records which showed income from 4 April, 1990, for instance, you could first copy the table and, then, delete the unwanted records. Figure 7.13 shows how the query form is filled in to delete records selected according to dates.

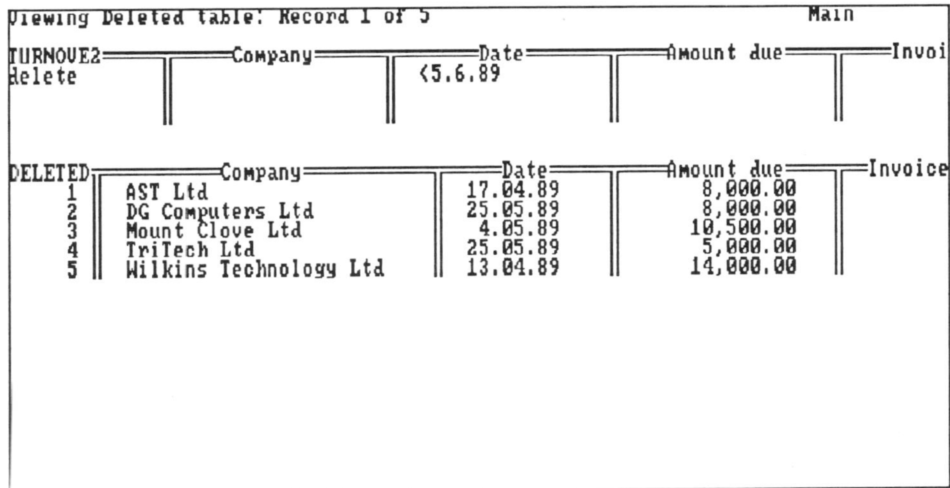

Figure 7.13: Deleting records

Notice that delete appears on the extreme left of the form and that it operates on complete records.

Similar to the Changed table produced when using changeto, the Deleted table shows all records removed. Deleted records can be reinstated by pressing **F10/T/M/A** in order to add records from the Deleted table to the queried table.

7.10 Calculations

Calculating new field values is possible using changeto. To some however, and particularly to the novice, altering field values directly may seem a little scary. Setting aside such fears, using changeto does have its limitations. For instance, check marks cannot be used, so, extracting particular field values to create a certain table is not possible.

To all intents and purposes, the calc operator is much more flexible as it can be integrated within normal query statements. Suppose it were necessary to show the overall effects of a 10% pay increase, as in the previous section, but to show both old and new salaries as well as the Name, NI and Salary fields. The following hands-on session shows how to do this using the calc operator.

7.10.1 Hands-on Session – using Calc

This session illustrates how to query the Employee table (created in Chapter 6) to show a 10% increase in salaries.

1. With Access the working directory, press **F10/A** to select Ask.

2. Press **<Enter>** and select the Employee table.

3. Press **F6** to include a check mark in the Name field.

4. Type the expressions shown in the Salary column in Figure 7.14.

5. Press **F2** to produce the Answer table.

Effects of the salary increase can now be examined.

7.10.2 Last words on Calc

When fully exploited, Calc becomes a useful operator. For instance, it can be used to calculate VAT, discounts, etc. It is particularly useful when playing What-if, to show effects of increases in services or products provided, increases in salaries or whatever. Coupled with graphs, such experimentation helps you to make informed, objective decisions.

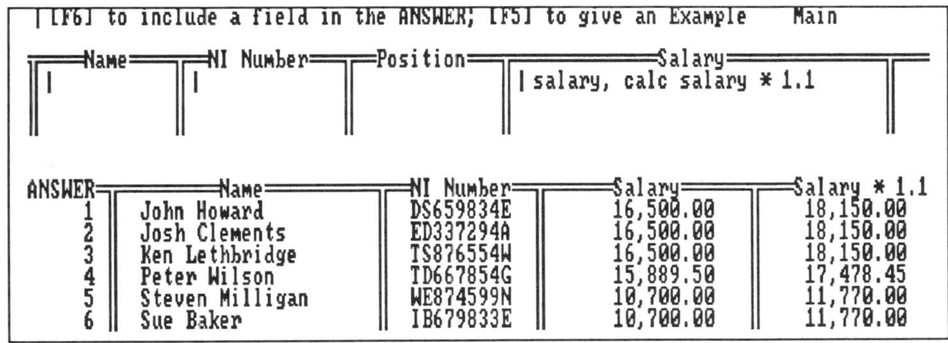

[F6] to include a field in the ANSWER; [F5] to give an Example			Main
Name	NI Number	Position	Salary
✓	✓		✓ salary, calc salary * 1.1

ANSWER	Name	NI Number	Salary	Salary * 1.1
1	John Howard	DS659834E	16,500.00	18,150.00
2	Josh Clements	ED337294A	16,500.00	18,150.00
3	Ken Lethbridge	TS876554W	16,500.00	18,150.00
4	Peter Wilson	TD667854G	15,889.50	17,478.45
5	Steven Milligan	WE874599N	10,700.00	11,770.00
6	Sue Baker	IB679833E	10,700.00	11,770.00

Figure 7.14: Using the calc operator

7.11 Insert Tables

Insert is used to add records from one table to another. It is more flexible than using Add (invoked by pressing **F10/T/M/A**) as tables of different structures can be added.

Take, for instance, a situation where you are working on the Client table created in Chapter 6, and you suddenly come across a similar table created with a different database, with additional client names. In such a circumstance, nine times out of ten, the imported table will be of a different format. Therefore, after importation using ExportImport, it is not possible to use Add to include the records.

To illustrate such a circumstance, take a look at the tables shown in Figure 7.15.

Editing Client table: Record 1 of 8 Edit

CLIENT	Company	ID	Name	
1	AST Ltd	107	John Farr	20 Tob
2	Brett Ltd	106	John Sawyer	7 Virg
3	DG Computers Ltd	109	Dave Trent	2 Morr
4	Morris Technology Ltd	105	Dave Arnfield	12 Gra
5	Mount Clove Ltd	101	Sue Phelps	Gordon
6	SouthGate Ltd	102	John White	10 Wal
7	TriTech Ltd	103	J Wallace	14 Wim
8	Wilkins Technology Ltd	104	Chris Wilkins	Gordon

CUSTOMER	Company	ID	First Name	Last Name
1	JSL Ltd	111	Jim	Cray
2	C scape Ltd	112	Alan	Mann
3	Band gap Ltd	113	Thor	Goldberg
4	Meiko Services Ltd	114	Gordon	Applebaum

Figure 7.15: Differing table formats

To convert the imported Customer table into a format suitable for addition to the Client table, obvious changes have to be made.

For example, the First Name and Second Name fields have to be united. Figure 7.16 shows how the Customer table is queried in order to add the Customer table to the Client table. Notice that, like delete, the insert operator appears on the left of the table.

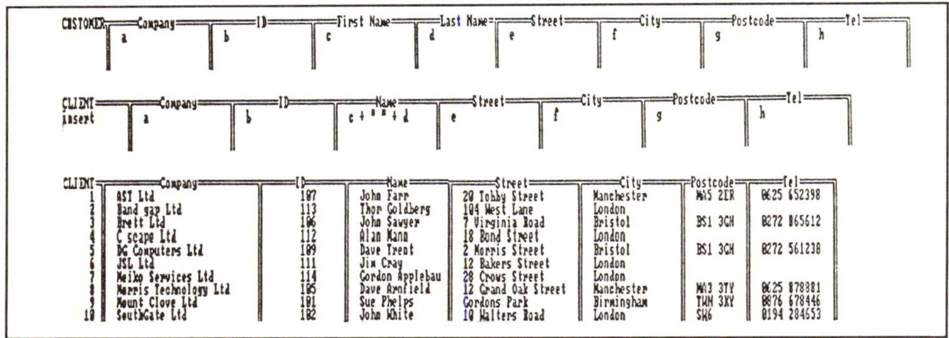

CUSTOMER	Company	ID	First Name	Last Name	Street	City	Postcode	Tel
	a	b	c	d	e	f	g	h

CLIENT	Company	ID	Name	Street	City	Postcode	Tel
insert	a	b	c + " " + d	e	f	g	h

CLIENT	Company	ID	Name	Street	City	Postcode	Tel
1	AST Ltd	107	John Farr	20 Tobby Street	Manchester	MA5 2ER	0625 652398
2	Band gap Ltd	113	Thor Goldberg	104 West Lane	London		
3	Brett Ltd	106	John Sawyer	7 Virginia Road	Bristol	BS1 3GH	0272 865612
4	C scape Ltd	112	Alan Mann	18 Bond Street	London		
5	DG Computers Ltd	109	Dave Trent	2 Morris Street	Bristol	BS1 3GH	0272 561238
6	JSL Ltd	111	Jim Cray	12 Bakers Street	London		
7	Meiko Services Ltd	114	Gordon Applebau	28 Crows Street	London		
8	Merris Technology Ltd	105	Dave Arnfield	12 Grand Oak Street	Manchester	MA3 3TY	0625 878881
9	Mount Clove Ltd	101	Sue Phelps	Gordons Park	Birmingham	TWN 3XY	0876 678446
10	SouthGate Ltd	102	John White	10 Walters Road	London	SW6	0194 284653

Figure 7.16: Using Insert

7.12 Find

Find, another operator which appears on the left of query forms, is, as its name suggests, used to find records. Essentially, it performs the same task as Zoom, invoked by pressing **Ctrl-Z.**

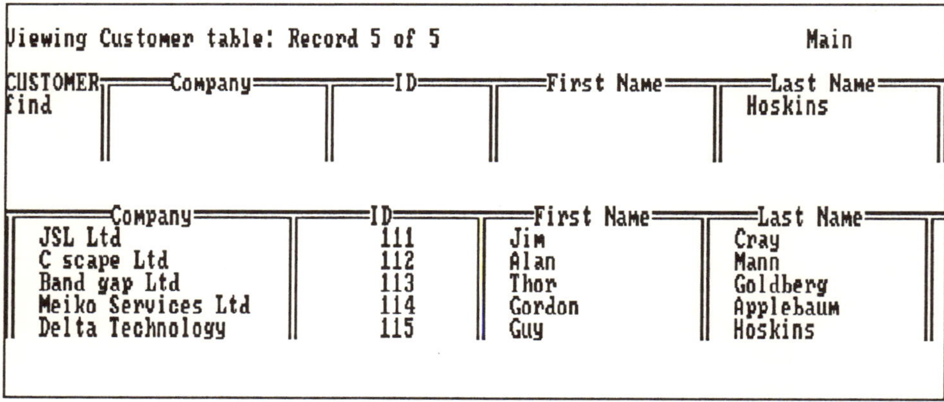

Viewing Customer table: Record 5 of 5 Main

CUSTOMER	Company	ID	First Name	Last Name
find				Hoskins

Company	ID	First Name	Last Name
JSL Ltd	111	Jim	Cray
C scape Ltd	112	Alan	Mann
Band gap Ltd	113	Thor	Goldberg
Meiko Services Ltd	114	Gordon	Applebaum
Delta Technology	115	Guy	Hoskins

Figure 7.17: Using Find

Using Find is fairly straightforward; you simply type find to the left of the query form, and then type the appropriate field value for which you are searching. Figure 7.17 shows an example where the name Hoskins is found.

7.13 Groups of Records

Querying can be extended to embody groups of records. Groups of records defined by a characteristic can be interrogated to find general trends. For example, the Turnover table could be queried to ascertain differences in spending between various clients. This kind of interrogation can help with decision making.

Querying groups of records requires the inclusion of Summary Operators shown in Table 7.1.

Operator	*Result*
average	produce average of values
count	total number of values
max	give highest value
min	give minimum value
sum	add all values

Table 7.1: Summary Operators

Of course, neither average nor sum can be used on alphanumeric fields. Also, sum cannot be used on date fields.

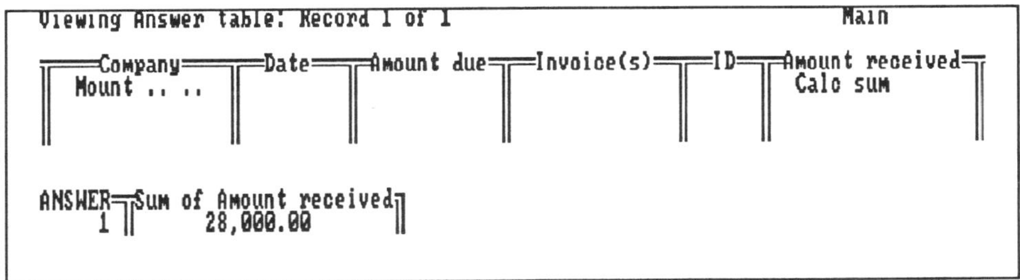

Figure 7.18: Calculating the sum of a group of values

To give a practical situation involving groups of records, consider a situation where, using the Turnover table (created in Chapter 6), you want to calculate the total amount received from Mount Clove Ltd.

Figure 7.18 shows exactly how such a query is tackled. Mount Clove Ltd has been entered in shorthand using wild card operators. With the group of records primed for selection using this common characteristic, the total amount received from this company is calculated by entering **calc sum** in the Amount received column.

Based upon the simple example shown, you have, no doubt thought of numerous ways in which such querying can help. Just remember the basic idea: specify a characteristic to unite a group of records, and then include expressions required. The following subsections cover some popular uses.

7.13.1 Calculating Sums of Groups

Turning, once again, to the Turnover table, suppose it were necessary to analyse total amounts received from each client – a common requirement when producing graphs. This involves including a check mark in the Company field, and the expression calc sum in the Amount received field. Figure 7.19 shows such a query.

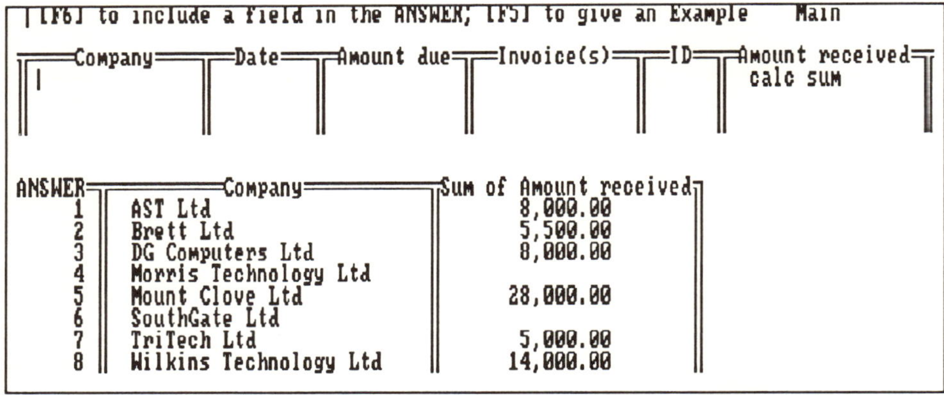

```
[F6] to include a field in the ANSWER; [F5] to give an Example     Main

Company    Date    Amount due    Invoice(s)    ID    Amount received
√                                                     calc sum

ANSWER  Company                    Sum of Amount received
   1    AST Ltd                         8,000.00
   2    Brett Ltd                       5,500.00
   3    DG Computers Ltd                8,000.00
   4    Morris Technology Ltd
   5    Mount Clove Ltd                28,000.00
   6    SouthGate Ltd
   7    TriTech Ltd                     5,000.00
   8    Wilkins Technology Ltd         14,000.00
```

Figure 7.19: Calculating sums of groups

The Answer table produced is ideal for generating a graph showing amounts received from each client. Position the cursor in the Amount received field of the Answer table and press **Ctrl-F7**.

7.13.2 Whole Group Calculations

When building tables of data which include numeric and currency field values, such as the Turnover table, it is all too easy to lose track of overall income and, more importantly, total expenditure. Monitoring such items is fundamental to running any business. It helps to produce profit and loss accounts, as well as to generate balance sheets. Figure 7.20 shows how turnover to the current date can be calculated, by including the simple expression, calc sum.

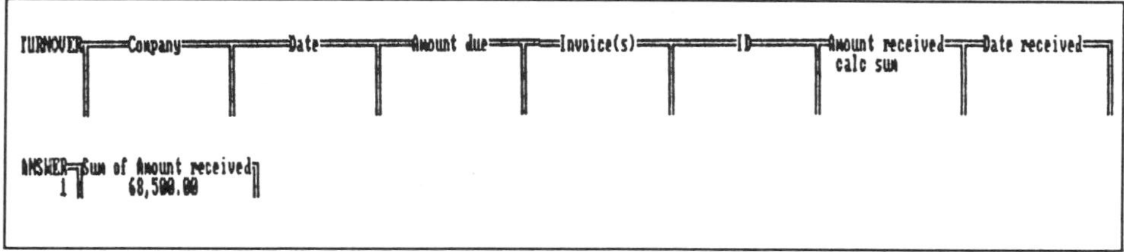

Figure 7.20: Calculating the sum of all field values

7.13.3 Calculating Sums in Renamed Fields

When creating graphs, by default, axes are labelled according to the field names. Therefore, changing a field name while querying is sometimes preferable. Figure 7.21 illustrates the use of the As operator to calculate sums and rename the field name in the Answer table:

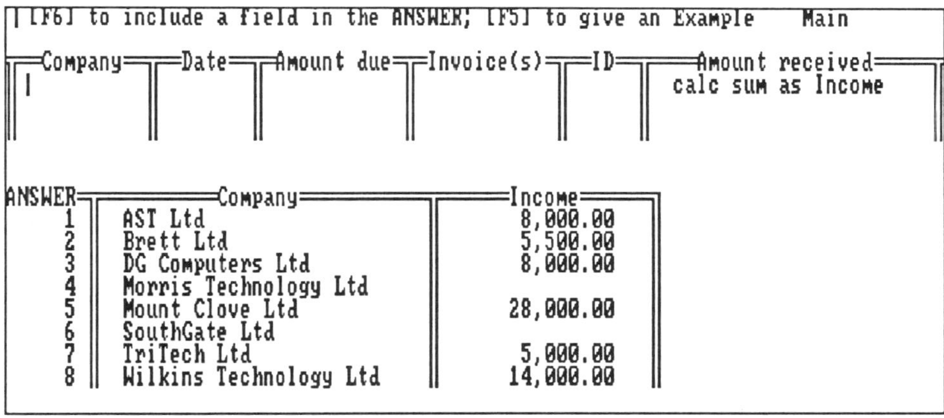

Figure 7.21: Calculating sums in renamed fields

7.14 Querying More Than One Table

So far, querying has been confined to single tables, giving you time to digest the general idea. QBE can be extended so as to ask questions about a number of tables.

Querying more than one table is a frequent requirement for the user that wants to exploit relational concepts. It can help when trying to generate a precise graph, to produce an additional table, and a whole host of other procedures.

The actual process is simple – all the operators and expressions discussed already are equally relevant. All you need remember is that tables must be appropriately linked by including a common example (entered by pressing **F5**).

Turning, once again, to the database solution developed in Chapter 6, consider the question: which London-based companies have purchased a single service costing £5,000 or more? To answer this question, both Client and Turnover tables have to be exploited – it is the only option as no single table contains enough information. Figure 7.22 shows how both tables can be linked to produce a single query.

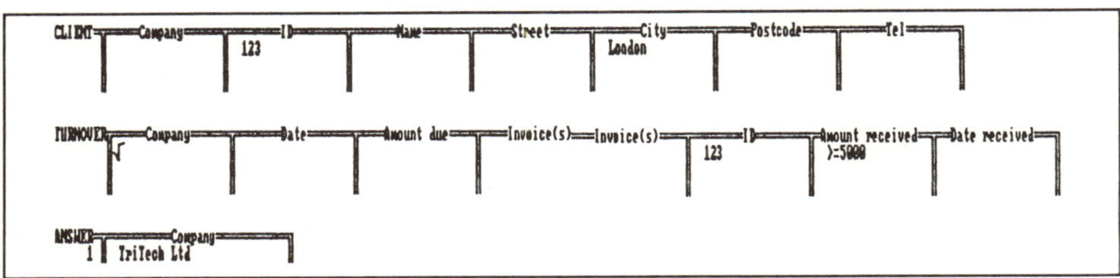

Figure 7.22: Querying two tables

The expression is a simple one; the check mark in the Company field causes selected fields to be listed in the Answer table; the example, 123, in both ID fields forms the vital link which jells the whole query together; London, in the City field confines the selection to London-based companies only; and >=5000 in the Amount received field ensures that only companies having purchased services of £5,000 or more are selected. Remember, 123 examples are entered after pressing F5.

To take things further consider a situation where the query just performed is developed. Instead of asking which London-based companies have purchased a single service costing £5,000 or more, the question becomes, what sort of service has been provided to companies purchasing services in excess of £5,000?

The answer to this slightly more complex question lies in three tables, ie the Work table which stores comments about projects, the Turnover table which holds all projects undertaken, and the Client table which indicates where clients are situated.

Breaking down the question further:

- ❑ The Client table is used to select London-based companies
- ❑ The Turnover table is used to narrow the selection to London-based companies that have purchased a single project costing £5,000 or more
- ❑ The Work table is called upon to provide comments for the services purchased.

Figure 7.23 shows how, exactly, the query is tackled.

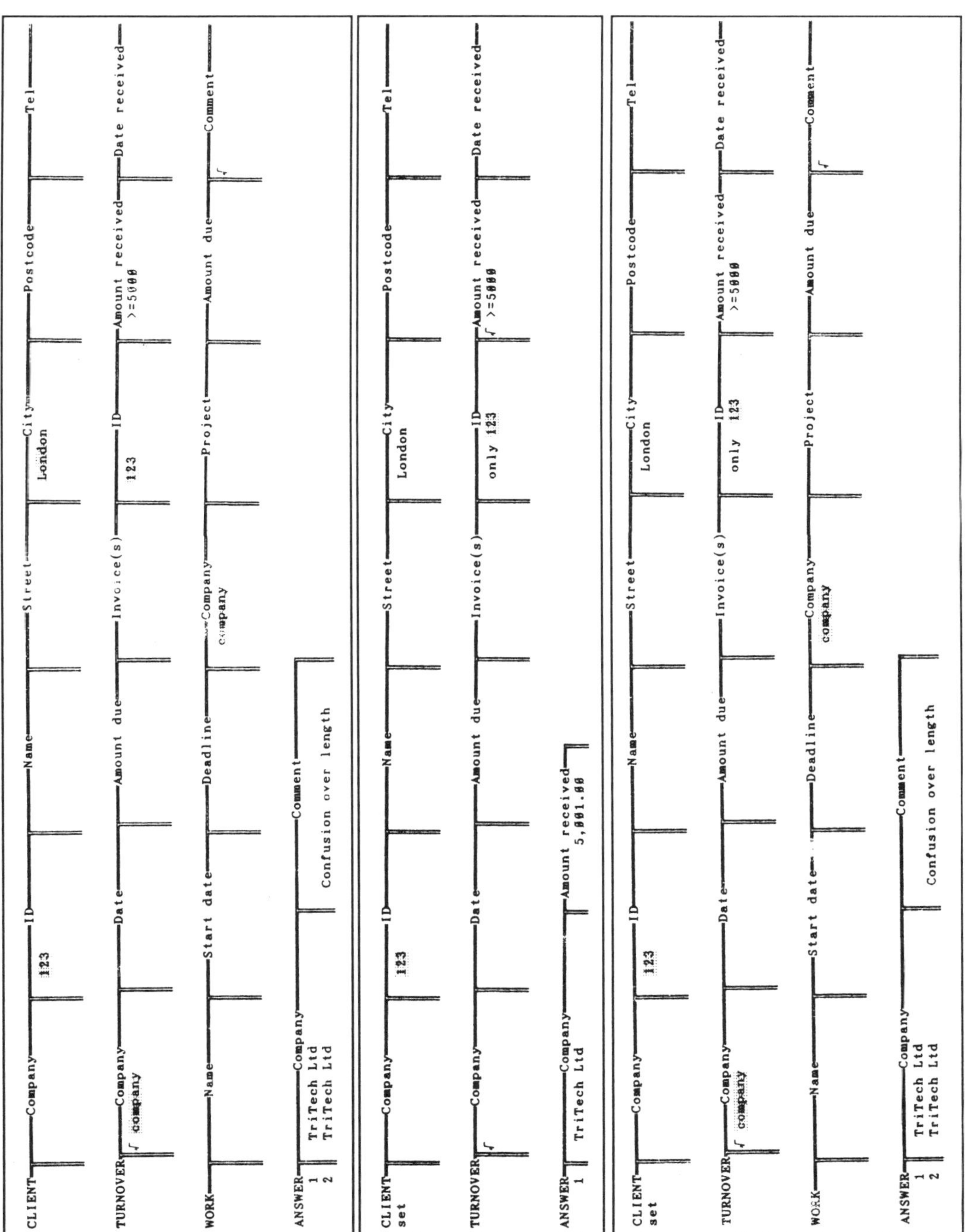

Figure 7.23: Querying three tables

Figure 7.24: Querying the Amount received

Figure 7.25: A set involving three tables

Notice how the tables are linked: 123 relates the Client and Turnover tables, while company binds Work and Turnover tables. Other than this minor difference, the process of querying three tables is markedly similar to querying two.

Remembering the simple procedures outlined here (and by referring to Table 7.2), it is possible to perform virtually any multi-table query.

7.15 Working with Sets of Records

QBE often involves 'nesting' queries, where an answer table may be queried several times to refine what you are looking for. Sometimes, however, a series of queries is best dealt with using **sets** of records. By first defining a **set** of records, it is possible to query the set as if it were a complete table, or group, of records. Not that a set is a group, but the concept is certainly similar. Using sets, questions which might otherwise take a number of queries can be generated in a single query.

The process basically involves three stages:

- ❑ Define a set
- ❑ Include expression which operates on the defined set
- ❑ Where necessary, include an expression to draw upon records from other tables.

Moving away from this unbridled abstraction, suppose you wanted to know which London-based companies had purchased a project costing £5,000 or more, as was done in the beginning of Section 7.14.

To obtain this information, using the Client table, we first define a set which includes all London based companies. Then by including the expression shown in Figure 7.24, the set itself is queried so as to produce only those London-based companies that have acquired a single service costing £5,000 or more.

The most important aspect of the query shown is the way in which reference is made to the set in the second query table; the example 123 in the ID field provides the essential link. Only 123 indicates that only those records of the set conforming to this example should be queried by the second query form. Take a close look at this example, as it is a concept worth getting to grips with.

If you analyse the advantage of using a set in the last example, you could be forgiven for thinking that sets yield little – a straightforward multi-table query would suffice. Personally, however, I would prefer to use a set, as it is easier to alter the overall query expression.

Sets of records can naturally be incorporated into queries where the question involves three tables. For example, cast your mind back to the final question asked in the previous example, ie what sort of service has been provided to London-based companies purchasing projects costing £5,000 or more? Figure 7.25 shows this query.

Notice that the initial set remains the same. All that has been done is to include the Work table which is linked to the Turnover table by the example, company. Note, it is quite legal to spread query statements over a number of lines. Sometimes this makes it easier to read and modify them.

Table 2: Summary of Query Operators

Reserved words:

√	list all field values in answer
√+	list all field values including duplications
√∇	list field values in descending order
G	specify group for set operators
calc	calculate new field
insert	insert new records
delete	delete selected records from queried table
changeto	change values in queried table
find	locate selected records (similar to Zoom feature)
set	define selected records as set

Arithmetic operators:

+	addition or concatenation of field values
-	subtraction
*	multiplication
/	division
( )	group operators in query expression

Range operators:

=	equal to
>	greater than
<	less than
>=	greater than or equal to
<=	less than or equal to

Wild cards:

@	any single character

Special operators:

as	change field name in Answer table
like	match field vaguely
blank	no value
today	current date
!	display all records in a field

Logical operators:

not	not match
or	either-or conditions
,	and conditions

Summary operators:

average	average of group of values
count	give number of values in group
max	highest value in group
min	lowest value in group
sum	total of values in group
all	calculate summary based on values irrespective of duplications
unique	calculate summary based on unique values in group

Set comparison operators:

every	list values that match all members of the defined set
exactly	list all records that exactly match members of the defined set
only	list all records that match members of the defined set
no	list all records that match no members of the defined set

8

All About Graphs

This chapter negotiates the particularly important aspect of using Paradox to generate graphs. The various graph types are examined together with how they are generated.

If you are moving up from Paradox 2, you will find a whole new world in graphs. And as Paradox will oblige by producing a graph in response to a single key press, their use has to be encouraged.

8.1 Introduction

Few would disagree that imparting numerical data in a lucid manner is best achieved using graphs. A business plan of any kind presented to a bank manager, financier, venture capitalist or whoever, becomes coherent when comprising graphs.

Setting aside such formal proposals, graphs are practical tools useful for breaking down and analysing data. For example, a previous week's or month's trading figures can be assessed and examined from numerous viewpoints. Paradox graphs offer sufficient flexibility so as to permit this. Bar graphs, rotated bar graphs, stacked bar graphs, pie charts, line graphs, marker graphs, area graphs, can all be created.

Graphs can also play an important role in decision making and playing what-if. For example, it is possible to compare various outcomes or trends.

8.1.1 Saving and Loading Graph Types

As graph types take some time to create, saving accompanying settings to disk can economise on keyboard operations. To save a graph type, press **I/G/S** to select Save, and enter the name of the graph. To load a graph type, press **I/G/L** to select Load, press <Enter> and select the graph required. It might be a good idea to save some of the graph types while negotiating this chapter.

8.1.2 Filing Graphs

With desktop publishing becoming more and more widespread, the importation of graphs (created with databases and spreadsheets) into newsletters or reports is an important requirement. Loading a Paradox graph into a word processor, or DTP program, is simply a matter of first filing the graph in an appropriate format, and then retrieving it as necessary. Before filing a graph, however, an appropriate file format must be selected. Encapsulated PostScript (or EPS) and Lotus PIC are available.

As WordPerfect is currently the most ubiquitous word processor, it should be said that EPS is one file type which cannot be imported, whereas PIC files can. At the time of writing, it is true to say that, PIC files are considerably more portable than their EPS counterparts, but things are changing. For Borland Sprint users, graph files must be in the EPS format. Loading graphs into Borland Sprint and WordPerfect 5.0 is discussed in Appendices 19 and 20.

To select a file format:

1. Press **I/G/M/F10** to invoke the Graph Design Menu.

2. Press **O/D/F** to choose an appropriate file type.

3. Press **P** to choose PIC file.

4. Press **F2.**

To write a graph to a file in the chosen format:

1. Position the cursor in the required numeric field.

2. Press **F10/I/G/V/F**, and enter an appropriate name for the graph. There is no need to include an extension as one is added automatically.

8.2 Graph Basics

You will remember that, prior to the successful generation of a graph, the cursor must be positioned amid an appropriate field type, ie a numeric or currency field. Using the menus a graph can be produced by selecting Image from the main menu; pressing **I/G/V** to select ViewGraph; and pressing **S** to output the graph to the screen. Alternatively, a less keyboard intensive alternative is achieved by simply pressing **Ctrl-F7**.

To recap, and just in case Power of Paradox is being used as a source of reference, the following hands-on session shows how to generate a standard bar graph.

8.2.1 Hands-on Session

This session uses the Turnover table to produce a bar graph.

1. With the Turnover table on screen, position the cursor in the Amount received field.

2. Press **Ctrl-F7** to produce the graph shown in Figure 8.1.

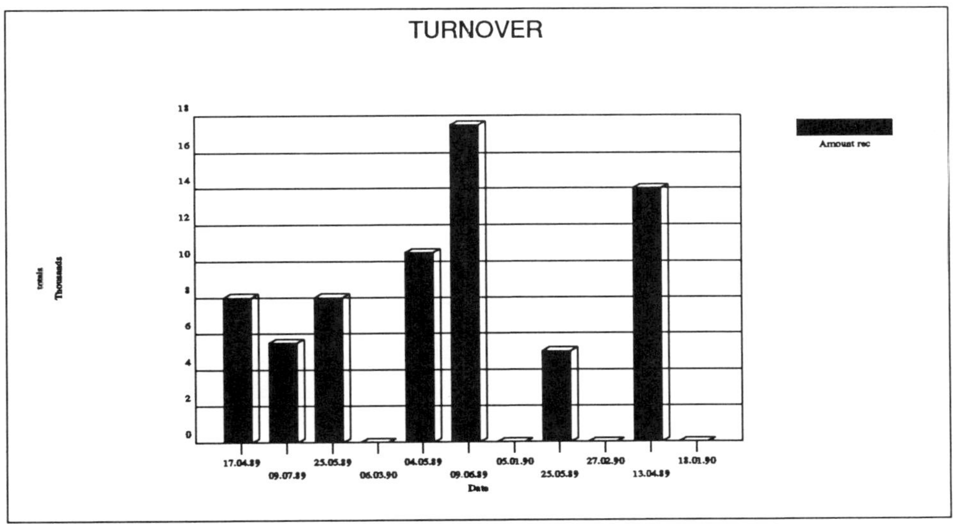

Figure 8.1: Bar graph produced from the Turnover table

(You will soon discover how to alter label sizes as shown.)

To print the Graph, press **Esc/F10/I/G/V/P**.

You have, no doubt, noticed something strange: the X-axis, instead of representing values from the first alphanumeric or date field (ie, the Company field), uses the Date field.

This is because the Company field and the Date field form a multi-field key. This being the case, the X-axis always shows values from the rightmost field making up the multi-field key.Remember, key fields have an asterisk (*) suffix, when the table structure is viewed. You can view a table structure by pressing **F10/T/I/S** to select Structure.

However, company names can be used as X-axis categories by querying. For example, by querying the Turnover table shown in Figure 8.2, the resultant Answer table can be used to produce the graph illustrated in Figure 8.3 where companies form X-axis categories.

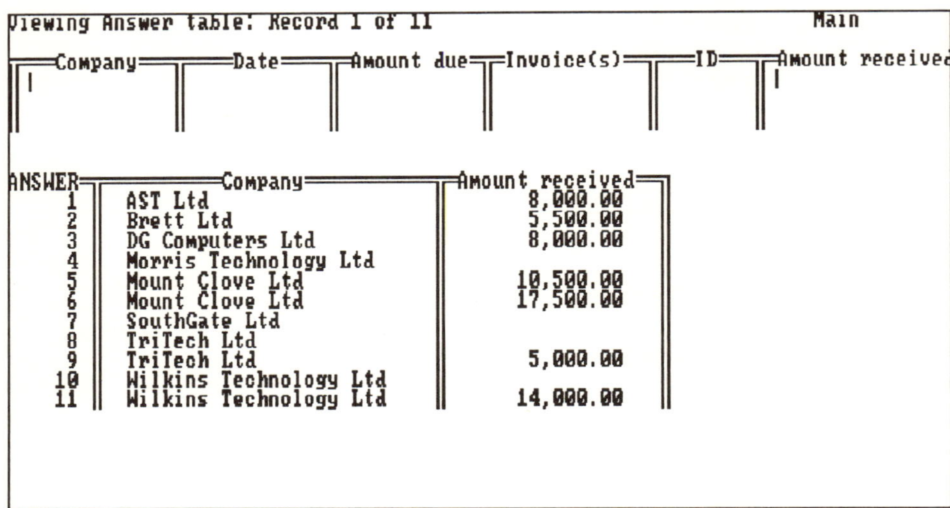

Viewing Answer table: Record 1 of 11 Main

Query: Company | Date | Amount due | Invoice(s) | ID | Amount received

ANSWER	Company	Amount received
1	AST Ltd	8,000.00
2	Brett Ltd	5,500.00
3	DG Computers Ltd	8,000.00
4	Morris Technology Ltd	
5	Mount Clove Ltd	10,500.00
6	Mount Clove Ltd	17,500.00
7	SouthGate Ltd	
8	TriTech Ltd	
9	TriTech Ltd	5,000.00
10	Wilkins Technology Ltd	
11	Wilkins Technology Ltd	14,000.00

Figure 8.2: Query to produce Company and Amount received fields

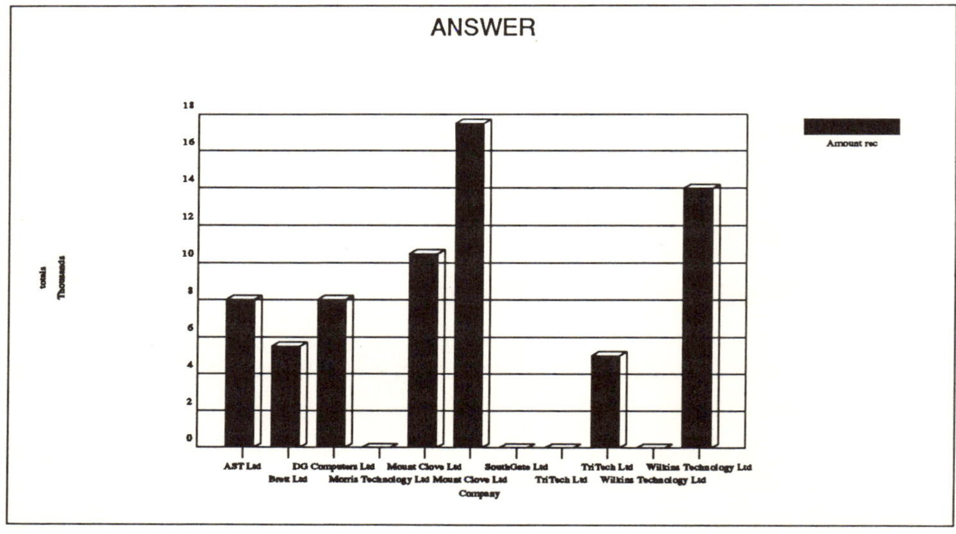

Figure 8.3: Bar graph generated from resultant Answer table

8.4 Rotated Bar Graph

Evidently, the graph produced shows individual amounts received, but company names making up X-axis categories are totally unreadable. You will soon discover that this can be remedied by altering the size of the axes titles. However, a rotated bar graph of the type shown in Figure 8.4 goes some way to offering a solution.

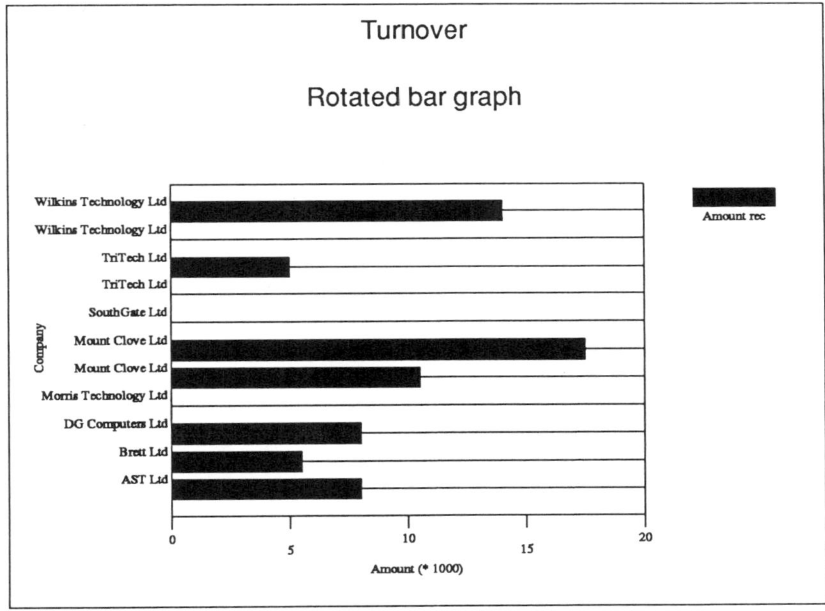

Figure 8.4: Rotated bar graph

The following hands-on session shows how to generate the rotated bar graph shown in Figure 8.4:

8.4.1 Hands-on Session – creating a rotated bar graph

1. Press **F10/I/G** to select Graph.

2. Press **M** to select Modify, giving the screen shown in Figure 8.5.

3. Press **R** to change the graph type to Rotated Bar.

4. Now labels for X and Y axes must be swapped: press **F10/O** to select Overall; press **T** to choose Titles.

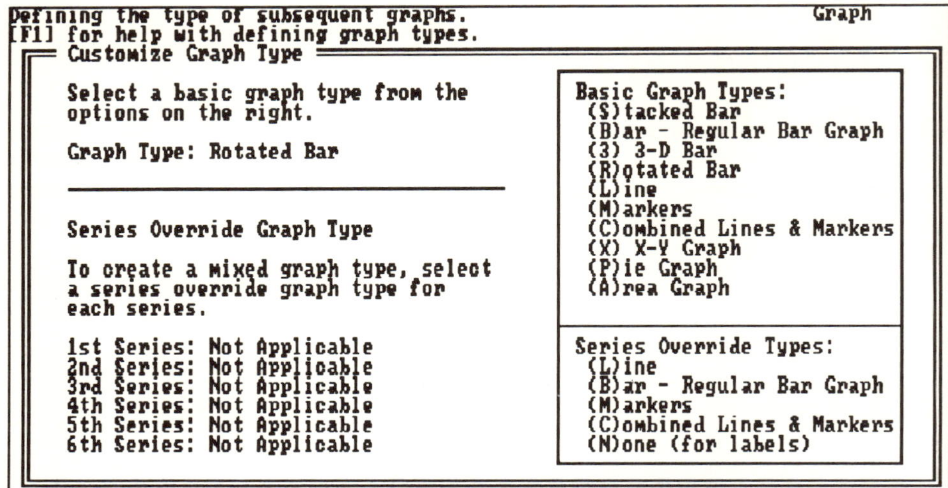

Figure 8.5: Modify

5. Complete the screen as shown in Figure 8.6.

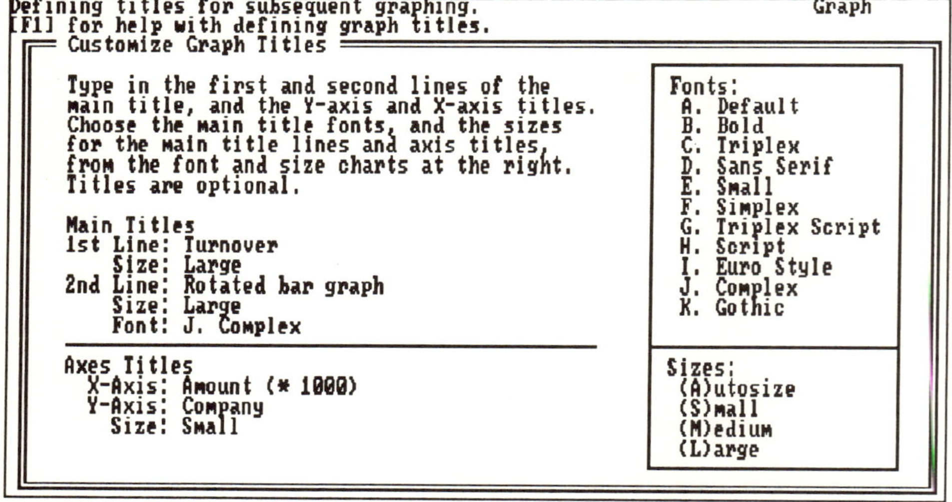

Figure 8.6: Customise graph titles

6. Press **F2** to record the settings.

With the Answer table on screen (produced in Hands-on 8.2.1), and with the cursor amid the Amount received field, invoke the rotated bar graph by pressing **Ctrl-F7**.

Refer to Chapter 6 about creating a script so as to automate the described process.

8.5 Pie Charts

Pie charts are useful for monitoring sizes of contributions, in terms of percentages, making up an overall Figure. This is advantageous when monitoring the performance of various contributors or contributory factors. Consider a situation where it is necessary to generate a pie chart which shows how each client contributes to the overall turnover. The following hands-on session shows how to generate such a pie chart.

8.5.1 Hands-on Session – generating a pie chart

1. Press **I/G/M** to select Modify.

2. Press **P** to seleect Pie Chart..

3. Press **F10/P/P** to indicate that pie slices are to be labelled in terms of percentages.

4. Press **F2** to record the graph type.

5. Query the Turnover table so as to isolate companies and the respective amounts paid.

6. With the cursor amid the currency field of the Answer table, press **Ctrl-F7** to generate the pie chart shown in Figure 8.7.

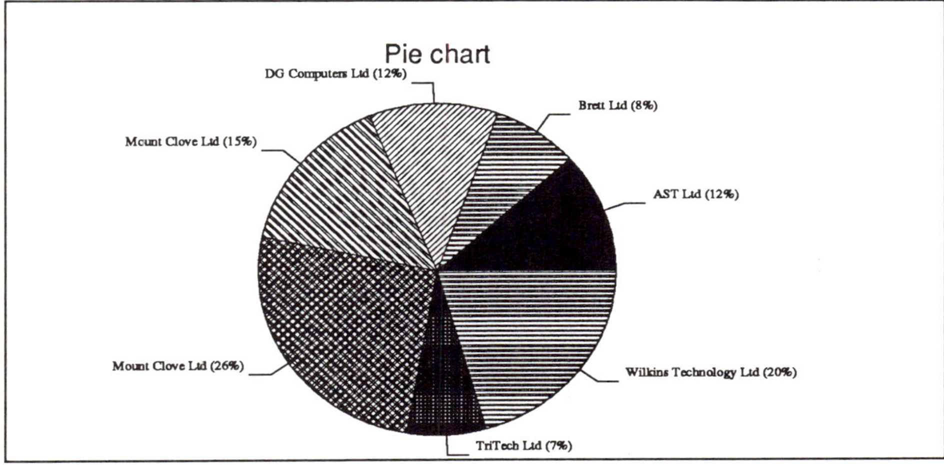

Figure 8.7: Pie chart (and pie chart settings)

8.6 Stacked Bar Graphs

The stacked bar graph, a development of the bar graph, can be used almost like a set of pie charts. For example, elements can be stacked one top of the other, which manifests contributions made by various fields. Take a look at the graph shown in Figure 8.8. This was created from the Repperf table contained in the Sample directory.

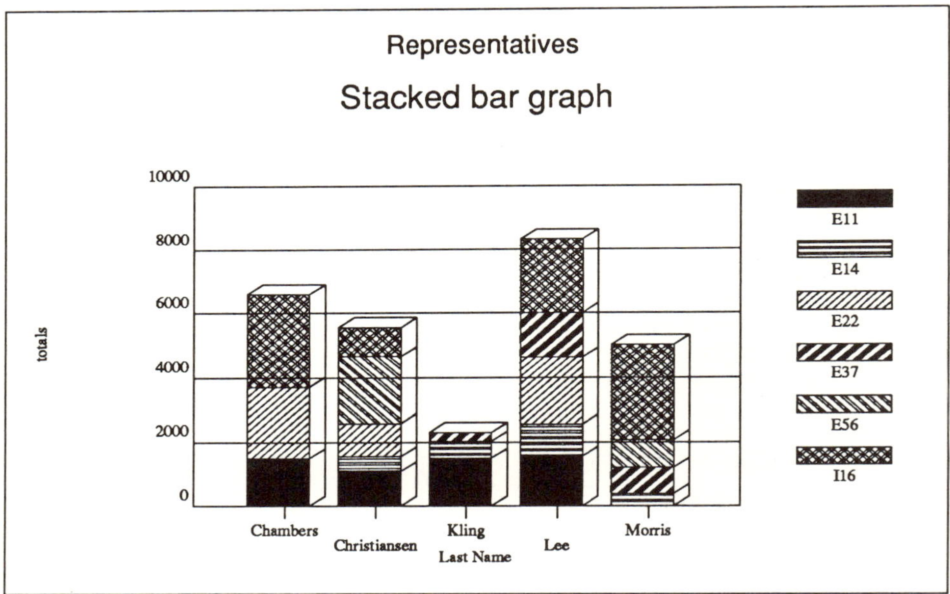

Figure 8.8: Stacked bar graph created using the Repperf table

Stacked bar graphs work by using the six fields beginning at the cursor field. Comparing the stacked bar graph with the Repperf table shown in Figure 8.9, you will notice that Last Name field values become X-axis labels, and that the first six numeric fields beginning at the cursor field become series elements.

REPPERF	Last Name	E11	E14	E22	E37	E56	I16	I24
1	Chambers	1,498.75	0.00	2,218.15	0.00	0.00	2,878.40	0.00
2	Christiansen	1,079.10	479.20	1,019.15	0.00	2,096.50	899.50	989.45
3	Kling	1,498.75	539.10	0.00	269.85	0.00	0.00	0.00
4	Lee	1,558.70	988.35	2,098.25	1,349.25	0.00	2,338.70	1,079.40
5	Morris	0.00	389.35	0.00	809.55	868.55	2,968.35	2,788.45

Figure 8.9: The Repperf table

The following hands-on session escorts you through the process of creating a stacked bar graph.

8.6.1 Hands-on Session – creating a stacked bar graph

1. First, it is a good idea to make Sample the working directory in order to provide easy access to the Repperf table, so press **F10/T/M/D** to select Directory.

2. Complete the directory path, so that it conforms to **c:\paradox3\sample**.

3. Press **<Enter>/O** to make sample the working directory. Press **I/G/M** and select Stacked Bar; press **F2**.

4. Enter **V** and select the Repperf table.

This table naturally shows representatives performances.

5. Position the cursor in the E11 field and simply press **Ctrl-F7** to produce the graph shown in Figure 8.8.

The series elements (such as E12 and so on) are selected because they form the first five elements to the right of the cursor. To change this simply move the cursor to the numeric field where you wish the six series elements to begin. Try this for yourself by pressing Escape, repositioning the cursor, and pressing **Ctrl-F7** once again.

The series elements of a stacked bar graph can be further rearranged by rotating fields. For example, position the cursor in the E11 field and press **Ctrl-R** to rotate it.

8.7 Marker Graphs

Marker graphs, as you would expect, consist of a number of markers, which represent single data points. When using series elements, trends and changes can be further accentuated by interconnecting lines which unite common markers. Such combined lines and marker graphs are often useful for making line graphs a little more coherent. In fact, where there are not too many intersections of associated lines, marker graphs are best combined with line graphs.

The following hands-on session illustrates how to generate a Marker graph using the Orders table.

8.7.1 Hands-on Session – creating a marker graph

1. Enter **V** and select the Orders table.

2. Press **F10/I/G/M** to choose Modify.

3. Press **M** to select (M)arkers.

4. Press **F2** to record the graph type.

5. Position the cursor in the Quant field and press **Ctrl-F7** to produce the graph shown in Figure 8.10.

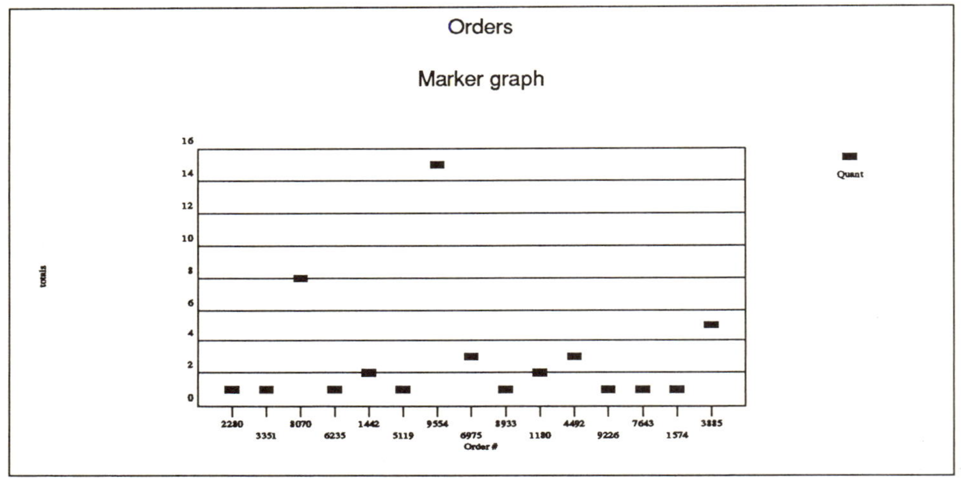

Figure 8.10: Marker graph

8.8 Line Graphs

The use of line graphs ranges from the breakdown of sales figures to tracking share prices over a given period. Because of the way line graphs manifest trends, they can be harnessed to give insights into the future by way of projection, rather like the Kondratieff waves in Chapter 1.

Line graphs are useful for showing slumps and peaks in performance. For example, consider the line graph shown in Figure 8.11, which shows a breakdown of orders according to dates.

It can be generated as follows:

❑ Modify the graph style to conform to that shown

❑ Produce a query form for the Orders table

❑ Rotate fields of the query form so as to place the Date field to the immediate left of the Quant field

❑ Place check marks in both Date and Quant fields

❑ Produce a graph from the resultant table.

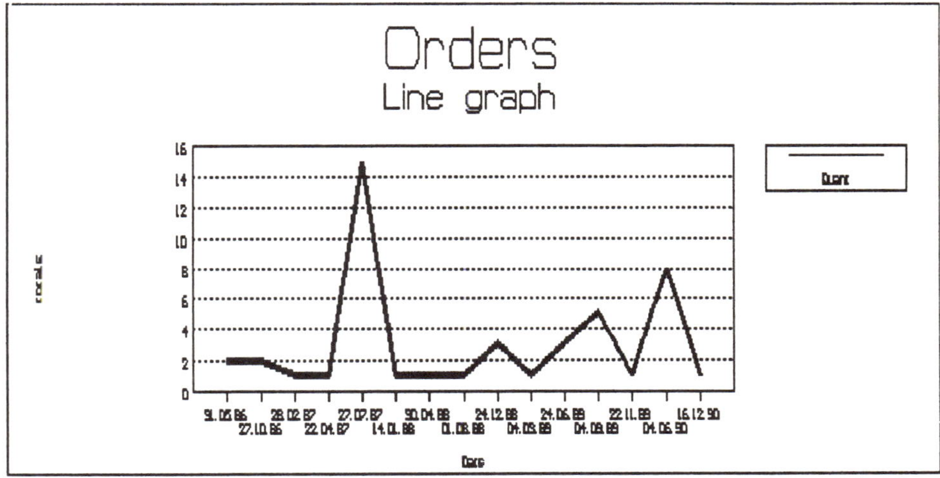

Figure 8.11: Line graph

The following hands-on session illustrates the generation of the line graph shown in Figure 8.11.

8.8.1 Hands-on Session – creating a line graph

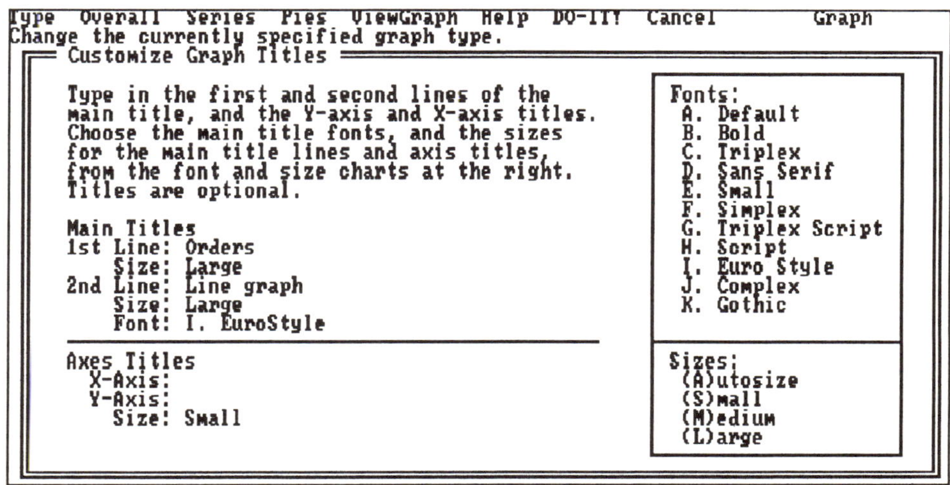

Figure 8.12: Customise Graph Titles screen

1. Enter **V** and select the Orders table.

2. Press **F10/I/G/M** to choose Modify.

3. Press **L** to select (L)ine.

4. Press **F10/O/T** to produce the Customise Graph Titles screen shown in Figure 8.12.

Complete the screen as shown, choosing the Euro Style font for the title, Orders. And choose Small size for Axes titles.

5. Press **F2** to record the newly created graph type.

It is now necessary to query the Orders table so as to produce the Answer table shown in Figure 8.13.

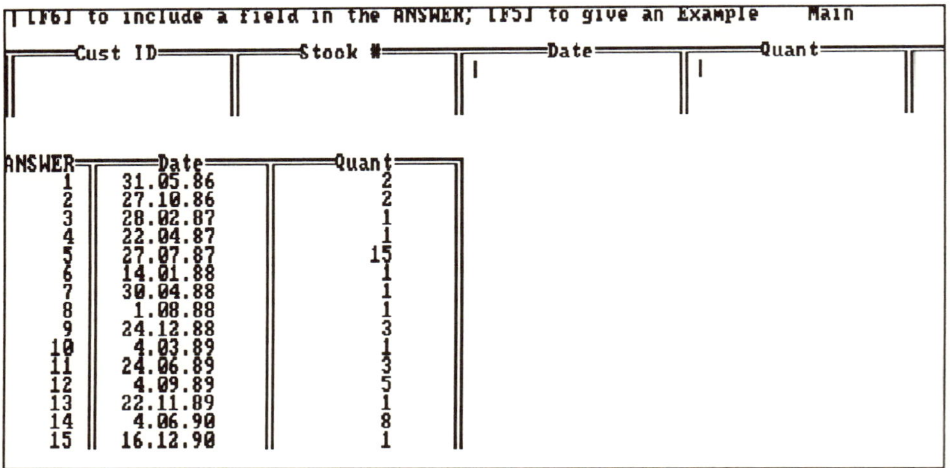

[F6] to include a field in the ANSWER; [F5] to give an Example   Main

Cust ID	Stock #	Date	Quant

ANSWER	Date	Quant
1	31.05.86	2
2	27.10.86	2
3	28.02.87	1
4	22.04.87	1
5	27.07.87	15
6	14.01.88	1
7	30.04.88	1
8	1.08.88	1
9	24.12.88	3
10	4.03.89	1
11	24.06.89	3
12	4.09.89	5
13	22.11.89	1
14	4.06.90	8
15	16.12.90	1

Figure 8.13: Querying the Orders table

Notice that dates are sorted in ascending order, so, we begin by sorting records according to the date field:

6. Press **F10/A** to select Ask.

7. Press **<Enter>** and select the Orders table.

8. Rotate the fields in the query form (by pressing **Ctrl-R**) so as to position the Quant field to the immediate right of the Date field. The most efficient method of achieving this is to position the cursor in the appropriate column and press **Ctrl-R** until the required field appears.

9. Press **F6** in both the Date and Quant fields. Press **F2** to implement query.

10. Finally, position the cursor in the Quant field of the Answer table and press **Ctrl-F7** to produce the graph shown in Figure 8.11.

8.9 XY Graphs

XY graphs display numeric values on both axes, and are naturally used to manifest links between two sets of values. Basically, XY graphs show how one set of values effects another. To offer one example of this, you could see how increases in product price effect sales.

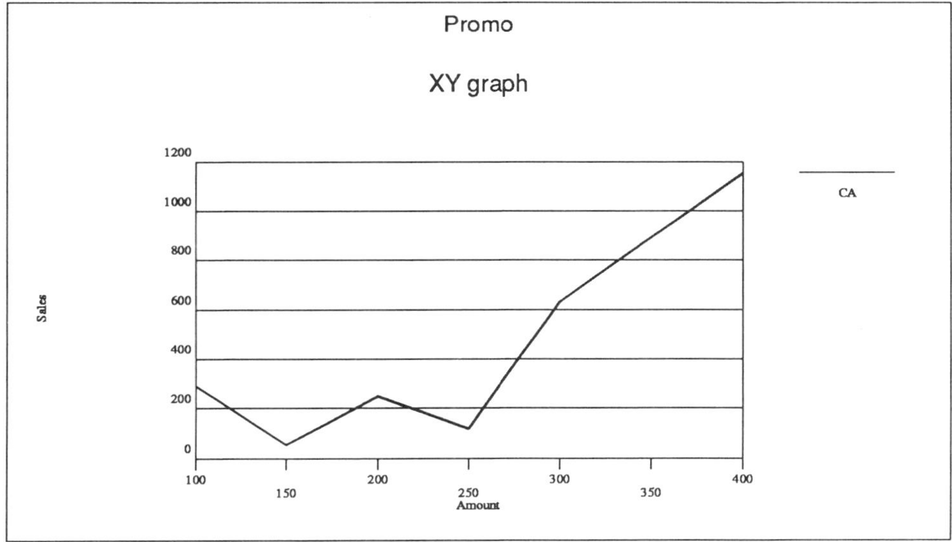

Figure 8.14: XY graph

Using XY graphs both the X and Y axes are scaled, where the X values are taken from the first numeric field in the table.

Figure 8.14 shows an XY graph generated from the Promo table, which illustrates how the amount spent on promotion effects sales in the State of California. The following hands-on session shows how to create this graph.

8.9.1 Hands-on Session – creating an XY graph

1. Press **F10/I/G/M** to select Modify.

2. Complete the screen as shown in Figure 8.15.

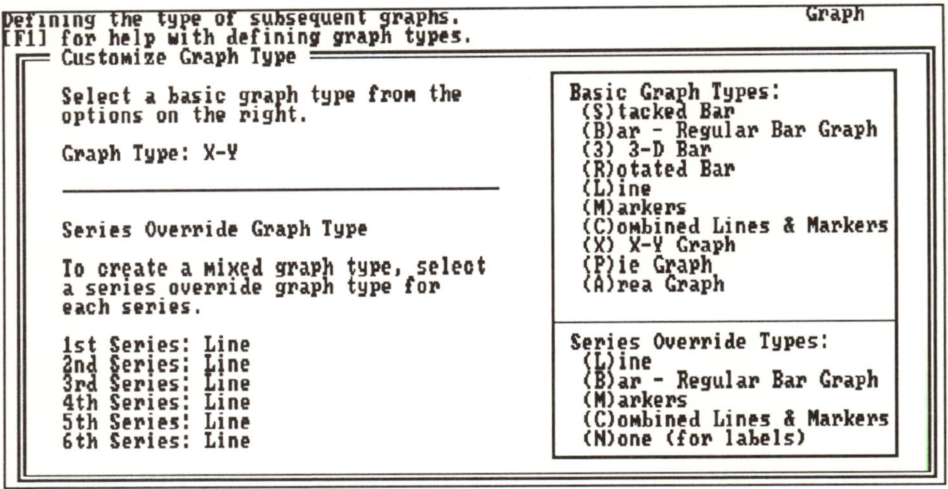

Figure 8.15: Modifying the Graph type

3. Press **F10/O/T** to select Titles, and complete the screen as shown in Figure 8.16.

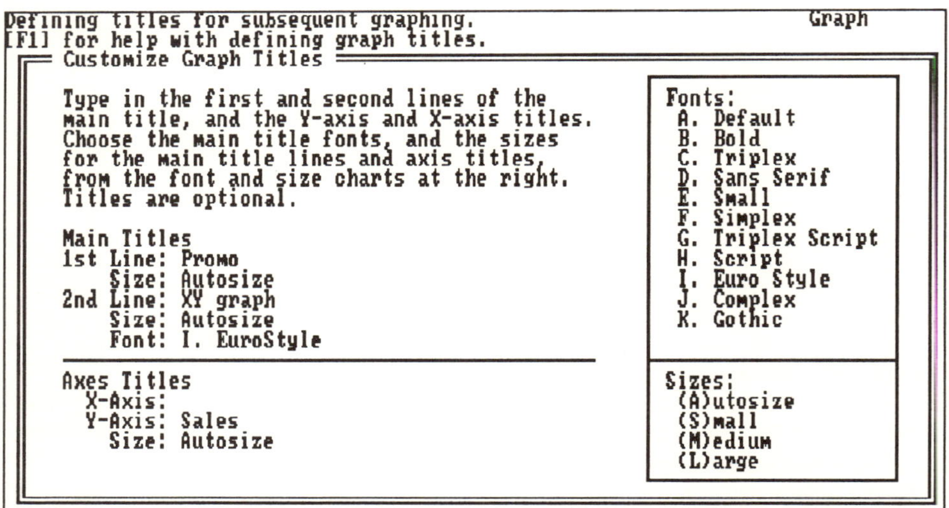

Figure 8.16: The Titles screen

4. Press **F2** to record the graph type.

5. Press **F10/V** followed by **<Enter>**, and select the Promo table.

6. Query the Promo table by placing check marks in the Amount and CA fields.

7. Position the cursor in the CA field of the resultant Answer table and press **Ctrl-F7** to produce the graph shown in Figure 8.14.

It should be said that, XY graphs work like stacked bar graphs, where fields to the right of the cursor become series elements.

8.10 Area Graphs

Area graphs offer the advantages of both bar graphs and line graphs. The filled area conveys quantity while lines manifest upswings and downswings.

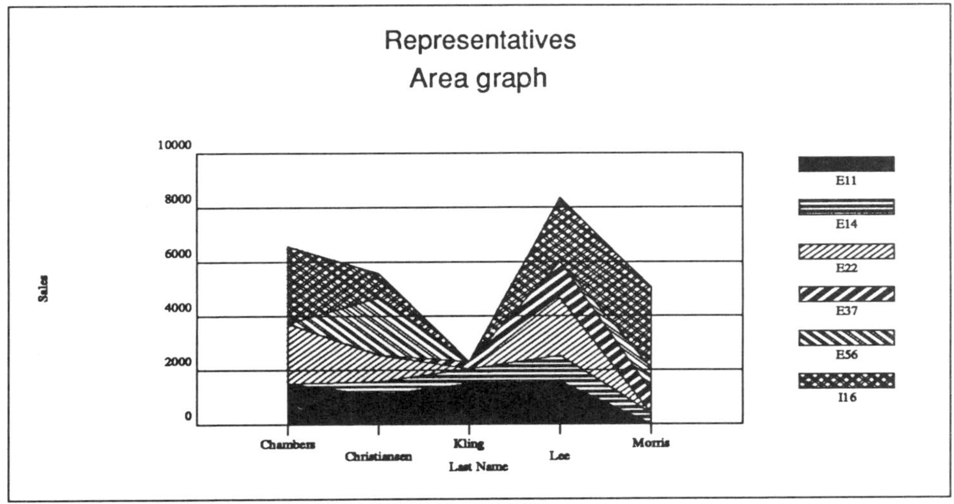

Figure 8.17: Area graph

The graph shown is generated from the Repperf table and shows the performance of each of the five representatives with regard to selling different product lines. Notice how trends can be reaped from such a graph. The following hands-on session shows how to generate the Area graph shown.

8.10.1 Hands-on Session – creating an area graph

1. Press **F10/I/G/M** to select Modify.

2. Complete the screen as shown in Figure 8.18 on the next page.

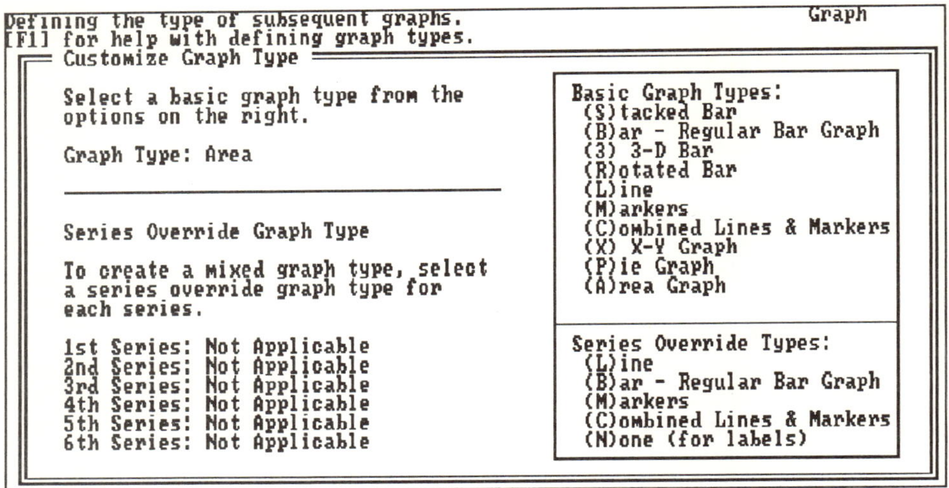

Figure 8.18: Modify the Graph type to Area

3. Press **F10/O/T** to select Titles, and complete the screen as shown in Figure 8.19.

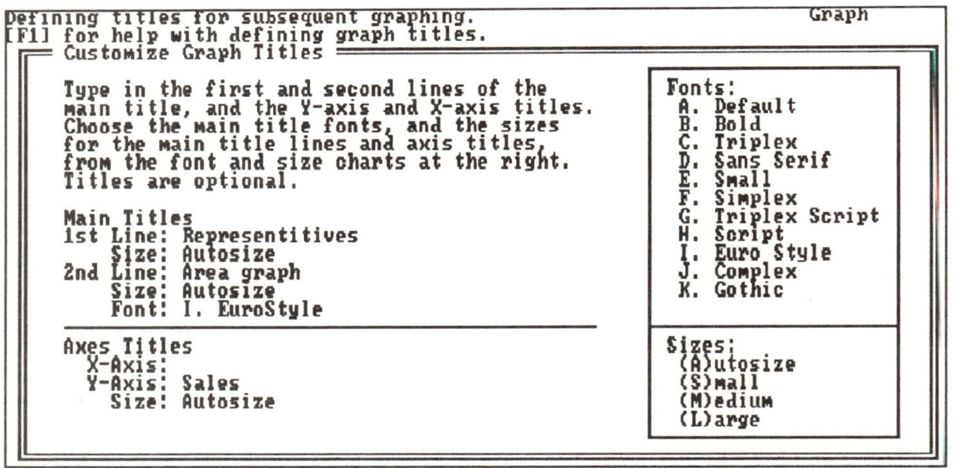

Figure 8.19: Titling the Area graph

4. Press **F2** to record the graph type.

5. Press **F10/V** followed by **<Enter>**, and select the Repperf table.

6. Position the cursor in the E11 field and press **Ctrl-F7** to produce the graph shown in Figure 8.17.

8.11 CrossTab

CrossTab can assist when preparing tables for the generation of graphs. Essentially, it permits the summarisation of a table to allow a more directed analysis via a graph.

Using CrossTab, it is possible to take columns of field values and convert them into field names. It opens up numerous mind boggling possibilities, allowing you to turn tables literally inside out. For example, consider the Masterbk table, where it is necessary to analyse sales to various clients over four years – like the graph shown in Figure 8.20. This graph was achieved by first isolating the Customer, Year and Total fields using QBE, and then generating an appropriate CrossTab.

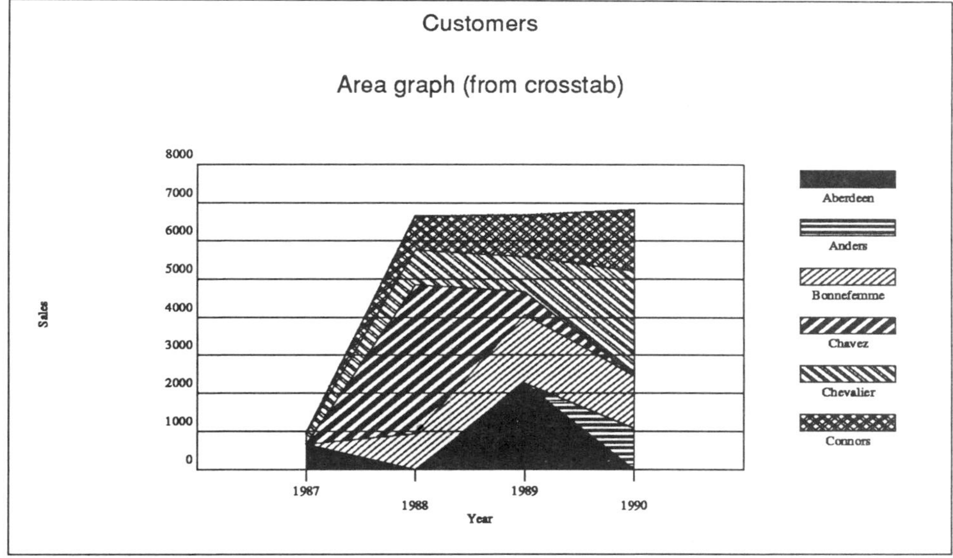

Figure 8.20: Graph generated from CrossTab

The following hands-on session shows how to generate the graph shown, illustrating how to analyse data in the Masterbk table over four years by using customer names as series elements.

8.11.1 Hands-on Session – using CrossTab

1. Press **F10/A** followed by **<Enter>**, and select the Masterbk table.

2. Press **F6** in the Customer field, the Year field, and type **calc sum as Total** in the Total field, as shown in Figure 8.21.

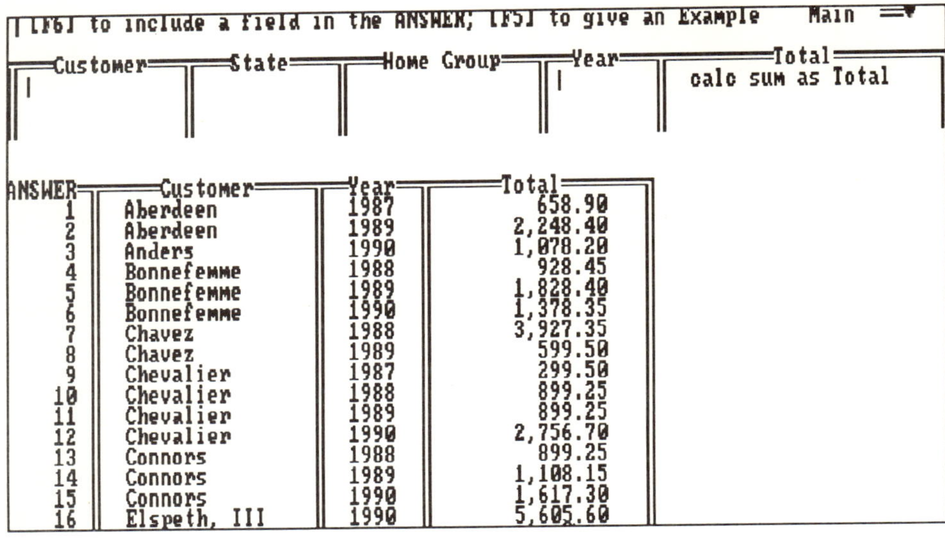

[F6] to include a field in the ANSWER; [F5] to give an Example Main

Customer	State	Home Group	Year	Total
✓			✓	calc sum as Total

ANSWER	Customer	Year	Total
1	Aberdeen	1987	658.90
2	Aberdeen	1989	2,248.40
3	Anders	1990	1,078.20
4	Bonnefemme	1988	928.45
5	Bonnefemme	1989	1,828.40
6	Bonnefemme	1990	1,378.35
7	Chavez	1988	3,927.35
8	Chavez	1989	599.50
9	Chevalier	1987	299.50
10	Chevalier	1988	899.25
11	Chevalier	1989	899.25
12	Chevalier	1990	2,756.70
13	Connors	1988	899.25
14	Connors	1989	1,108.15
15	Connors	1990	1,617.30
16	Elspeth, III	1990	5,605.60

Figure 8.21: Querying the Masterbk table

3. Press **F2** to produce the Answer table.

4. The field which will form the CrossTab row labels must now be moved to the left of the table. Press **Ctrl-R** to rotate columns until the arrangement shown in Figure 8.22 is achieved.

Viewing Answer table: Record 1 of 56 Main

ANSWER	Year	Customer	Total
1	1987	Aberdeen	658.90
2	1989	Aberdeen	2,248.40
3	1990	Anders	1,078.20
4	1988	Bonnefemme	928.45
5	1989	Bonnefemme	1,828.40
6	1990	Bonnefemme	1,378.35
7	1988	Chavez	3,927.35
8	1989	Chavez	599.50
9	1987	Chevalier	299.50
10	1988	Chevalier	899.25
11	1989	Chevalier	899.25
12	1990	Chevalier	2,756.70
13	1988	Connors	899.25
14	1989	Connors	1,108.15
15	1990	Connors	1,617.30
16	1990	Elspeth, III	5,605.60
17	1987	Fahd	899.25
18	1988	Fahd	449.25
19	1989	Fahd	899.25
20	1990	Fahd	1,349.25
21	1987	Farouk	599.50
22	1988	Farouk	299.50

Figure 8.22: Rotated columns of Answer table

5. Press **F10/I/G/C** to select CrossTab.

6. Press **<Enter>** to select 1) Sum.

7. With the cursor in the Year field, press **<Enter>** to make these values CrossTab row labels.

8. Move the cursor to the Customer field and press **<Enter>** once again, to make these values CrossTab column labels.

9. Move the cursor to the Total field and press **<Enter>** to make these the CrossTab values. The CrossTab shown in Figure 8.23 will then be generated.

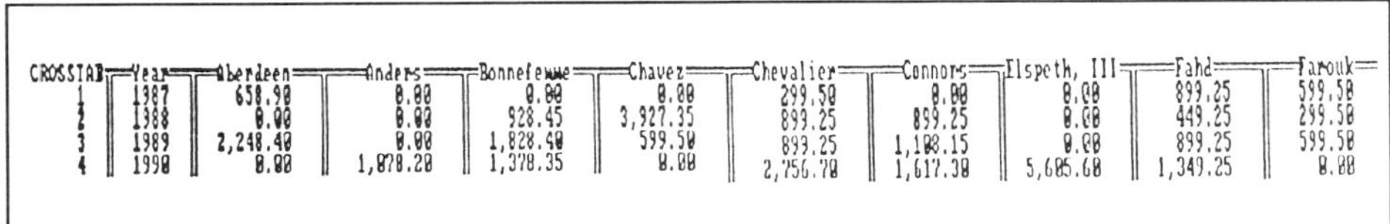

CROSSTAB	Year	Aberdeen	Anders	Bonnefemme	Chavez	Chevalier	Connors	Elspeth, III	Fahd	Farouk
1	1987	658.90	0.00	0.00	0.00	299.50	0.00	0.00	899.25	599.50
2	1988	0.00	0.00	928.45	3,927.35	899.25	899.25	0.00	449.25	299.50
3	1989	2,248.40	0.00	1,828.40	599.50	899.25	1,108.15	0.00	899.25	599.50
4	1990	0.00	1,878.20	1,378.35	0.00	2,756.70	1,617.30	5,685.60	1,349.25	0.00

Figure 8.23: CrossTab generated from the Masterbk table

10. Establish graph settings to conform to the Area graph shown in Figure 8.20. The main title is in EuroStyle, while axes titles are Medium size.

11. To generate the graph, position cursor in the Aberdeen field and press **Ctrl-F7**.

Of course, any six customers can be used as series elements by moving the cursor to the appropriate field, or by rearranging the table.

8.11.2 CrossTab Shortcut

Though CrossTab can be selected using the menus without too much difficulty, **Alt-X** represents a shortcut you might like to use.

This shortcut works in an uncompromising way, where:

❑ The cursor field is used as the row labels

❑ The rightmost column is used as the CrossTab values

❑ The field to the immediate left of this is used for column labels.

Provided you are prepared to restructure or rotate columns appropriately, **Alt-X** can save time.

8.12 Modifying Tables for Graphs

Modifying tables for the generation of graphs is, as you have seen, a frequent requirement; few tables in standard form give rise to suitable graphs. It is important, therefore, to become acquainted with the basic techniques making up this prelude, and to appreciate what, exactly, can be reaped from them:

- Querying, the heart of Paradox, is possibly the most fruitful, allowing the interrogation of tables so as to give the appropriate table for the creation of a graph (see Chapter 7)

- Rotate Column (**Ctrl-R**), permits columns to be rotated and generally rearranged

- Restructuring, often the last resort, is a little permanent for many users, but remains one method of creating a required graph.

8.13 Printing Graphs

Apart from the default, landscape orientation, graphs can be printed precisely to requirements. It is possible to print in portrait orientation, specify width and height, and set left and right margins.

Before taking advantage of these options, however, it is imperative that you install your printer using the CCP, otherwise specified printer settings will be ignored. The following series of steps show how to install your printer:

1. With the main menu on screen and with paradox3 the working directory, press **S/P** followed by **<Enter>**, and select Custom.

2. Press **G** to choose Graphs.

3. Press **P** to select Printers.

4. Press **<Enter>** to choose 1stPrinter.

5. Press **T** to select TypeOfPrinter.

6. Move the cursor to the make of your printer and press **<Enter>**. If you make a mistake, press Escape to return to the previous screen.

7. In the same manner, select the printer model.

8. The number of graphics modes on screen naturally depends upon your printer. Appropriately select one of these. Bear in mind, however, that the higher the resolution, the slower graphs will be printed.

9. Press **R** three times to return to the main CCP menu.

10. Press **F2.**

11. Press **H** to write the changes to hard disk.

12. Enter **paradox3** to reload the program.

When printing a graph, by pressing **I/G/V/P**, you will now see the Make and model of your printer as well as the graphics mode chosen. For example:

Graph Printer: Epson – LQ 2500 (all)

Mode: B & W 180 x 180 dpi Med.

Press <ESC> to cancel printing

8.13.1 Layout

Defining the layout for printing graphs is simplicity itself. By way of illustration, the following session shows how to customise the graph layout for printing.

8.13.2 Hands-on Session – customising layout for printing

1. Press **F10/I/G/M** to select Modify.

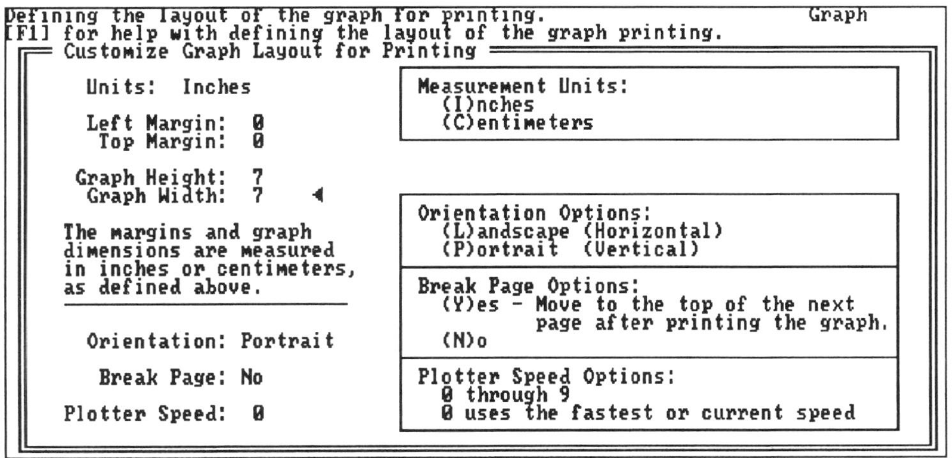

Figure 8.24: Specifying printer layout

2. Press **F10/O/P** to choose PrinterLayout, giving the screen shown in Figure 8.24.

3. As you can see, the screen is fairly self explanatory. Enter the shown Graph width and height of 7 inches.

4. Press **F2** to record the setting.

5. Now try printing a graph as previous described, and notice that it is 7 inches wide and 7 inches high.

8.13.3 Default Printer Layout

Like many other operations, the layout described in the previous hands-on session is temporary. A more permanent layout is achieved by running the CCP.

Assuming you are not using *Power of Paradox* for reference, you should now be aware of how to run the CCP. However, to shed more light on the process, the following hands-on session shows how to create a default printer layout.

8.13.4 Hands-on Session

1. With the main menu on screen and with paradox3 the working directory, press **S/P** followed by **<Enter>**, and select Custom.

2. Press **G** to choose Graphs.

3. Press **G** to select GraphSettings.

4. Press **F10/O** to choose Overall.

5. Press **P** to select PrinterLayout.

6. Complete the layout required.

7. Press **F2**.

8. Press **R** to return to the main CCP menu.

9. Press **F2**, once again.

10. Press **H** to write the changes to hard disk.

11. Enter **paradox3** to reload the program.

8.14 Default Graph Settings

The default settings – those which are present when Paradox is loaded – can be established using the Paradox Custom Configuration Program (or CCP). You can revert to the default graph settings at any time by pressing **F10/I/G/R** to select Reset.

The following session shows how to use the CCP to specify default graph settings.

8.14.1 Hands-on Session – declaring default graph settings

1. With Paradox3 the working directory, run the CCP by pressing **S** to select Scripts from the main menu, then **<Enter>** and select Custom.

2. Press **G** to select Graphs from the main menu.

3. Press **G**, once again, to choose GraphSettings.

4. You will then be confronted by a familiar screen – the Customise Graph Type screen; press **Esc.** As such, it is now possible to establish any of the graph settings discussed in this chapter, if required.

5. When satisfied with graph settings, press **F2** to record your graph settings.

6. Press **Esc** to return to the main menu.

7. Press **F2**, once again.

8. Press **H** to write the settings to your disk, if not using a network that is.

9. Enter **paradox3** to reload the program.

Table 8.1: Key references

Operations	*Key(s)*
CrossTab	Arrange table/**F10/I/G/C** or **Alt-X** (see text)
Default graph settings	**F10/S/P/<Enter>**/select Custom/**G/G** (see Session 8.14.1)
Graph types	
Area grap	**F10/I/G/M/A/F2**
Bar graph	**F10/I/G/M/B/F2**
Line graph	**F10/I/G/M/L/F2**
Marker graph	**F10/I/G/M/M/F2**
Pie chart	**F10/I/G/M/P/F2**
Rotated bar graph	**F10/I/G/M/R/F2**
Stacked bar graph	**F10/I/G/M/S/F2**
XY graph	**F10/I/G/M/X/F2**
Load graph type	**F10/I/G/L/<Enter>**/select graph type
Print graph	**F10/I/G/V/P** (position cursor in numeric field. See Section 8.13)
Default layout	See Hands-on Session 8.13.4
Printer layout	**F10/I/G/M/F10/O/P** (see Session 8.13.1)
Select printer	See Section 8.13
Save/File graph	**F10/I/G/V/F/filename/<Enter>**
File type	**F10/I/G/M/F10/O/D/F/** select file type
Save graph type	**F10/I/G/S/graph name/<Enter>**
View graph on screen	**Ctrl-F7** or **F10/I/G/V** (position cursor in numeric field)
View table structure	**F10/T/I/S**

9

All About Forms

This chapter escorts you through the particularly important aspect of using Paradox to generate forms. Simple forms are described as well as the more complex multi-table variety, able to reap records/fields from more than one table. Multi-record forms are also discussed.

In some instances, to illustrate the creation of forms, sections from Chapter 6, *A Typical Application*, are reproduced. Incidentally, you might find forms described in the context of a real application, as in Chapter 6, easier to understand.

9.1 Designing Forms

For some users, editing and viewing data via tables can become confusing, particularly where field names wander off screen. In light of this, many prefer forms which show where each field value should be entered. For example, the form shown in Figure 9.1 overleaf makes it manifestly obvious where various field values are entered. Many database programmers incorporate such forms with field names and prompts in an attempt to make applications user-friendly.

Designing a form is markedly similar to designing a report, but unlike reports forms are never committed to paper. The appearance of personally designed forms is, of course, a matter of preference. But if advice could be offered, forms should be uncluttered, but yet comprise adequate textual help, particularly where field names are concerned. In regard to borders, and there are several different types available, these are often useful for creating the illusion of pre-printed forms.

Though the process of designing forms is intuitive, the following hands-on session shows how to create the one shown in Figure 9.1.

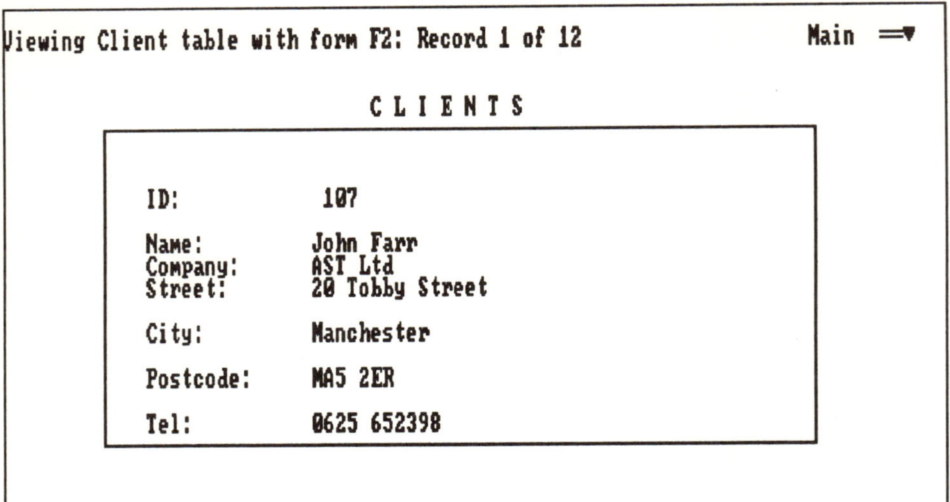

Figure 9.1: Form for the Client table

9.1.1 Hands-on Session – creating a simple form

1. Press **F10/F** to select Form.

2. Press **D** to choose Design.

3. Press **<Enter>** and select the Client table.

4. Select an unused form.

5. Enter **DataIn** in response to, *Form Description:*

6. Press **F10/F/P/R** to place a regular field; and select the Name field.

7. Move the cursor approximately to the location shown in Figure 9.1. Press **<Enter>** twice.

8. Repeat stages 6 and 7, and place the remaining fields as shown in Figure 9.1.

9. Press **Ins,** and type the field names illustrated. (Hint – positioning the cursor amid a field causes the field name to be shown.) Close up gaps that appear between the field names and the fields by pressing Backspace as you would with a word processor.

(Remember, fields can be erased and relocated from the Field menu. Also, if a field is placed incorrectly, press **F10** before pressing **<Enter>** for the second time.)

10. Press **F10/B/P** to begin placing a Border.

11. The border style is a matter of preference. For this example, however, press **S** to choose Single-line.

12. Position the cursor in the top-left corner of the border and press **<Enter>**.

13. Move the cursor to the bottom-right of the border and press **<Enter>**. (Note, a border cannot intersect a field; it can be erased by pressing **F10/B/E**.)

14. Type an appropriate title for the form, like that shown.

15. Press **F2** to record the form.

Press **V** to view the Client table and press **F10/I/P**; then select the DataIn form. See Chapter 5 for information about using forms for data entry. Once a form is 'picked' during a Paradox session, pressing **F7** (Form Toggle) produces that form.

9.2 Multi-record Forms

Comprising records in a tabular format, multi-record forms are rather like a window in which sections of a table can be viewed or edited. The multi-record form illustrated in Figure 9.2 relates to the Turnover table.

Viewing Turnover table with form F5: Record 1 of 11 Main =▾

T U R N O V E R

Company	ID	Amount received	Date
AST Ltd	107	8,000.00	17.04.89
Brett Ltd	106	5,500.00	9.07.89
DG Computers Ltd	109	8,000.00	25.05.89

Figure 9.2: Multi-record form

The creation of a multi-record form varies little from a standard form. It involves placing a multi-record region together with appropriate fields. The following hands-on session shows how to create the form shown in Figure 9.2.

9.2.1 Hands-on Session – creating a multi-record form

1. Press **F10/F/D** to begin designing a form.

2. Press **<Enter>** and select the Turnover table.

3. Move the cursor to the right until you find an unused form and press **<Enter>**.

4. Enter **turnover** in response to *Form description:*

5. Press **F10** to invoke the menu.

6. Press **M** to select Multi – this will permit the creation of a multi-record form.

7. Press **R** to select Records.

8. Press **D** to begin defining a multi-record region.

9. Move the cursor to the top left corner of the region shown in Figure 9.3 and press **<Enter>**.

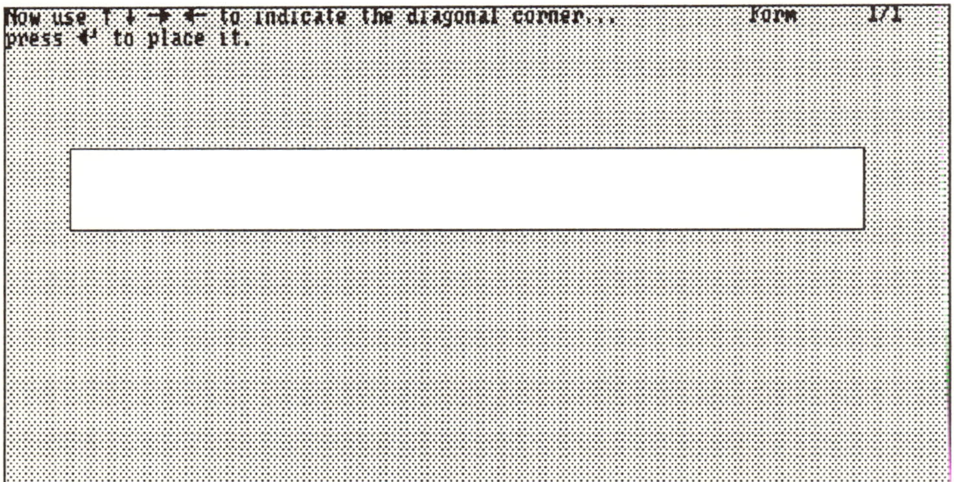

Figure 9.3: Left corner of multi-record region

10. Press **<down-arrow-key>** twice, and press **<left-arrow-key>** repeatedly until a highlighted rectangle appears of the sort shown in Figure 9.3.

(Remember, if you make a mistake, press **<Escape>** to cancel that operation.)

11. Press **<Enter>**. Basically, you have now created a region which, though **2** lines deep, will accommodate a single record. To determine just how many records are included in this multi-record region, press the **<down-arrow-key>**; cover approximately half the screen as shown in Figure 9.4, and press **<Enter>**.

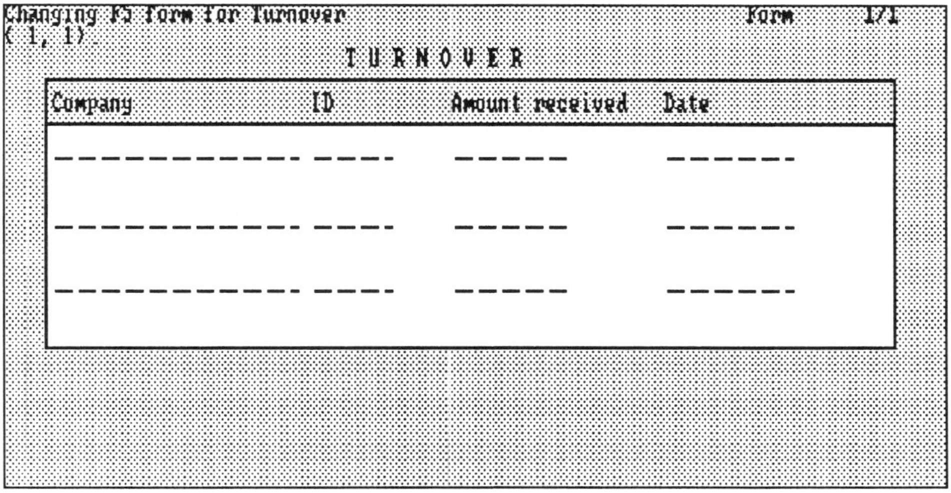

```
Changing F3 form for Turnover                                  Form    1/1
( 1, 1)
                          T U R N O V E R
   Company                 ID         Amount received  Date

   ------------ ----     -----         -------

   ------------ ----     -----         -------

   ------------ ----     -----         -------
```

Figure 9.4: Multi-record form

12. Press **F10** to invoke the menu.

13. Press **F/P/R** to place a regular field.

14. Select the Company field.

15. Move the cursor to the top left of the multi-record region, and press **<Enter>**. You will then see a column of lines appear in the region.

16. Size the field using the arrow keys and press **<Enter>**.

17. Repeating steps 12 – 16, place ID, Amount received and Date received fields, as shown in Figure 9.4. Resize your fields to correspond with those illustrated.

18. Press **Ins** and type the field names and title shown in Figure 9.4.

(Bear in mind that you can delete and resize fields using Erase and Reformat.)

19. Press **F2** to record the form.

This multi-record form can be invoked, like any other, by using PickForm. You can edit and move about such a form using all the techniques discussed so far (see Chapters 5 and 6).

(The most significant disadvantage of using multi-record forms is the inability to place fields outside the multi-record region.)

9.3 WordWrap

Where field values become too large to be confined to a specific area of a form, WordWrap allows you to spread them over more than one line. There are no petty limitations when harnessing WordWrap, it can be used on both multi-table and multi-record forms.

Using WordWrap is simplicity itself:

1. Within the form design screen (see Hands-on Session 9.2.1), press **F10** to produce the menu.

2. Press **F** to select Field.

3. Press **W** to choose WordWrap.

4. Move the cursor to the field to be wrapped and press **<Enter>**.

5. Enter the number of lines over which the field is to be wrapped.

When using WordWrap, you must ensure that there is adequate space for the field to spread over the specified region. As such, using WordWrap with multi-record forms often requires adjustment of the multi-record region by pressing **F10/M/R/A** to select Adjust. If there is not enough space for the field to be wrapped, you will be informed after pressing **F2**.

Wrapped fields can be moved or erased by first pressing **F10/A** to select Area, and then appropriately choosing Move or Delete. After selecting the area over which the field is wrapped, press **<Enter>** to delete it, or use the arrow keys to move to a new location.

9.4 Changing Forms

Often, form design is an iterative process – the novice will rarely get a form right first time. As such, forms can be redesigned or simply modified using Change, like this:

1. With the main menu on screen, press **F/C** to select Change.

2. Select the appropriate table.

3. Finally, choose the form you wish to change. All standard features pertaining to form design are unleashed.

9.4.1 Changing or Designing

As forms can be copied, it is possible to design a new form by Changing an existing one. Naturally, this can save a considerable amount of time and effort. The process of copying a table is initiated by pressing **F10/T/C** to select Copy. After copying a form, press **F10/F/C** to begin changing it.

9.5 Multi-table Forms

Forms dedicated to a single table, of the type created in the previous hands-on sessions, are limited in many applications.

Beyond these simple forms, multi-table forms permit fields to be reaped from more than one table. Figure 9.5 illustrates the basic idea of a multi-table form.

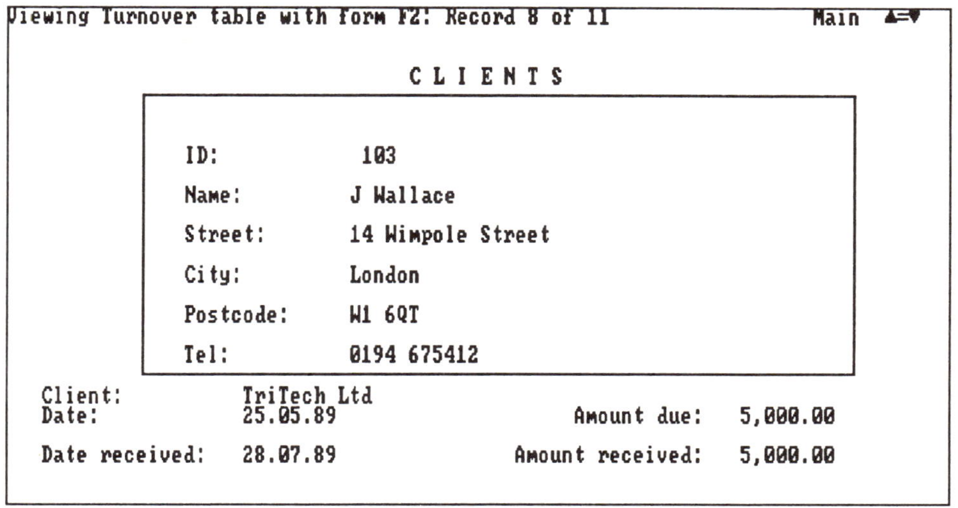

Figure 9.5: Multi-table form

Tables making up multi-table forms can be linked or unlinked. Usually, multi-table forms behave like a number of entirely separate forms where it is necessary to press **F3** (Up Image) and **F4** (Down Image) to move between fields which emanate from different tables.

A multi-table form (comprising two tables) requires a master table and a detail table. The detail table is used to generate a single form which is embedded in the form created using the master table (as shown in Figure 9.5). Essentially, then, the design of a multi-table form is, initially, a matter of designing a number of individual forms.

9.5.1 Constraints on Multi-table Forms

Before going any further, there are a number of constraints that must be brought out into the open, the most important of which is the fact that a multi-record form cannot be a master form. Naturally, therefore, multi-record forms must emanate from detail tables only. Two other possibly less encumbering constraints, are: embedded forms cannot be multi-page; and, embedded forms cannot contain other embedded forms.

9.6 Links

When a multi-table form embodies linked tables, records from different tables become logically related. Linking tables is achieved by homing in on a common field, or a number of common fields. You will recall the concept of linking tables from your experiences with QBE.

The multi-table form shown in Figure 9.5 uses the Company field to establish a logical link between two tables. Such common fields are called link keys, for obvious reasons.

9.7 Link Keys

Embedded forms must not contain link keys. In fact, this is how Paradox detects link keys, and then asks you to select a field, or fields, in the master table so as to complete a link during the design of a multi-table form.

Before discovering how to establish such links, it is necessary to say something about the various types of link that can be established.

9.8 Types of Link

Based upon how tables are keyed, there are four possible kinds of link. As the type of link depends upon such factors, it is sometimes necessary to restructure tables in order to achieve the link required. Don't panic about all this talk of different types of links, as, more often than not, your tables will lead to adequate links, without having to carry out modifications. The following subsections describe the four types of link.

9.8.1 One-to-One Link

A one-to-one link is the simplest of all, existing where each master record is linked to just one detail record. As such there must be no duplication of link fields in neither master nor detail tables.

For such a link to occur, key fields in the detail and master tables must match exactly. For this reason, the one-to-link is most likely to occur where master and detail tables each comprise one key field.

The one-to-one link will be indicated by the words, (1-1 Group), on screen.

9.8.2 One-to-Many Link

Indicated by (1-M Group) on screen, a one-to-many link exists where each master record is linked to a number of detail records.

Such a link will often occur when not all key fields in the detail table are used to establish a link with the master table.

9.8.3 Many-to-One Link

Shown as (Group) on screen, the many-to-one link indicates that groups of master records are linked exclusively to a single detail records.

The many-to-one link will often occur where all of the detail table's key is matched to master table fields that can contain duplicate values.

9.8.4 Many-to-Many Link

Illustrated on screen as simply (Group), the many-to-many link relates groups of master records to groups of detail records.

The many-to-many link will often occur when the detail key is matched to master fields that can contain duplicate values.

9.9 Creating Multi-table Forms

Consider using a form to enter data into the Turnover table. Updating the Client table to include new clients would be difficult. Not only would you not know if a new Client was being entered, but you would also have to edit the Client table or form separately.

This problem can be solved using a multi-table form which can link the Client table to the Turnover table. This makes data entry considerably easier; for as you input Company names into the Turnover table, new clients will be spotted immediately, as they will not show up on the form.

Take a look at the multi-table form shown in Figure 9.5. This shows a form which provides the type of link necessary to make the process of data-entry less haphazard.

The following hands-on session shows how to create the multi-table form shown in Figure 9.5.

9.9.1 Hands-on Session – creating a multi-table form

Here, the form DataIn, (see Figure 9.1) will be embedded in a master form assigned to the Turnover table. Before it can be embedded, however, the Company field, the link field which relates it to the Turnover table, must be erased. Yes, this is a peculiar requirement for the creation of a multi-table form.

The Company field can be deleted as follows:

1. Press **F10/F** to select Form.

2. Press **C** to choose Change.

3. Press **<Enter>** and select the Client table.

4. Select the DataIn form.

5. Press **<Enter>** to leave the form description unchanged.

6. Press **F10/F/E** to choose Erase.

7. Position the cursor amid the company field and press **<Enter>**.

8. Press Ins and delete the field name, Company.

9. Press **F2** to record changes made.

Now to design the master form:

10. Press **F10/F/D** to select Design.

11. Press **<Enter>** and select the Turnover table.

12. Press **1** or select an alternative unused form.

13. Arbitrary, of course, enter **Input** in response to the prompt, *Form description:*

14. Press **F10** to invoke the Design menu.

15. Press **M/T** to begin embedding the DataIn form.

16. Press **P/L** to Link the Client table.

17. Press **<Enter>** and appropriately select the Client table.

18. Press **1** or whichever number corresponds to the form you used.

19. In response to, *Select TURNOVER field to match Company in CLIENT,* simply choose Company. The Company field is, of course, the link field.

20. Presented with a large block, which reflects the DataIn form of the Client table shown in Figure 9.1, position it the upper half of the screen, and press **<Enter>**. Left on the screen will be shaded area indicating where, exactly, the form will be embedded.

21. As with the design of the previous form, fields from the Turnover table can be included in the normal manner. Try placing the fields such as those shown in Figure 9.5. (Remember to reduce the width of the currency fields).

22. Type an appropriate name for the form.

23. Finally, press **F2** to record the multi-table form.

To actually use the form for editing or viewing data, make the Turnover table the current image, and select the Input form.

If there is one slight disadvantage with this multi-table form, it must be the need to press **F4** and **F3** (Up Image and Down Image) to move between fields from different tables.

This drawback is outweighed by obvious advantages: records from both the Client table and Turnover table can be viewed or edited simultaneously.

To demonstrate this, using the Input form, try entering a company name which is not in the Client table, and press **F3** (Up Image) or **Ctrl-L**. Such an entry is immediately met with blank fields, indicating that there is a new client and, therefore, appropriate information must be entered. Furthermore, there is no possibility of duplicating clients using such a multi-table form.

Table 9.1: Key references

Operation	*Key(s)*
Design and change form	
Adjust multi-record region	**F10/M/R/A**
Change form	**F10/F/C**
Design form	**F10/F/D**
Embed/Link table	**F10/M/T/P/L** (see Session 9.9.1)
Erase border	**F10/B/E**
Erase field	**F10/F/E**
Erase wrapped field	**F10/A/E**
Link table	**F10/M/T/P/L** (see Session 9.9.1)
Place border	**F10/B/P**
Place multi-record region	**F10/M/R/D**
Place regular field	**F10/F/P/R** (see Session 9.2.1)
Type text	**Ins**
Wrap field	**F10/F/W** (see Section 9.3)
Edit form	**F9** (with form on screen)
Form Toggle	**F7**
Invoke form	**F10/I/P**/select form

10

All About Reports

This chapter explains and discusses the design, creation and use of tabular and free-form reports. Beginning with simple reports, which gather records from just one table, multi-table reports are discussed. To illustrate certain aspects, excerpts from Chapter 6 are reproduced.

Finally, it must be stressed that examples contained herein are practical ones, and only essential operations are described.

10.1 Introduction

Uses of reports vary from the common, such as printing receipts and invoices (as in Chapter 6), to the more specialised, such as mail merging (also discussed in Chapter 6). Occasionally, reports are used to simply back up information.

There are two kinds of report: free-form and tabular. Tabular reports closely relate to tables and, as such, are predominantly used for printing or summarising tables. Tabular reports are useful for producing hardcopies of tabular presentations you would expect to find on multirecord forms.

Free-form reports are like (normal) forms, where fields can be placed anywhere in the report area.

At this point, it should be said that, though Paradox is particularly flexible when it comes to restructuring tables, modified fields are sometimes erased from accompanying reports.

For instance, if the Company field in the Client table were altered using Restructure, it would disappear from the address in the Invoice report, in which case it would have to be reinserted. In light of this, do not design reports before absolutely satisfied with table structures.

10.2 Creating a Report

The process of creating a report is markedly similar to that of creating a form. Operations such as placing fields and borders are exactly the same. In terms of multi-table reports, these are in actual fact easier to generate than multi-table forms.

To illustrate the creation of a report, consider the form letter shown in Figure 10.1. Each field shown emanates from the Client table, and the body of the letter is simply typed.

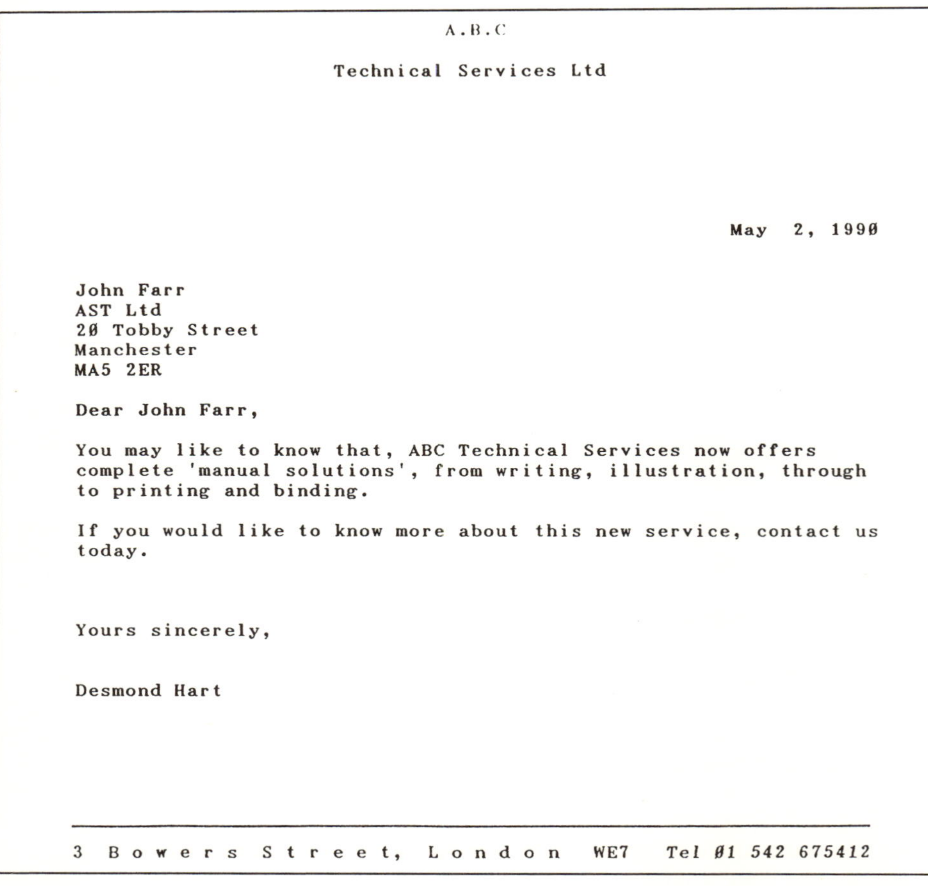

A.B.C

Technical Services Ltd

May 2, 1990

John Farr
AST Ltd
20 Tobby Street
Manchester
MA5 2ER

Dear John Farr,

You may like to know that, ABC Technical Services now offers complete 'manual solutions', from writing, illustration, through to printing and binding.

If you would like to know more about this new service, contact us today.

Yours sincerely,

Desmond Hart

3 Bowers Street, London WE7 Tel 01 542 675412

Figure 10.1: Report – form letter

This form letter, you will remember, was used to illustrate mail merging in Chapter 6. As such, the following hands-on session also emanates from that chapter.

10.2.1 Hands-on Session – creating a report

It should be said that, though the following form letter is a simple one, it is possible to include fields within the text itself – which helps personalise letters by including the addressee's name where necessary.

1. Press **R** to select Report from the main menu.

2. Press **D** to select Design.

3. Press **<Enter>** and select the Client table.

4. Press **<right-arrow-key>** until you find an unused report.

5. Press **<Enter>** to select the report.

6. Enter **Advert**.

7. Press **F** to select Free-Form.

8. Press **F10** to call up the menu.

9. Delete the Tel field by first pressing **F/E**, then move the block cursor to the field and press **<Enter>**. Press **Ins** and delete the field name, Tel.

10. Repeat step 9 to delete the Company field and the ID field. Also, delete the header using Erase and the delete keys, or, simply press **Ctrl-Y**.

11. Align all address fields to the left using the Backspace key.

12. Move the cursor to the beginning of the Street field and press **<Enter>**.

13. Press **F10/F/P/R** and select the Company field.

14. Position the cursor directly beneath the Name field and press **<Enter>** twice.

15. With Ins shown in the top right of the screen, using **<Enter>** position the cursor beneath the address and type **Dear.**

16. Place the Name field directly after Dear:, press **F10/F/P/R** and select the Name field. Move the cursor to the appropriate point and press **<Enter>** twice.

17. Type the form letter shown and include an address if not using headed note paper.

18. Include the date: press **F10/F/P/D**; select the date format required and place it as you would a regular field.

19. After completing the text, press **F2**.

(See Chapter 6 about mail merging.)

10.3 Printing Free-form Reports

Printing reports so as to confine each to a single page is, naturally, an important aspect of using Paradox. Though this can be a process of trial and error, a technique can be refined using Setting on the Report menu. However, with a printer on-line print the form letter: press **F10/R/O** followed by **<Enter>**; select the Client table; select the Advert report; finally, press **P**. You can temporarily halt output by pressing **Ctrl-Break**.

Form letters will be printed in a continuous stream where, no doubt, they will have spilled over from one page onto another. Also, the comma will be detached from the name after Dear (see Subsection 10.3.2)

10.3.1 Setting a Page Size

To demonstrate how a page size can be set, return to the form letter (just created):

1. Type **F10/R/C** to select Change.

2. Press **<Enter>** and select the Client table.

3. Select the Advert report.

Press **Ctrl-V** to give a vertical ruler, so as to indicate the length of the report.

By first pressing **Ins**, it is possible to introduce space between the form band and the top and bottom of the page. By carefully matching the number of lines on each page to those printed, it is possible to print reports exactly as required.

For example, you can set the page length of 65 lines by pressing **F10/S/P/L** and entering **65**. Then, use the vertical ruler to set a corresponding page length in the report. If necessary you can pause between pages by pressing **F10/S/W/Y**. Press **F2** to record the changes made. Note: Escape can be used to abandon printing.

10.3.2 Eliminating Horizontal Space

When outputted, the Name field is accompanied by leading and trailing blanks. Such horizontal space is eliminated by using FieldSqueeze, in the following manner:

1. Press **R** to select Report from the main menu.

2. Press **C** to select Change.

3. Press **<Enter>** and select the Client table.

Remember, to select the Client table in this manner, Access must be the working directory, as previously discussed.

4. Select the Advert report.

5. Press **<Enter>** to leave the report description unchanged.

6. Press **F10/S** to select Setting.

7. Press **R** to choose RemoveBlanks.

8. Press **F/Y** to remove all field blanks in the form band.

9. As always, press **F2** to complete the operation.

10.3.3 Filing Reports

Conveniently, reports can be written to disk in the form of Dos Text files, opening up the possibility of exporting reports to word processors and DTP packages. Coupled with the fact that graphs can be saved in PIC and EPS file formats, it is possible to incorporate any amount of your information within documents.

To file a report:

1. Press **F10/R/O** to select Output.

2. Press **<Enter>** and choose the appropriate table.

3. Select the appropriate report, and press **F**.

4. Enter a file name (without an extension). The report will be saved with the default RPT extension.

When loading reports into word processors and DTP programs, treat the RPT report as an ASCII file. If using WordPerfect 5 or WordPerfect 5.1, load Reports as Dos Text files

10.4 Creating Multi-table Reports

Consider the report shown Figure 10.2. This typical invoice reaps fields from both the Client and Turnover tables and is, therefore, a multi-table report.

Because the invoice links two tables, the report can be accommodated within families of either one. For the sake of logic, however, and hopefully to make report design slightly more intuitive, the report will be an object of the Turnover table.

```
******************************************************************************
*                              I N V O I C E                                 *
******************************************************************************
ABC Technical Services, 3 Bowers Street, London WE7.  Tel 01 542 675412
VAT 07868236321

Company: AST Ltd
         John Farr
         20 Tobby Street
         Manchester

Amount: 8,000.00

Date: 17.04.89

******************************************************************************
```

Figure 10.2: Report – invoice

The following hands-on session shows how to create the multi-table report (invoice) shown in Figure 10.2:

10.4.1 Hands-on Session – creating a multi-table report

1. Select Report from the main menu.

2. Press **D** to select Design.

3. Press **<Enter>** and select the Turnover table.

4. Press **<right-arrow-key>** and find an unused report.

5. Press **<Enter>** to select the report.

6. Enter **Invoice**.

7. Press **F** to select Free-Form.

8. Press **F10** to call up the menu.

9. Press **F/L** to choose Lookup.

At this point we are going to link the Turnover table to the Client table, for reasons previously discussed.

10. Press **L** to select Link; press **<Enter>** and select the Client table.

11. The prompt, *Select TURNOVER field to match Company in Client,* indicates that the common field is Company, so, choose the Company field.

Having successfully established the link between Turnover and Client tables, fields from either table can be placed in the report.

12. Press Ins to invoke a full-screen editor in insert mode – this is confirmed by Ins in the top right of the screen.

Now establish the asterisks, company name and address as shown in Figure 10.3. The design chosen is arbitrary but it must exist somewhere within the report form band.

```
Changing report R1 for Turnover table                             Report     1/1
Form Band, Field Squeeze
....+...10....+...20....+...30....+...40....+...50....+...60....+...70....+...8*

▼page
▼form
********************************************************************************
*                               I N V O I C E                                  *
********************************************************************************
ABC Technical Services, 3 Bowers Street, London WE7.  Tel 01 542 675412
VAT 07868236321

Company: AAAAAAAAAAAAAAAAAAAAAAA
         AAAAAAAAAAAAAAAAAAAA
         AAAAAAAAAAAAAAA
         AAAAAAAAAAAAAAA

Amount: (999,999,999.99)

Date: dd.mm.yy

********************************************************************************
▲form
```

Figure 10.3: Report design screen

13. Delete the Amount received field: press **F10/F/E**; position the block cursor amid the bracketed nines which represent the field; then press **<Enter>**.

14. With Ins shown in the top right of the screen – achieved by pressing Ins – delete Amount received using the Delete keys.

15. Repeat steps 13 and 14 to erase ID and Date received fields.

16. Again with Ins shown in the top right of the screen, position the cursor immediately following the Company field and press **<Enter>** three times so as to make space for the additional fields.

17. Press **F10/F/P/R** to place a regular field.

18. Highlight the linked table [<Client>], and press **<Enter>** to produce a list of fields contained in that table.

19. Highlight Street and press **<Enter>**.

20. Position the cursor beneath the company field and press **<Enter>** to place the Street field. Resize the field as required using the arrow keys and press **<Enter>**, once again.

21. Repeat stages 17 to 20 placing the fields City and Postcode as shown in Figure 10.3.

22. If necessary, delete the header by pressing **Ctrl-Y.**

23. Finally, as always, press **F2** (Do-It!).

If the design of a report has to be abandoned midway, press **F2** and return to it by pressing **F10/R/C** to select Change, and then retrace the main steps by pressing **<Enter>** at the appropriate points.

10.5 Printing a Single Free-form Report

To illustrate how to print single reports, we focus on the invoice created in the previous hands-on session.

Depending upon the size of a business, the need to print invoices from a whole table is an uncommon one. Indeed, it is more conventional to print a single invoice.

Consider, for one moment, viewing the Turnover table and realising that Southgate Ltd (record number 7 in this case) should be invoiced. This can be done as follows – before beginning, ensure that each invoice is printed on a single page – see subsection 10.3.1:

1. View the Turnover table on screen. It is important that you do this, as this will show the record number which naturally corresponds to the page number which needs to be printed, provided each invoice is confined to its own page – as is common.

2. Press **F10** to produce the main menu.

3. Press **R/R** to select RangeOutput.

4. Press **<Enter>** twice to select the Turnover table. Note, if you have switched off your computer after changing to the Access directory, you will have to make Access your working directory once again.

5. Select the Invoice report.

6. Press **P** to send the report to the printer. Of course, for the purposes of experimentation it is quite practical to select Screen.

7. As record number 7 is required – which will be printed on page 7, press **Backspace** and enter **7** in response to the prompt, *Beginning page number:*

8. Enter **7** in response to, *Ending page number:*

9. Because a pause exists between pages, it is necessary to press any key seven times before the actual invoice is printed – this will not be the case if the report is output to the screen.

The inconvenience of having to press any key a number of times to correspond with the record number is eliminated by removing the pause between pages. If uncertain as to how this is achieved, the following steps will help:

1. Press **R** to select Report from the main menu.

2. Enter **C** and select the Turnover table; select the Invoice report.

3. Press **F10/S** to select Setting.

4. Press **W/N/F2**.

10.6 Tabular Reports

As already mentioned, tabular reports are similar to the columnar arrangements that tables are so dependent upon. Understandably, tabular reports are used to produce hardcopy of tables, often in summary form.

For example, a tabular report can be used to generate a list of clients in terms of name, company and telephone number, like that shown in Figure 10.4.

The following session shows how to create and print such a report:

Name	Company	Tel
John Farr	AST Ltd	Ø625 652398
Thor Goldberg	Band gap Ltd	
John Sawyer	Brett Ltd	Ø272 865612
Alan Mann	C scape Ltd	
Dave Trent	DG Computers Ltd	Ø272 561238
Jim Cray	JSL Ltd	
Gordon Applebau	Meiko Services Ltd	
Dave Arnfield	Morris Technology Ltd	Ø625 878881
Sue Phelps	Mount Clove Ltd	Ø876 678446
John White	SouthGate Ltd	Ø194 284653
J Wallace	TriTech Ltd	Ø194 675412
Chris Wilkins	Wilkins Technology Ltd	Ø876 678423

Figure 10.4: Simple tabular report

10.6.1 Hands-on Session – creating a simple tabular report

1. Press **R** to select Report from the main menu.

2. Press **D** to choose Design.

3. Press **<Enter>** and select the Client table.

4. Press **<right-arrow-key>** until you find an unused report and then press **<Enter>**.

5. Enter **Table** in response to, Report description:

6. Press **T** to select Tabular. You will then be confronted by the sort of Report design screen shown in Figure 10.5.

Notice how the default report reflects the columnar arrangement of the Client table. To see how field names, and their order, correspond exactly, press **Ctrl-<right-arrow-key>** to see all fields.

When the cursor is moved into the second screen, a new page is being viewed/edited as indicated in the top right corner. Use **Ctrl-<left-arrow-key>** to move back to page 1. Naturally, therefore, if this report were printed, the table would be divided over two pages.

To preview on screen how the report is printed press **F10/O/S**. Press any key to move through the pages, and observe the unsatisfactory way in which the table is divided – this problem will be addressed later. Press any key to return to the design of your report.

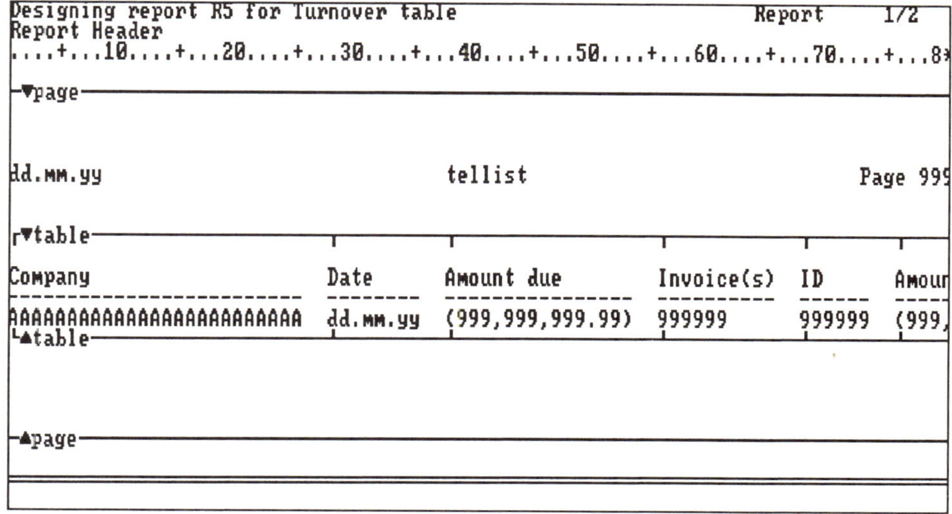

Figure 10.5: Report design screen

Delete unwanted columns together with fields:

7. Press **F10/T/E** to choose Erase.

8. Move the cursor to the ID field and press **<Enter>**.

Note, use **Ctrl-<arrow-key>** to move half a screen at a time.

9. Repeat stages 7 and 8 to delete the columns, Street, City and Postcode.

10. Rearrange the fields: Position the cursor in the Company field and rotate columns by pressing **Ctrl-R** until you encounter the Name field. Rotate the Tel field so that the first three fields conform to the order: Name, Company, Tel.

11. Finally, press **F2** to record the Report.

To print the report: press **F10/R/O**, select the Client table, choose the appropriate report, and press **P**, or, if you want to output to the screen press **S**.

10.7 Multi-table Tabular Reports

Multi-table tabular reports, which permit fields to be reaped from more than one table, are created in exactly the same way as their free-form equivalents.

Returning to the database solution developed in Chapter 6, suppose it were necessary to produce a report showing all orders together with appropriate telephone numbers. To produce this multi-table report, both Client and Turnover tables are required. Figure 10.6 shows a multi-table tabular report which offers a solution.

Company	Tel	Date	Amount due	ID	Amount received	Date receive
AST Ltd	0625 652398	17-Apr-89	8,000.00	107	8,000.00	20-Jun-89
Brett Ltd	0272 865612	9-Jul-89	5,500.00	106	5,500.00	29-Aug-89
DG Computers Ltd	0272 561238	25-May-89	8,000.00	109	8,000.00	27-Jul-89
Morris Technology Ltd	0625 878881	6-Mar-90	6,000.00	105		
Mount Clove Ltd	0876 678446	4-May-89	10,500.00	101	10,500.00	6-Jul-89
Mount Clove Ltd	0876 678446	9-Jun-89	17,500.00	101	17,500.00	4-Aug-89
SouthGate Ltd	0194 284653	5-Jan-90	9,000.00	102		
TriTech Ltd	0194 675412	25-May-89	5,000.00	103	5,000.00	28-Jul-89
TriTech Ltd	0194 675412	27-Feb-90	4,500.00	103		
Wilkins Technology Ltd	0876 678423	13-Apr-89	14,000.00	104	14,000.00	15-Jun-89
Wilkins Technology Ltd	0876 678423	18-Jan-90	5,000.00	104		

Figure 10.6: Multi-table tabular report

The following hands-on session shows how to generate the multi-table tabular report shown in Figure 10.6.

10.7.1 Hands-on Session

1. Press **F10/R/D** to begin designing the report.

2. Press **<Enter>** and select the Turnover table.

3. Press **<Right-arrow-key>** until you encounter an unused report, and press **<Enter>**.

4. Enter **TelList** in response to, *Report description:*

5. Press **T** to choose Tabular. You will then be confronted by a design screen of the sort shown in Figure 10.7.

It is now necessary to link the Client table:

6. Press **F10/F/L** to select Lookup.

7. Press **L** to choose Link.

8. Press **<Enter>** and select the Client table.

9. Choose the Company field in response to, *Select TURNOVER field to match Company in CLIENT.*

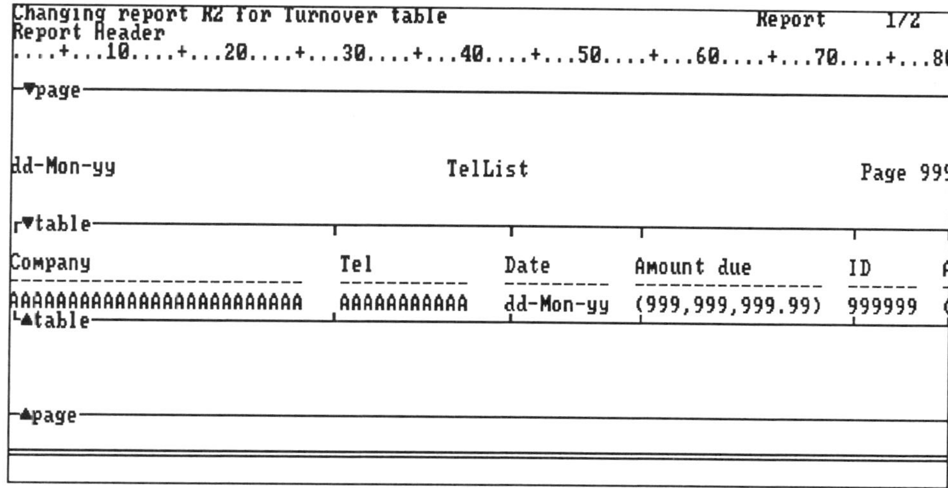

Figure 10.7: Report design screen

You are now free to place fields from the Client table. However, before an additional field can be placed, an extra column must be included:

10. Press **F10/T** to select TableBand.

11. Press **I** to choose Insert.

12. Within the Table Band move the cursor to the Date column and press **<Enter>**, inserting a new column.

Note, columns can be erased by pressing **F10/T/E**.

To place the Tel field:

13. Press **F10/F/P/R** to place a regular field.

14. Highlight [Client->] and press **<Enter>**, producing a list of fields in the Client table.

15. Select the Tel field.

16. With the cursor in the newly created column, press **<Enter>**.

17. Use the arrow keys to resize the field and press **<Enter>** once again.

18. Press **Ins** and complete the column by typing the field name, Tel, and then underline it.

Before pressing **F2** to record the report, one slight problem has to be surmounted, namely, columns on the right will be printed on a separate page. To remedy this it is necessary to modify the page layout as follows:

19. Press **Ctrl-<right-arrow-key>** until the page width border is in the middle of the screen.

20. Press **F10/S/P** to select PageLayout.

21. Press **W** to select Width.

22. Adjust the default page width of 80 by entering **125.**

23. Press **F2** to record the report.

This tabular report can be printed in the conventional way.

10.8 Calculations

Several spreadsheet-type methods of performing calculations were discussed in Chapter 7 Asking Questions. An alternative method of calculating such items as VAT, effects of increases in salary, lie in Calculated fields.

To illustrate one example of Calculated fields, suppose the Amounts shown in the Turnover table did not include VAT, and, naturally, it was necessary to incorporate a field which added the appropriate amount of VAT for each order. Such a report is shown in Figure 10.8.

Company	Date	Amount due	Invoice(s)	ID	Date received	Amount received	Inc VAT
AST Ltd	17.04.89	8,000.00	2	107	20.06.89	8,000.00	9,200.00
Brett Ltd	9.07.89	5,500.00	2	106	29.08.89	5,500.00	6,325.00
DG Computers Ltd	25.05.89	8,000.00	1	109	27.07.89	8,000.00	9,200.00
Morris Technology Ltd	6.03.90	6,000.00		105			
Mount Clove Ltd	4.05.89	10,500.00	1	101	6.07.89	10,500.00	12,075.00
Mount Clove Ltd	9.06.89	17,500.00	2	101	4.08.89	17,500.00	20,125.00
SouthGate Ltd	5.01.90	9,000.00		102			
TriTech Ltd	25.05.89	5,000.00	1	103	28.07.89	5,000.00	5,750.00
TriTech Ltd	27.02.90	4,500.00		103			
Wilkins Technology Ltd	13.04.89	14,000.00	1	104	15.06.89	14,000.00	16,100.00
Wilkins Technology Ltd	18.01.90	5,000.00		104			

Figure 10.8: A report to calculate VAT

The following hands-on session shows how to create the report shown in Figure 10.8.

10.8.1 Hands-on Session – using calculated fields

1. Press **F10/R/D** to select Design.

2. Press **<Enter>** and select the Turnover table.

3. Press **<Right-arrow-key>** until you encounter an unused report, and press **<Enter>**.

4. Enter **Turnover** in response to, *Report description:*

5. Press **T** to choose Tabular. You will then see a design screen of the sort shown in Figure 10.5.

6. Press **F10/T** to select TableBand.

7. Press **I** to choose Insert.

8. Within the Table band move the cursor to the Date received column and press **<Enter>**, inserting a new column.

Note, if necessary, columns can be erased by pressing **F10/T/E.**

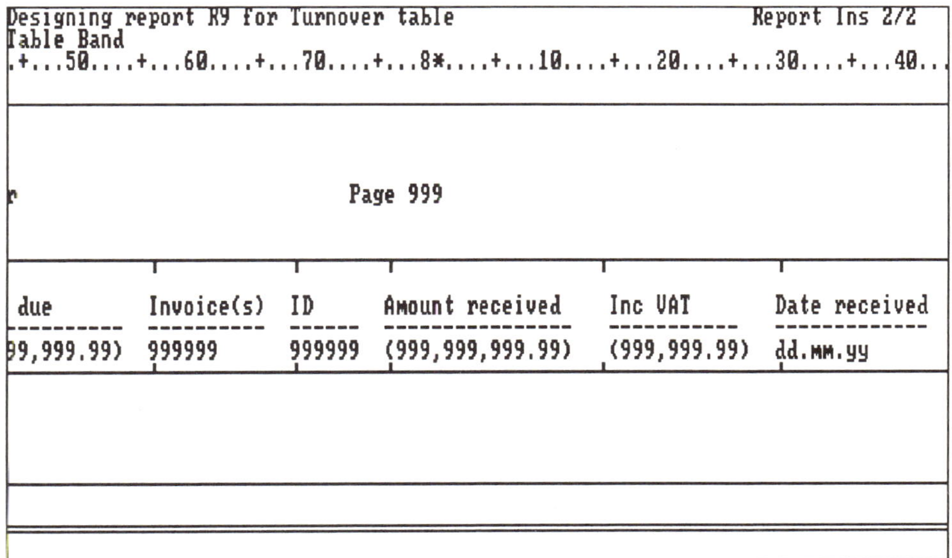

Figure 10.9: Report design screen

Now, to establish the calculated field:

9. Press **F10/F/P/C** to create and place a calculated field.

10. It is now necessary to enter an expression, so, enter: **[Amount received] * 1.15**

11. Press **<Enter>** and place the field as shown in Figure 10.9.

Use the arrow keys to adjust the number of digits shown, and press **<Enter>**. Use the arrow keys once again to ensure that amounts are shown to two decimal places.

If you place the calculated field wrongly, press **F10/F/E** to erase it and place it once again.

12. Press Ins and type the field name, Inc VAT, and underline it as shown.

13. Using **Ctrl-R**, rotate the last three columns so the order conforms to: Date received, Amount received, Inc VAT.

As with the generation of the report in Hands-on Session 10.7.1, the page width must be altered, so:

14. Press **F10/S/P** to select PageLayout.

15. Press **W** to select Width.

16. Adjust the default page width of 80 by entering **125**.

17. Press **F2** to record the report.

10.9 Using Summary

Complementary to Calculated fields, Summary allows you to perform calculations which embody complete fields of a report, such as the total amount received for instance. Summary can also be used to:

❑ Average values of a field

❑ Count the number of values in a field

❑ Show the highest value in a field

❑ Show the lowest value in a field.

Take a look at the report shown in Figure 10.10. This is a variation of the report created in the previous Hands-on Session, but shows the total amount received.

Company	Date	Amount due	Invoice(s)	ID	Date received	Amount received	Inc VAT
AST Ltd	17.04.89	8,000.00	2	107	20.06.89	8,000.00	9,200.00
Brett Ltd	9.07.89	5,500.00	2	106	29.08.89	5,500.00	6,325.00
DG Computers Ltd	25.05.89	8,000.00	1	109	27.07.89	8,000.00	9,200.00
Morris Technology Ltd	6.03.90	6,000.00		105			
Mount Clove Ltd	4.05.89	10,500.00	1	101	6.07.89	10,500.00	12,075.00
Mount Clove Ltd	9.06.89	17,500.00	2	101	4.08.89	17,500.00	20,125.00
SouthGate Ltd	5.01.90	9,000.00		102			
TriTech Ltd	25.05.89	5,000.00	1	103	28.07.89	5,000.00	5,750.00
TriTech Ltd	27.02.90	4,500.00		103			
Wilkins Technology Ltd	13.04.89	14,000.00	1	104	15.06.89	14,000.00	16,100.00
Wilkins Technology Ltd	18.01.90	5,000.00		104			
						Total	78,775.00

Figure 10.10: Report with Summary field

The following hands-on session shows how to change the Turnover report to incorporate this added feature.

10.9.1 Hands-on Session – using summary fields

1. Press **F10/R/C** to select Change.

2. Press **<Enter>** and select the Turnover table.

3. Press **<Right-arrow-key>** until you encounter the Turnover report just created, and press **<Enter>**.

4. Press **<Enter>** once again.

Now, to establish the Summary field:

5. Press **F10/F/P/S** to select Summary.

6. Press **C** to choose Calculated.

7. It is now necessary to enter an expression, so, enter: **[Amount received] * 1.15**

8. Press **S** to select Sum.

9. Press **O** to select Overall.

10. Place the field as shown in Figure 10.11.

Use the arrow keys to adjust the number of digits shown and press **<Enter>**. Use the arrow keys once again to ensure that amounts are shown to two decimal places. Press **Escape** to cancel either of these actions.

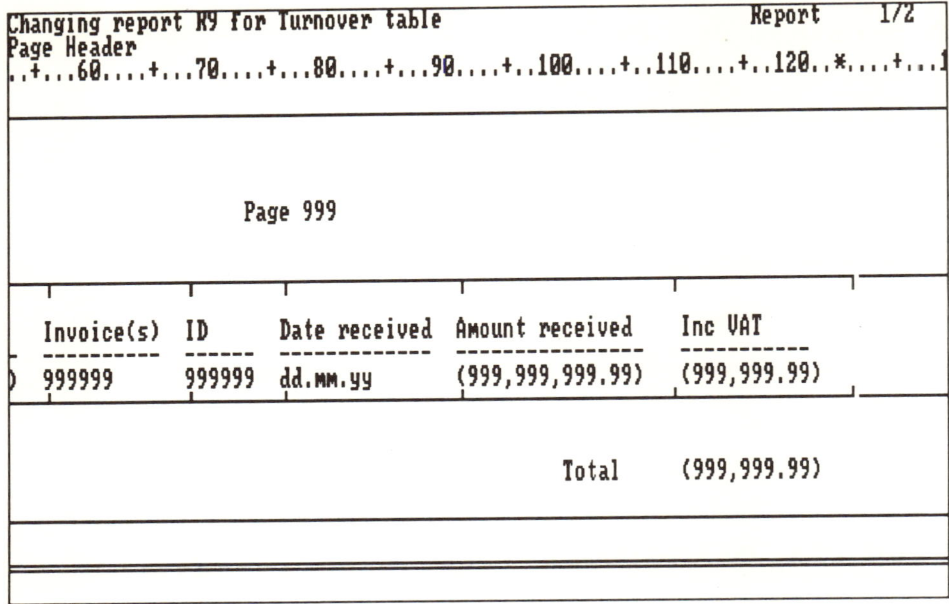

Figure 10.11: Placing the VAT field

If you place the calculated field wrongly, press **F10/F/E** to erase it and place it once again.

15. Press **Ins** and enter **Total**, as shown in Figure 10.11.

16. Press **F2** to record the report.

In this session, Summary/Calculated was used to add all field values. However, using regular fields, Summary/Regular can be used.

10.10 More about Calculations

There are numerous possibilities when entering expressions for calculated/summary fields. Available are the standard arithmetic operators: +, -, *, / and (). Summary operators include, Average, Count, High, Low and Sum. It is also possible to include constant values, like the 1.15 used in the previous hands-on session.

Though the operators are used in a conventional manner, the following expressions illustrate their use, where you will no doubt gather, all field names are enclosed in square brackets:

Product of Quantity and Amount fields :

[Quantity] * [Amount]

Show average value of Amount field:

Average ([Amount])

Halve Amount field, and add 15% VAT:

([Amount]/2) * 1.15

Multiply Quantity field (from linked Orders table) by Amount:

[Orders->Quantity] * [Amount]

Table 10.1: Key References

Operation	*Key(s)*
Change free-form/tabular report	**F10/R/C/<Enter>**/select table /select report
Design report	
Design free-form report	**F10/R/D/<Enter>**/select table/ select report/enter name/**F**
Design tabular report	**F10/R/D/<Enter>**/select table/ select report/enter name/**T**
Eliminate horizontal space (FieldSqueeze)	**F10/S/R/F/Y**
Erase field	**F10/F/E**/position cursor/**<Enter>**
Erase tabular column	**F10/T/E**/position cursor amid unwanted column/**<Enter>**
Insert tabular column	**F10/T/I**/move cursor to appropriate position/**<Enter>**
Link table	**F10/F/L/L/<Enter>**/select table/ choose appropriate field
Menu	**F10**
Move cursor to bottom of report design page	**End**

Move cursor to top of report design page	**Home**
Move screen left or right one half screen	**Ctrl-<arrow-key>**
Page width	**F10/S/P/W**/number of characters/ **<Enter>**
Pause between pages	**F10/S/W/Y** or **N**
Place and establish calculated field	**F10/F/P/C**/enter expression/ move cursor to desired location/**<Enter>** /use arrow keys to specify number of digits shown/**<Enter>**/use arrow keys to specify number of decimal places shown/**<Enter>**
Place and establish summary field	(see Section 10.9)
Place regular field	**F10/F/P/R**/select field/move cursor/**<Enter>**/size field/**<Enter>**
Record report	**F2**
Rotate tabular column	**Ctrl-R**
Type (insert-mode)	**Ins**
Eliminate horizontal space(FieldSqueeze)	**F10/R/C/<Enter>**/select table /select report/**<Enter>/F10/ S/R/F/Y**
File report (as .RPT Dos Text)	**F10/R/O/<Enter>**/select table /choose report/**F**/enter filename
Output report to screen	**F10/R/O/<Enter>**/select table /choose report numbe**r/S**
Printing	
Pause between pages	**F10/R/C**/select table/select report/**<Enter>/F10/S/W/Y/F2**
Print report	**F10/R/O/<Enter>**/select table /choose report numbe**r/P**
Print page range	**F10/R/R/<Enter>**/select table /select report/**P/ Backspace**/ Beginning page numbe**r/<Enter>** /Ending page number (see section 10.5)
Stop printing	**Escape**
Stop printing temporarily	**Ctrl-Break**

Page size (in report design screen)

Page length	**F10/S/P/L**/number of lines/ **<Enter>**
Vertical ruler	**Ctrl-V**

11

Programming Applications using the Personal Programmer

DON'T ABANDON THIS CHAPTER BECAUSE YOU'VE SEEN THE WORD PROGRAMMING!

Well it had to be said, because so many people suffer from programming phobia. Here, however, you will discover the ultimate cure!

This chapter discusses and explains the Paradox Personal Programmer. It should be said that this is essentially a tool which permits you to program Paradox without knowledge of its indigenous programming language, PAL (Paradox Application Language). In fact, the Paradox Personal Programmer produces PAL listings automatically.

Here, tailoring Paradox to your exact requirements for particular applications is discussed. Even PAL programmers are addressed, as the Personal Programmer is ideal for prototyping applications.

Finally, the database solution devised in Chapter 6 is used to illustrate how to use the Personal Programmer.

11.1 Introduction

The concept of programmable databases has been with us for a long time. It is not one of those optional extras or, worse still, a gimmick to sell software – of which there are many. It is a necessity, largely because a standard database which offers a blanket solution to all users is simply not possible – well not today, at least.

Consequently, databases such as Paradox are, in one sense, database development tools, which can be used to generate applications. Used in this context, an application is a collection of instructions which Paradox understands and can interpret. In actual fact, an application is best thought of as customised database, designed to satisfy particular needs.

Previously, programming applications often meant using a database language, which was invariably a high-level language, where single statements initiate complex internal computations. Though high-level languages are easy to use, Borland has taken things a step further with Paradox. The Personal Programmer allows you to program applications without knowledge of PAL, the Paradox Application Language, nor programming in general.

Packages which perform the duty of the Personal Programmer are often referred to as applications generators. In the past, these have usually been expensive and, in some instances, they have demanded a certain level of programming skills.

Things are changing fast, however, and tools such as the Paradox Personal Programmer hammer home the inescapable fact that, one day, the majority of database applications will be generated this way.

Developing applications using the Personal Programmer offers three fundamental advantages:

- You need not be familiar with programming to develop an application
- The application can be modified with ease – modifying programs often means hours of shuffling code
- Developed applications can be executed using Paradox Runtime, giving the possibility of running applications on machines where Paradox3 is not installed.

11.2 Installing the Personal Programmer

Before the Personal Programmer can be installed, at least 2 Mbytes of disk space must be available. Confirming this, the Personal Programmer can be installed as follows:

1. With the Installation/Sample Tables Disk in drive A, enter **a:install.** (If you place the disk in drive b, use **b:install**).

2. Press **<Enter>** and select 3) Optional Software Installation, and press **<Enter>**, once again.

3. Press **<Enter>** to verify that the source drive is A: (If the Installation/Sample Tables disk is in drive B, then enter **B**.)

4. Press **<Enter>** to select C as the destination drive.

5. Press **<Enter>** to indicate that Paradox is installed in the Paradox3 directory. (Enter an alternative directory, if you did not install Paradox in the Paradox3 directory.)

6. Enter **3** to select 3) PPROG – Paradox Personal Programmer Installation.

7. Press **<Enter>** to install the Personal Programmer in the Pprog directory.

8. Sequentially, you will then be asked to insert Personal Programmer Disks 1 to 6. Finally, you will see: *Paradox Personal Programmer successfully installed.*

9. When the Optional Software Installation menu reappears, select Exit.

11.3 Developing Applications

As was demonstrated in Chapter 6, developing a database solution requires careful design and planning. We will not recap, but just remember the points about first obtaining a descriptive algorithm and then working your way down to an overall solution, following the route of top-down analysis (see Chapter 6). In this chapter, the bulk of this solution will be converted into an application.

Figure 11.1 shows the structure of the simple application created in this chapter using the Personal Programmer.

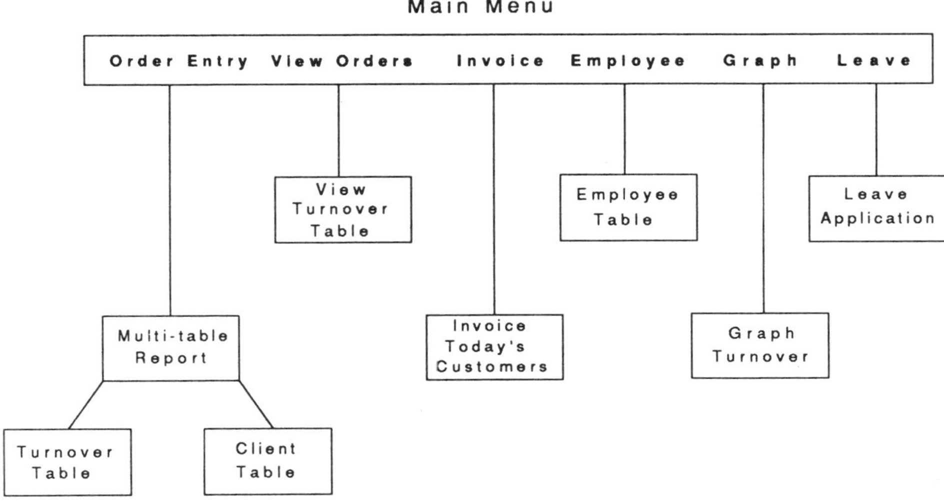

Figure 11.1: Application

Tables, objects and scripts making up a complete application can be developed from within the normal Paradox environment (within a single directory). The Personal Programmer is then used to gel these building blocks into an application.

The process of creating an application can be condensed to the following:

❑ Design tables and objects (see Chapter 6)

❑ Create a new directory for the application

❑ Develop tables and objects in normal Paradox3 environment

❑ Create a new directory within Pprog directory

❑ Copy tables and objects to directory within Pprog directory

❑ Run Personal Programmer

❑ Create Application

❑ Iterate by modifying application as necessary.

(Note, the need to enter a password before an application is run provides a reasonable degree of security. Passwords are discussed in Chapter 6.)

11.4 Using the Personal Programmer

Using the Personal Programmer is very much like using Paradox itself. Menu items are selected by pressing the appropriate key, or by highlighting them and then pressing **<Enter>**. The Escape key retains its role of backing out of menu selections. **F2** (Do- It!) also remains active. In many instances **F10** can be used to invoke the main menu.

Because menu names manifest their purpose, you should find using the Personal Programmer intuitive. For example, menu items such as Create, Modify etc should now be familiar to you. Finally, try to keep an eye on the information boxes shown in the lower half of the screen – these provide invaluable help.

11.5 Preparations

Previously, the database solution in Chapter 6 was confined to the Access directory, a subdirectory of the paradox3 directory. This cannot be used here, because applications must occupy directories within the Pprog directory. Naturally, therefore, all building blocks, ie tables and objects, must be copied to a new directory.

To do this, first make a new directory called Techno:

1. Press **T/M/T** to go to Dos.

2. Enter: **md c:\paradox3\pprog\techno**

3. Change to this directory by entering: **cd c:\paradox3\pprog \techno**

Having created the directory it is now necessary to copy all the building blocks, such as tables, forms, reports and scripts, (created in Chapter 6) from the Access directory to the Techno directory, so:

4. Enter: **copy c:\paradox3\access*.* c:\paradox3\pprog\techno**

5. Enter: **exit** to return to Dos.

11.6 Starting the Personal Programmer

The Personal Programmer must be run from Dos in the following manner:

1. Change to the Pprog directory by entering: **cd c:\paradox3\pprog**

3. Enter: **pprog.**

(Note, though it is possible to add an appropriate Dos path so as to enable the Personal Programmer to be run from any directory, we shall assume that it is necessary to change to the appropriate directory each time the Personal Programmer is run.)

11.7 Creating an Application

With all tables and respective families copied to the Techno directory, it is now possible to begin developing the application within the Personal Programmer. The following subsections divide the process into a number of phases, so as to isolate important procedures.

First, to say a little more about the application about to be created: to begin with, the main menu will be as follows:

OrderEntry ViewOrders Invoice Employee Leave

These menu items will lead to the following operations:

❑ **OrderEntry:** permit orders and new clients to be entered, using a multi-table form, Input (created in Chapters 6 and 9)

❑ **ViewOrders:** view the Turnover table, showing orders placed

❑ **Invoice:** print invoices entered on current date

❑ **Employee**: view employee records

❑ **Leave:** leave application.

(Later another menu item to produce graphs will be added.)

11.7.1 Selecting Tables

The first step in creating an application is to select all tables making up that application. Additionally, a concise description must be added to each. This straightforward process is dealt with via the ensuing stages:

1. Start the Personal Programmer as described in Section 11.6.

2. To change to the Techno directory, press **T** to select Tools; press **D** to select Directory; select Directory, once again; enter **techno**.

3. Press **C** to begin creating the application.

4. In response to the prompt, *Application name:*, enter **Tech**.

Unfortunately, there is limit of just five characters for application names. Now, the required tables will be selected:

5. Press **E** to select ExistingTable, and press **<Enter>** to list all tables in the Techno directory.

6. Highlight the Client table and press **<Enter>**.

7. Repeat stages 5 – 6 and select Employee and Turnover tables. (Note, only three of the five tables are required for this application.)

8. Press **F2** to record the selected tables as part of the application.

9. Now, it is necessary to include a concise description of each table. Enter the following remarks for each table:

Client	Clients' names and addresses
Employee	Employee records
Turnover	Amounts received.

Before moving on to create the main menu, a few words . . .

11.7.2 Building the Main Menu

Building the main menu is a particularly satisfying aspect of using the Personal Programmer; you can create Paradox-style menus according to precise requirements or tastes.

Though it is important to give the main menu design careful consideration, menu items and descriptions can be edited to a reasonable extent. Menu items can be up to 20 characters long, and descriptions up to 60 characters.

The basic operations when creating and editing a main menu are as follows:

❑ Enter an appropriate menu item; enter the description for that menu item.

❑ To edit a menu item, highlight it using the cursor keys, press **F9**, and then press **Backspace** or **Ctrl-Backspace** to erase characters – to move on and edit an accompanying description press **<Enter>**. **Del** is used to erase a menu selection.

When designing the main menu, or indeed submenus, it is preferable to choose items which begin with different letters, so that they may be selected by pressing a single key. For this application the following main menu (and descriptions) are required:

OrderEntry Enter a new order from client

ViewOrders View orders placed

Invoice Invoice a client

Employee Employee records

Leave Leave tech application

Interestingly, there is no need to include the Leave item (which acts like Exit), as the Personal Programmer has the intelligence to add it automatically.

Moving on from steps outlined in subsection 11.7.1, we now create the main menu:

1. Enter the menu item **OrderEntry**, and then enter the accompanying description, **Enter order from client.**

2. Repeat step 1 and enter the remaining menu items and descriptions, *except for Leave.*

(Note: You can use **Ins** to insert a new item amid the menu and the cursor keys to move around.)

At this point, we are going to leave the Personal Programmer, to demonstrate the ease with which you can go return to creating an application:

1. Press **F2** twice

2. We will not design a 'splash screen' yet (a splash screen is simply an introductory screen shown each time an application is run), so, press **N** to select NoSplashScreen.

3. Press **F2**, once again, to generate and save the application so far – this may take some time. You will see a number of PAL scripts grace the screen – all of which have been created without programming a single line of code!

4. Finally, press **E/Y** to leave the Personal Programmer.

11.7.3 Menu Actions

What has been achieved so far? Well, not much in actual fact, you have merely selected tables and created the main menu. The next logical step, therefore, is to include the appropriate menu actions listed in Section 11.7.

To continue working on the application, run the Personal Programmer (see Section 11.6), then change to the Techno directory (see stage 2 of subsection 11.7.1).

The application can be modified so as to embody the OrderEntry selection as follows:

1. Press **M** to select Modify.

2. Enter the name of the application, ie **tech**.

Before the Tech application can be modified, Paradox checks for password-protected tables – if present, you will have to enter the appropriate password(s).

3. At this stage it is possible to implement any type of modification. However, here, menu actions have to be defined, so, press **M** to select MenuAction.

4. Ensure OrderEntry is highlighted, and press **F10** to invoke the menu.

5. With OrderEntry blinking, press **A** to select Action.

To defined an action for the OrderEntry selection:

6. Press **D** to select Define.

7. As this item involves entering and editing data, press **E** to choose Edit.

8. Press **S** to choose SelectTable, and select the Turnover table.

9. Satisfied that the correct table has been chosen, press **F2**.

10. Press **A** to choose AllRecords.

To include the multi-table form, Input:

11. Highlight FormView and press **<Enter>**.

12. Press **B** to select Borrow. Borrow will enable you to use the multi-table form, Input, created in Chapters 6 and 9.

13. Press the **<right-arrow-key>** until you encounter the Input form, then press **<Enter>**.

14. Press **I** to select InsertDelete.

15. Press **I/Y** to allow the user to insert and edit records.

16. Press **F2** to record the menu selection.

17. Press **F10/F2** to save changes.

18. Press **F2**, once again – you will have to wait some time while scripts are generated and saved.

11.7.4 Summarising an Application

When creating an application, it is all too easy to focus on particular aspects, ignoring the overall picture. As with the design of any application, or indeed computer program, standing back to achieve an overall picture is a compulsory requirement.

For example, when the building blocks were designed in Chapter 6, a structure was drafted which helped gain such an overall view. Equally, before designing the nuts and bolts of an application, it is a good idea to summarise the menu structure. It has to be said that, in this instance the menu structure is so simple, it hardly needs to be summarised.

However, to illustrate how to use Summarize:

1. Press **S** to select Summarize from the main Personal Programmer menu.

2. Enter the name of the application, **tech**.

3. Press **T** to choose Tree.

4. You can send the summary to the printer, screen or file. Summaries are written as

Dos Text files with an RPT extension – just like tables, in fact. Press **S** to output to the screen, producing the tree shown in Figure 11.2.

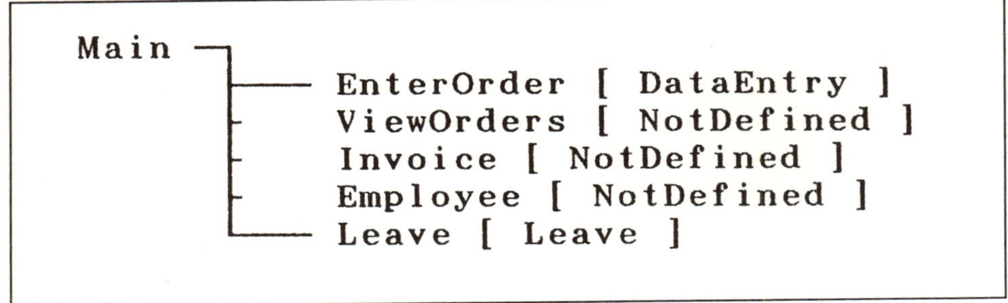

Figure 11.2: Summarise – Tree structure

11.7.5 Adding a Menu Action for ViewOrders

We now look at how to assign the action of viewing the Turnover table to the ViewOrders selection:

1. Press **M** to select Modify, and enter **Tec.** Press **M** to select MenuAction.

2. Highlight ViewOrders and press **F10** to invoke the menu.

3. Press **A** to choose Action.

4. Press **D** to select Define.

5. As this is a **View** item, press **V** to choose View.

6. Press **S** to choose SelectTable.

7. Select the Turnover table.

8. Press **F2**.

9. Press **A** to use all fields in the Turnover table.

10. Press **A**, once again, to use all records in the Turnover table.

11. Press **T** to select TableView.

11.7.6 Invoicing

You will remember that in Chapter 6, the particularly important topic of invoicing was discussed. Of course, using the complete Paradox configuration, as in Chapter 6, QBE can be used to select and print any invoice required.

Using the Personal Programmer is slightly more restrictive, so, the Invoice item will simply print invoices with the current date. At the end of each day, invoices can then be printed.

Needless to say, such a method of invoicing is best implemented using a table which contains a date field indicating when a client should be invoiced.

1. Highlight the Invoice menu item and press **F10** to invoke the menu.

2. Press **A** to select Action.

3. Press **D** to choose Define.

4. Press **R** to select Report, because we want to print Invoices.

5. Press **S** to choose SelectTable.

6. Press **T** to choose the Turnover table.

7. Press **F2**.

8. Press **S** to choose SelectRecords – in order to invoice selected customers.

9. Fill in the query form by simply entering **today** in the Date field – this will cause invoices with the current date to be printed.

10. Press **F10/T** to try the query – Query was successful will be shown temporarily in the bottom right of the screen.

11. Press **F2**.

12. Press **B** to Borrow an existing report.

13. Using the arrow keys find the Invoice report and press **<Enter>**.

14. Press **P** to send invoices to the printer.

11.7.7 The Employee table

The following series of steps show how to add the action of viewing the Employee table.

1. Highlight the Employee selection, and press **F10** to invoke the menu.

2. Press **A** to select Action.

3. Press **D** to choose Define.

4. Press **V** to select View.

5. Press **S** to choose SelectTable.

6. Press **E** to select the Employee table.

7. Press **F2**.

8. Press **A** to select AllFields.

9. Press **A** to choose AllRecords.

10. Press **T** to select TableView.

11. Press **F10/D** to select Do-It! and save all changes made so far.

11.7.8 Adding a SplashScreen

The splash screen is simply an introductory screen displayed when the application is run. The process of designing a splash screen is very much like designing a form – in actual fact, a splash screen is a cut-down form. As such, you should be able to design one merely by recalling, or observing, the process of creating forms.

Press S to select SplashScreen, then press **F10** to produce the menu.The splash screen shown in Figure 11.3 opposite is purely optional.

11.7.9 Saving (and Generating) complete Applications

Having created the application, it is now necessary to save and generate it. This is, naturally, achieved by simply pressing D to select Do-It! from the Personal Programmer menu.

11.7.10 Reviewing Applications

Using Review from the Personal Programmer main menu, it is possible to browse through the menu structure of the application, like so:

1. Press **R** to invoke Review.

2. Enter the name of the application, ie **Tech**.

Select items as normal and press **F2** when you have finished.

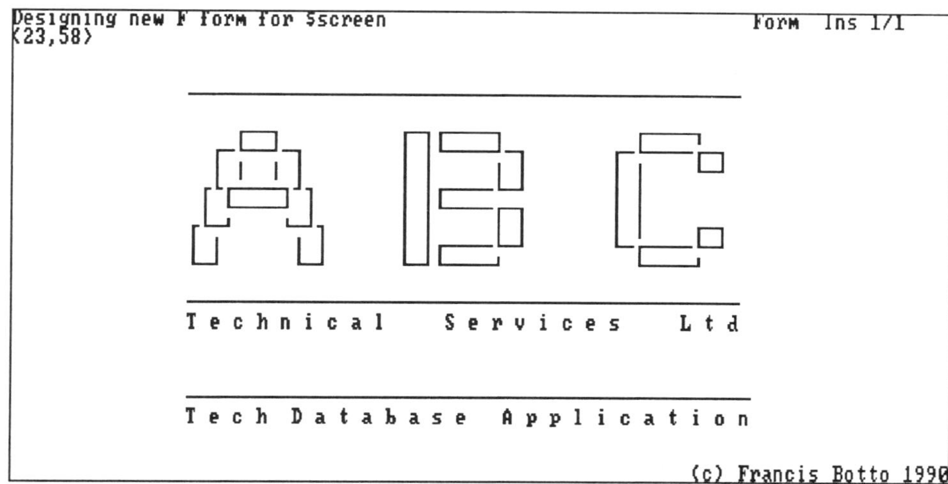

Figure 11.3: Splash screen for Tech application

11.7.11 Playing the Application

The Tech application can be played directly from within the Personal Programmer, as follows:

1. Press **P** to select Play.

2. Enter **Tech**.

You will then be confronted by the splash screen, and asked to enter any passwords if tables are protected.

You will then see the main menu:

OrderEntry ViewOrders Invoice Employee Leave

Enter a new order from client

Experiment with the application – convince yourself that it works! For example, press **O** to select OrderEntry, and enter a record with the current date (in the Date field), press **F2**, and then use Invoice to generate the invoice corresponding to that record.

Press **L/Y** to leave the Tech application. Finally, leave the Personal Programmer by pressing **E/Y**.

Congratulations you have created a new application!

11.8 Running Applications

Outside the confines of the Personal Programmer, there are three ways of running an application:

❑ From within Paradox itself

❑ From Dos

❑ Using Paradox Runtime.

The following subsections address each of these methods.

11.8.1 Running Applications from Paradox

Running an application from within Paradox requires that you change to the appropriate Pprog directory and then play the application as you would a script. For example, to run the Tech application:

1. Press **T/M/D** to select Directory.

2. Enter **pprog\techno**, and press **O**

3. Press **S/P** to choose Play.

4. Press **<Enter>** and select the Tech application.

11.8.2 Running Applications from Dos

The beauty of creating applications with the Personal Programmer, or indeed using PAL, is that end-users need not be familiar with Paradox. For example, running an application from Dos essentially leads to an entirely different database.

To run the Tech application from Dos:

1. Make Techno the default directory using the CCP, as discussed in Chapter 6.

2. Each time you want to run the application from Dos, enter: **paradox3 tech**.

11.8.3 Running Applications using Paradox Runtime

You will understand that applications can only be run when Paradox is actually present. Technically, therefore, applications can only be distributed to systems where Paradox is installed.

Paradox Runtime, however, allows applications to be developed which do not require the presence of the Paradox program. Under a special licence agreement Paradox Runtime can be used to distribute applications. You can find out more about Paradox Runtime from Borland.

11.9 More About Menus

The Menu structure of the Tech application created in section 11.7, was as simple as one could possibly achieve. A single menu was included, which provided routes to only the most essential features. Beyond such a simple array of selections, more complex menu structures can be created, which also incorporate submenus. When submenus are assigned to menu selections, the Personal Programmer will not automatically include a Cancel item so as to return to the main menu, as the Escape key will do this.

Submenus are created in exactly the same way as main menus. To begin creating a submenu ensure that the action menu, ie:

Menu View Report DataEntry Edit Script Help NotDefined Cancel

is on screen, and that the menu item to which leads to the submenu is blinking.

Before continuing to develop an application, the Personal Programmer demands that you define each of the selections on the submenu. However, to continue with an application, include a NotDefined action to the (main) menu selection.

11.10 Adding Help

When using Paradox the Help key, **F1**, provides invaluable help to the novice, or to the inexperienced user. Like splash screens, Help screens are created in a similar manner to custom forms – see subsection 11.7.8 on designing a splash screen.

Unfortunately, F1, the Help key, will not invoke help from within an application.

Suppose it were necessary within the Tech application to include a help screen within the Tech application, which indicated the main purpose of the application and what each of the main menu items permitted. Such a screen could be achieved from within the Personal Programmer as follows:

(Note, a Help selection must be included in the main menu of the Tech application.)

1. With the action menu on screen, ie:

Menu View Report DataEntry Edit Script Help NotDefined Cancel

and with the Help selection blinking, press **H** to select help.

2. Using the techniques described in subsection 11.7.8, create an appropriate help screen.

3. Finally, press **F2** to save the Help screen.

(See Section 11.7.1 about saving an application and leaving the Personal Programmer.)

11.11 Graphs and Scripts in Applications

The importance of graphs was fully explained in Chapter 8, where the various graph types were discussed. You may have noticed that including a graph within an application is not directly possible using the Personal Programmer. The answer is to include a script.

Suppose, for example, it was necessary to include a menu item which generated a graph showing amounts received from the various clients. In Chapter 6, where the building blocks for the Tech application were developed, a script capable of doing this was created (see subsection 6.11.2).

That script simply queried the Turnover table to isolate the Client and Amount received fields, renamed the resultant Answer table Income, and then produced a graph according to the default settings.

The following hands-on session shows how to add this script to the Tech application.

11.11.1 Hands-on Session

This session shows how to include the script, Income, created in subsection 6.11.2. If you have not created the Income script, return to Chapter 6 and do so now.

1. Run the Personal Programmer and, if necessary, change to the Techno directory.

2. Press **M** to select Modify.

3. Enter **Tech**.

4. Press **M** to choose MenuAction.

We now need to include the Graph selection:

5. Highlight the Leave selection, and press **F10**. Press **M** to select Menu, then press **<Ins>**.

6. Enter **Graph**.

7. Enter the description: **Show graph of turnover**. The main menu will appear:

OrderEntry ViewOrders Invoice Employee Graph Leave Show graph of turnover

8. Press **F2** to save the selection.

9. Press **F2**, once again, to save changes so far.

10. Press **M** to select MenuAction.

11. Using the arrow keys, highlight Graph.

12. Press **F10** to produce the menu.

13. Press **A** to select Action.

14. Press **D** to choose Define.

15. Press **S** to select Script.

16. Press **<Enter>** and select the **Income** script.

17. Press **F2** to save changes.

18. Press **D** to select Do-It!

19. Finally, press **E/Y** to leave the Personal Programmer.

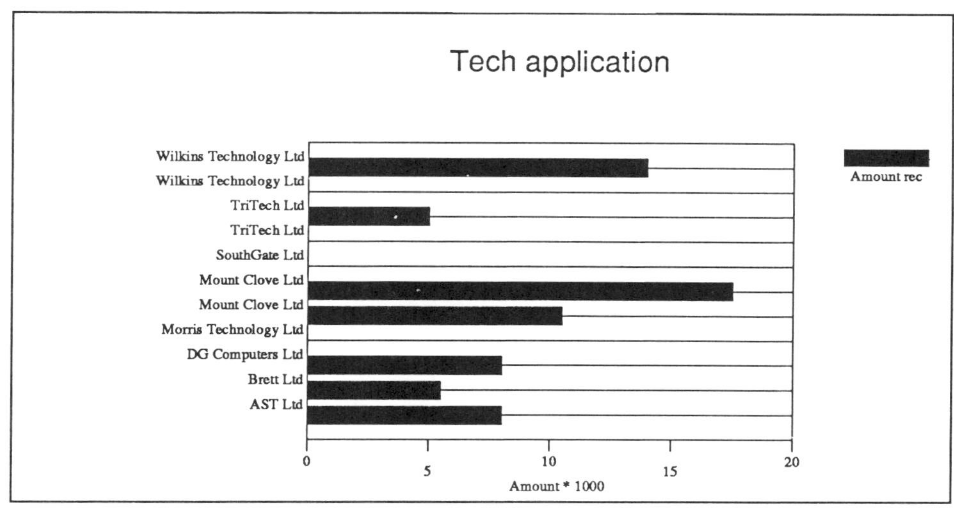

Figure 11.4: The resulting graph from the tech application

You may find that graphs are not generated when applications are run from within the Personal Programmer.

Run the script from within Paradox, and press G to select Graph giving the rotated bar graph (see Chapter 8 about graph settings) shown in Figure 11.4. on the next page.

Note, in terms of compatibility, there is a bitter pill to be swallowed when applications comprise graphs. Pre-Paradox 3 releases will not support selections which generate graphs.

11.12 Final Words

As you will have seen reading this chapter, it is quite easy to return to the Personal Programmer and modify any part of an application. Though the operation of the Personal Programmer lacks what might be called lightening speed, it is considerably easier to use than programming line after line of code.

For programmers, and those developing serious applications for distribution via Paradox Runtime, the Personal Programmer is an ideal prototyping tool. It is also useful for laying down the foundations for further programming using PAL. The limitation of just 16 tables might present an obstacle, but by no means an insurmountable one, as the idea of merging a number of Paradox scripts is quite possible.

One day, all applications will be generated using programs like the Personal Programmer!

Appendix

Paradox Operations

The Main Menu

View	view table on screen
Ask	QBE (query by example)
Report	design, write report to printer or screen
Create	create table structure
Modify	edit, sort, restructure table
Image	resize and reformat table; move to field or record; pick form; graph table.
Forms	design or change form
Tools	rename tables, forms, reports; export and import data; copy and delete tables, forms, reports and scripts; speed up queries; add and subtract records; protect tables and scripts; set user names and refresh interval; change directory; go to Dos.
Scripts	record and play scripts
Help	context sensitive help, or choose topic
Exit	leave Paradox

Important Function Keys

F1	produces context sensitive help and help on specified topics
F2	invokes Do-It! which digests changes or data entered

F3	(Up Image) move from one table to the table above
Alt-F3	record an instant script
F4	(Down Image) move from one table to table below
Alt-F4	play instant recorded script
F5	enter example while filling in query form (see Chapter 7)
Alt-F5	(Field View) converts field value into full editor; useful for viewing hidden parts of field value
F6	(Check mark for querying) causes field values to be listed (see Chapter 7)
Alt-F6	(Check Plus for querying) lists field values including duplicates (see Chapter 7)
Ctrl-F6	(Check Descending for querying) lists field values in descending order (see Chapter 7)
F7	toggle between form and table
Alt-F7	produce standard report in tabular format
Ctrl-F7	produce graph
F8	clear current image
Alt-F8	clear all images in workspace
F9	edit table – used for switching to edit mode while viewing table(s)
Alt-F9	co-edit tables
F10	main menu

Important Shortcuts

Alt-C	switch colour palette on or off during form design
Ctrl-D	copy value from record above cursor
Ctrl-F	equivalent to Alt-F5, switches on field view
Ctrl-L	resynchronise records on a multi-table form
Alt-L	lock or unlock record
Ctrl-O	equivalent to ToDos from Tools
Alt-O	equivalent to ToDos from Tools
Ctrl-R	rotate columns in table (or tabular report)
Alt-R	update screen to reflect changes made by network users
Ctrl-U	undo changes made to a table
Ctrl-V	display vertical ruler which shows line numbers
Alt-X	CrossTab (see Chapter 8)
Ctrl-Y	delete line in report, script or form
Ctrl-Z	locate specified field value in table
Alt-Z	locate next occurrence of field value in table
Ctrl-Backspace	delete word/field at cursor while editing
Tab	move between fields when viewing/editing table

Query Operators

Reserved words:

√	list all field values in answer
√+	list all field values including duplications
√∇	list field values in descending order
calc	calculate new field
changeto	change values in queried table
delete	delete selected records from queried table
find	locate selected records (similar to Zoom feature)
G	specify group for set operators
insert	insert new records
set	define selected records as set

Arithmetic operators:

+	addition or concatenation of field values
-	subtraction
*	multiplication
/	division
()	group operators in query expression

Range operators:

=	equal to
>	greater than
<	less than
>=	greater than or equal to
<=	less than or equal to

Wild cards:

..	any sequence of characters
@	any single character

Special operators:

as	change field name in Answer table
like	match field vaguely
blank	no value
today	current date
!	display all records in a field

Logical operators:

not	not match
or	either-or conditions
,	and conditions

Summary operators:

average	average of group of values
count	give number of values in group
max	highest value in group
min	lowest value in group
sum	total of values in group
all	calculate summary based on values in group irrespective of duplications
unique	calculate summary based on unique values in group

Set comparison operators:

every	list values that match all members of defined set
exactly	list all records that match members of the defined set exactly
only	list all records that match members of the defined set
no	list all records that match no members of defined set

Editing/data entry with forms

Move cursor

Down one field	**Down arrow**
First field of current record	**Ctrl-Home**
First record of table	**Home**
Last field of current record	**Ctrl-End**
Last record of table	**End**
Next record	**PgDn**
Next field	**Right arrow**
Previous field	**Left arrow**
Previous record	**PgUp**
Same field of next record	**Ctrl-PgDn**
Same field of previous record	**Ctrl-PgUp**
Up one field	**Up arrow**

Edit form

Delete field	**Ctrl-Backspace**
Delete record	**Del** (on numeric keypad)

Insert record	**Ins**
Store editing session	F2 (Do-It!)
Toggle between table and form	**F7**

Forms

Design and change form

Adjust multi-record region	**F10/M/R/A**
Change form	**F10/F/C**
Design form	**F10/F/D**
Embed/Link table	**F10/M/T/P/L** (see Hands-on 9.9.1)
Erase border	**F10/B/E**
Erase field	**F10/F/E**
Erase wrapped field	**F10/A/E**
Link table	**F10/M/T/P/L** (see Hands-on 9.9.1)
Place border	**F10/B/P**
Place multi-record region	**F10/M/R/D**
Place regular field	**F10/F/P/R** (see Hands-on 9.2.1)
Type text	**Ins**
Wrap field	**F10/F/W** (see Hands-on 9.3)
Edit form	**F9** (with form on screen)
Form Toggle	**F7**
Invoke form	**F10/I/P**/select form

Graphs

CrossTab	first arrange table/**F10/I/G/C** or **Alt-X**
Default graph settings	**F10/S/P/<Enter>**/select Custom/**G/G**

Graph types

Area graph	**F10/I/G/M/A/F2**
Bar graph	**F10/I/G/M/B/F2**
Line graph	**F10/I/G/M/L/F2**
Marker graph	**F10/I/G/M/M/F2**
Pie chart	**F10/I/G/M/P/F2**
Rotated bar graph	**F10/I/G/M/R/F2**
Stacked bar graph	**F10/I/G/M/S/F2**
XY graph	**F10/I/G/M/X/F2**

Load graph type	**F10/I/G/L/<Enter>**/select graph type
Print graph	**F10/I/G/V/P** (position cursor in numeric field – see Section 8.13)

Default layout	(Hands-on 8.13.4)
Printer layout	**F10/I/G/M/F10/O/P** (Hands-on 8.13.1)
Select printer	(see Section 8.13)
Save	
File graph	**F10/I/G/V/F/filename/<Enter>**
File type	**F10/I/G/M/F10/O/D/F**/select file type
Graph type	**F10/I/G/S/file name/<Enter>**
View graph on screen	**Ctrl-F7** or **F10/I/G/V** (position cursor in numeric field)
View table structure	**F10/T/I/S**

Reports

Change free-form/tabular report	**F10/R/C/<Enter>**/select table/select report
Design report	
Design free-form report	**F10/R/D/<Enter>**/select table/select report/**enter name/F**
Design tabular report	**F10/R/D/<Enter>**/select table/select report/**enter name/T**
Eliminate horizontal space (FieldSqueeze)	**F10/S/R/F/Y**
Erase field	**F10/F/E**/position cursor/**<Enter>**
Erase tabular column	**F10/T/E**/position cursor amid unwanted column/**<Enter>**
Insert tabular column	**F10/T/I**/move cursor to appropriate position/**<Enter>**
Link table	**F10/F/L/L/<Enter>**/select table/choose appropriate field
Menu	**F10**
Move cursor to bottom of report design page	**End**
Move cursor to top of report design page	**Home**
Move screen left or right one half screen	**Ctrl-<arrow-key>**
Page width	**F10/S/P/W/no of characters/<Enter>**
Pause between pages	**F10/S/W/N**
Place and establish calculated field	**F10/F/P/C/enter expression/** move cursor to desired location/**<Enter>**/use

	arrow keys to specify number of digits shown/**<Enter>**/use arrow keys to specify no. of decimal places/**<Enter>**
Place and establish summary field	(see Section 10.9)
Place regular field	**F10/F/P/R**/select field/move cursor/ **<Enter>**/size field/**<Enter>**
Record report	**F2**
Rotate tabular column	**Ctrl-R**
Type (insert-mode)	**Ins**
Eliminate horizontal space (FieldSqueeze)	**F10/R/C/<Enter>**/select table/select report/**F10/S/R/F/Y**
File report (as .RPT Dos Text)	**F10/R/O/<Enter>**/select table/choose report/**F/enter filename**
Output report to screen	**F10/R/O/<Enter>**/select table/choose report number/**S**
Printing	
Pause between pages	**F10/R/C**/select table/select report/ **F10/S/W/Y/F2**
Print report	**F10/R/O/<Enter>**/select table/choose report number/**P**
Print page range	**F10/R/R/<Enter>**/select table/select report/**P/Backspace/Beginning page number/<Enter>/Ending page number** (see Section 10.5)
Stop printing	**Escape**
Stop printing temporarily	**Ctrl-Break**
Page size (in report design screen)	
Page length	**F10/S/P/L/number of lines/<Enter>**
Vertical ruler	**Ctrl-V**

Input/Output Operations

Using SideKick to import screen data from Paradox

SideKick users can import screen data from Paradox into the notepad. This operation can be useful for copying reports into a word processor.

Screen data can be copied as follows:

1. Produce the screen data you wish to copy and then press **Alt-Ctrl** to activate SideKick and select the notepad. Press **F4** – the notepad will disappear, leaving the cursor in the top left of the screen.

2. Position the cursor in the top left of the block you want to copy and press **F7**.

3. Mark the data using the arrow keys and press **<Esc>** to return to the Notepad.

4. Press **Ctrl-K/C** to paste data into the notepad.

Using SideKick to paste data into Paradox

You can paste text from SideKick as follows:

1. Mark the block of text on the SideKick notepad, marking its beginning by pressing **F7**, and its the end by pressing **F8**.

2. Press **Ctrl-K/E**. Press **Ctrl-F1** to assign the block of text to this key combination. Then press **B** to indicate that it is a block of text. Note, take care not to re-define existing Paradox shortcuts.

3. To insert the block into a Paradox report, for example – be sure to press **Ins,** and simply press **Ctrl-F1**.

Loading graphs into the Borland Sprint word processor

Note, to load graphs into Borland Sprint, the graph must be stored in the Encapsulated PostScript (EPS) file format (see Chapter 8, Subsection 8.1.2 for details). Furthermore, a postscript printer is required, else the graph cannot be printed.

1. Press **Alt-F** to pull down the File menu.

2. Press **F** to select the File Manager.

3. Press **C** to select Change directory, and enter the name of the Paradox3 directory where the EPS file is stored. Enter: **c:\paradox3\access**, for example.

4. Press **Shift-Esc** to remove all menus from the screen.

5. Position the cursor at the relevant point in the document, and press **Alt-S** to pull down the Style menu.

6. Press **G** to select Graphics.

7. Press **E** to choose EPS Picture.

8. In response to *Name of EPS picture to place here:*, enter the name of the graph file. There is no need to include the EPS extension.

9. It is advisable to press **Y** to opt to scale the graphic – this will help prevent any overspill, so, press **Y**.

10. Enter **6.25** inches for the width, and, once again, **6.25** inches for the height. It is quite all right, Sprint understands units of measurement such as inches!

11. The following formatter commands will then appear in the document:

EPS "TREND.EPS", width = 6.25 inches, height = 6.25 inches

12. If you wish, you can preview the graphic on screen by either pressing **Alt-F/S**, or, by using the shortcut **Ctrl-F8**. All you will see is, **[graphic TREND.EPS goes**, which illustrates the beginning of the graph, and **here]**, which indicates its end.

13. With a postscript printer on line, print the document and graph: press **Alt-P/G**.

Loading graphs into WordPerfect 5.0

Note, to load graphs into WordPerfect 5, the graph must be stored in the PIC file format (see Chapter 8, Subsection 8.1.2 for details)

1. Position the cursor where the graph is required and press **Alt-F9**.

2. Press **1** to select Figure.

3. Press **1** to choose Create.

4. Press **1** and enter the name of the file required. Remember that, if you are not in the correct directory, you must specify a full pathname and file extension. For example, to load a file called graph from the Access directory, you would enter **c:\paradox3\access\graph.pic**.

5. Size the graph as required. Also, you might like to scale it by pressing **8**.

6. Press **F7** to return to your document; press **Ctrl-F7/V** to view the document and graph on screen.

File Handling

Moving Files or Programs (using Dos)

If less than certain that a file or program will not be needed again while making room on hard disk, it is advisable to move it to floppy disk. By way of example, consider the hypothetical situation where it is necessary to move the Letter.spr file from the root directory of a hard disk to a floppy disk. The ensuing steps show how this is achieved:

1. Ensure that a C> prompt is on screen. If not, enter **c:**

2. If necessary, enter **cd** to change to the root directory.

3. With a floppy disk in drive A, enter **copy letter.spr a:**

Now that a copy of the file has been made on floppy disk, you can delete the Letter.spr file as discussed in the next section.

To move files from directories other than the root directory demands that the subdirectory name be included in the Dos command statement, or, that you simply change to the appropriate directory before issuing the Dos copy command.

The former method, which represents the easier of the two, is best illustrated by example: suppose it was necessary to move the Letter.spr file from the Sprint directory to floppy disk. The following steps show how to do this:

1. Ensure that you have a C> prompt on screen. If not, enter **c:**

2. Enter **cd\sprint** to change to the Sprint directory.

3. With a floppy disk in drive A, enter **copy letter.spr a:**

(It is possible to skip stage 2 entirely and include a complete pathname when using the Dos copy command. For example, you might find it easier simply to enter **copy c:\sprint\letter.spr a:**)

Deleting Files (from Dos)

When absolutely certain that a file or program on hard disk is no longer required, perhaps after it has been copied, it can be deleted using the Dos command, del. Note that, even though you may have a program running, such as a word processor, spreadsheet, integrated package or whatever, you should find that you are able to issue a command which will allow you to interact with Dos without having to abandon your current program/application. Check the relevant manual to find out how to achieve this.

Suppose it was necessary to delete the Letter.spr file in the root directory:

1. Ensure that the C> prompt is on screen. If not, enter **c:**

2. Enter **cd** to change to the root directory.

3. Enter **del c:\letter.spr**.

To delete files in directories other than the root directory demands that you either change to the appropriate directory before issuing the del command, or, that you include the directory name in the Dos command statement.

The following steps illustrate a situation where the Letter.spr file is deleted from the Sprint directory:

1. Ensure that the C> prompt is on screen. If not, **enter c:**

2. Enter **cd\sprint** to change to the Sprint directory.

3. Enter **del letter.spr**.

Alternatively, a pathname can be included:

1. Ensure that there is a C> prompt on screen. If not, enter **c:**

2. Enter **del c:\sprint\letter.spr**.

Files Necessary for Installation

If you boot (start) your system by inserting a floppy (Dos startup) disk, or you use a hard disk other than the one on which you wish to install Paradox, you may have to carry out some simple filing chores. This section of the appendix also applies if you are using a single hard disk as two virtual disks where you boot your system from virtual disk C but you wish to install Paradox on virtual disk D.

The installation program makes use of the CONFIG.SYS file, which is used by Dos to store setup parameters that dictate how your system is configured after booting. For example, it has a parameter to set the maximum number of files that can be opened.

In most instances, it is not necessary to modify the CONFIG.SYS file, as it will already satisfy the requirements that FILES=20 and BUFFERS=20. Two easy ways of modifying the CONFIG.SYS file so that it comprises these statements stem from the use of a word processor or Dos. Both methods are addressed in the following appendix sections.

Modifying the CONFIG.SYS file (using Borland Sprint and WordPerfect 5)

Most professional word processors such as Borland Sprint and WordPerfect will allow you to read and edit the CONFIG.SYS file directly. Whichever word processor you use, simply remember that the CONFIG.SYS file should be treated as either a Dos Text file or an Ascii file, and it should be edited so that it contains the following statements: **FILES=20, BUFFERS=20.**

Using Borland Sprint you can open, edit and save the CONFIG.SYS file as follows:

1. Press **F10/F/F** to produce the File Manager menu. If the default directory shown on the dividing horizontal line is not where the CONFIG.SYS file may be found, press **C** and enter the appropriate directory.

2. Press **Shift-Esc** to cancel all menus.

3. Press **Alt-F** to call up the File menu.

4. Press **T** to select Translate.

5. Press **I** to select Import.

6. Press **A** to select Ascii.

7. Press **<Enter>**, position the selection bar over CONFIG.SYS and press **<Enter>**, once again.

8. Edit the file making sure that FILES and BUFFERS equate to 20.

9. To save your edited CONFIG.SYS file press **Alt-F/T/E/A** and then press **<Enter>**. Change the ASC extension to SYS, and press **<Enter>**, once again. Press **Y** to overwrite the old CONFIG.SYS file.

10. Quit Sprint.

11. Re-boot your system by pressing **Ctrl-Alt-Del**.

Using WordPerfect 5, it is possible to load, edit and save the CONFIG.SYS file as follows:

1. Press **F5**. Enter the appropriate directory. For example, if your stratup disk is inserted into drive A enter **a:**

2. Position the bar over CONFIG.SYS using the cursor keys.

3. Press **5** to load the file.

4. Edit the file making sure that both FILES and BUFFERS equal 20.

5. Press **Ctrl-F5/1** to select Dos Text.

6. Press **1** to select Save, and press **<Enter>.**

7. Finally, press **Y** in order to overwrite the existing CONFIG.SYS file.

8. Exit WordPerfect.

9. Re-boot your system by pressing **Ctrl-Alt-Del.**

Modifying the CONFIG.SYS file (using Dos)

Here we will add FILES=20 and BUFFERS=20 to the CONFIG.SYS file:

1. Insert your Dos system disk into drive A if necessary, or change to the root directory by entering **cd**

2. Enter **copy a:config.sys+con a:config.sys**, if Dos is on floppy disk, or enter **copy c:config.sys+con c:config.sys**, if Dos is on hard disk.

3. Enter **files=20** and **buffers=20.**

4. Press **Ctrl-Z.**

5. Finally, press **<Enter>**, and reboot your system by pressing **Ctrl-Alt-Del.**

File Extensions of Paradox Objects

.DB	Table
.F or F?	Form
.G	Graph specification
.PX	Primary index
.R or R?	Report
.SC	Script
.SE	Image setting
.VAL	Validity checks
.X??	Query speedup
.Y??	Query speedup

? represents a single character

The Custom Configuration Program (CCP)

Running the CCP

The Paradox Custom Configuration Program, or CCP, is automatically copied to the

Paradox3 directory of your hard disk during installation. So, naturally, the working directory must be Paradox3 before the CCP can be run. The easiest way to run the CCP is from within Paradox itself; press S to choose Scripts from the main menu; press P to select Play; press **<Enter>** and choose Custom. Press y or n to indicate whether or not a monochrome monitor is being used.

To run it from Dos simply enter paradox3 custom in the paradox3 directory. It is inadvisable to run the CCP by pressing Ctrl-O to resort to Dos as many machines with under 1 MByte of memory will cause the *Insufficient memory* prompt to appear.

Changing Default Directories using the CCP

After the CCP is run, the default directory can be changed as follows:

1. Press **D** to select Defaults.

2. Press **<Enter>** to choose Defaults once again.

3. Press **S** to select SetDirectory.

4. Enter **directory name**.

5. Press **R** to return to the main menu.

6. Press **D** to select Do-It!

7. Highlight Do-It! and press **<Enter>**.

8. Press H to write the configuration to your hard disk.

9. Return to Paradox by entering **paradox3**.

Modifying the AutoSave feature using the CCP

1. Run the CCP and press **D** to select Defaults

2. Press **<Enter>** to select Defaults once again.

3. Press **A** to select AutoSave.

4. Press **Y** to enable frequent automatic saving to disk, or press **N** to auto save occasionally.

5. Press **R** to return to the CCP main menu.

6. Press **D** to select Do-It!.

7. Highlight Do-It!, press **<Enter>** to select it once again.

8. Press **H** to write the configuration to your hard disk.

9. Enter **paradox3** to rerun Paradox.

Making fields in Answer tables sensitive to Query Forms

1. Run the CCP as outlined in the previous section.

2. Press **D** to select Defaults.

3. Press **<Enter>** to select Defaults once again.

4. Press **Q** to choose QueryOrder.

5. Press **I** to select ImageOrder.

6. Press **R** to return to the main menu.

7. Press **D** to invoke Do-It!

8. Invoke Do-It! once again, by highlighting it and pressing <Enter>.

9. Press **H** to write the configuration file to hard disk, if you are not using a network that is.

By configuring Paradox so as to make Answer tables compatible with query forms, gives control over the resultant sort order of a query – columns in the Query form can be rotated and arranged so as to produce the sort order required.

The UK Data Protection Act

Databases may have given you a slight feeling of *déjà vu*, if you have read George Orwell's 1984. Faceless bureaucrats keeping tabs on us makes us all feel a little uneasy. The year of 1984 passed by quite unlike Orwell's vision of it, but, nonetheless, the public was made aware of the ease with which personal information can be kept and, more importantly, misused.

The early part of the 1980s was graced by a plethora of press reports regarding misuse of personal data by employers, and numerous other data users. And despite the 'general press' living up to its reputation of being absolutely incompetent when reporting computer related stories, an important matter was successfully put across. The fact that the public had no right to see its personal information, and that there was no Act to govern the conduct of data users, simply had to be remedied.

However reluctantly it might have appeared, officialdom was finally persuaded to take action, with the Data Protection Act (or DPA) receiving Royal Ascent in July, 1984. The DPA was designed to govern the conduct and manner of data users, in other words individuals or establishments utilising computers to store personal information. More than this, the Act was aimed at protecting the rights of individuals.

As expected, a logical starting point was to catalogue all data users, by requesting them to apply for registration. In the brief registration period from November 1985 to May 1986, little over half of Britain's data users registered. This was in keeping with similar ventures implemented elsewhere in Europe. According to the Act, such data users failing to register risked fines of up to £2,000 in the lower Courts.

Eric Howe, the Data Registrar, laid down eight principles in order to set the Act's objectives in motion:

1. The information to be contained in personal data shall be obtained and personal data shall be processed, fairly and lawfully.

2. Personal data shall be held only for specified and lawful purposes.

3. Personal data held for any purpose or purposes shall not be disclosed in any manner incompatible with that purpose or those purposes.

4. Personal data held for any purpose or purposes shall be adequate, relevant and not excessive in relation to that purpose or those purposes.

5. Personal data shall be accurate and, where necessary, kept up to date.

6. Personal data held for any purpose or purposes shall not be kept for longer than is necessary for that purpose or those purposes.

7. An individual shall be entitled at reasonable intervals and without undue delay or expense:

❑ To be informed by any data user whether he holds data of which the individual is a subject

❑ To access to any such data held by a data user

❑ Where appropriate, to have such data corrected or erased.

8. Appropriate security measures shall be taken against unauthorised access to, or alteration, disclosure or destruction of, personal data and accidental loss or destruction of personal data.

To coincide with the full introduction of the Data Protection Act on November 11,

1987, I reported on the Act for *Popular Computing Weekly.* I felt I had to be sceptical, finding fault with the fact that subjects had to pay to see their information (Principle 7). Furthermore, pinpointing who, exactly, lay behind the misuse of a subject's information seemed to be an impossible task.

I later wrote another article for *Personal Computing Today* (then *Personal Computing with the Amstrad*) in which I briefly interviewed Francis Aldhouse, the Deputy Registrar, and discovered that as few as 16 part-time investigators were employed. Though the Act has since evolved, many feel that it still lacks teeth.

Registering as a Data User

The burning question must now be, should you register?

If you intend using Paradox to store personal information about employees, or other individuals, then you will almost certainly have to register.

In many respects, however, the Act is sensibly aimed, so not all Paradox users who store personal information are required to register. You may not need to register if you store information about members of your family for other than professional purposes. Personal information pertaining to members of your computer club, or similar organisation, can gain you exemption too, provided that each and every member of your club approves of his or her personal data being stored. Certain payroll and accountancy operations are also exempt.

If you are unsure about whether or not you should register, it is perhaps advisable to contact the Registrar's office for further information: Data Protection Registrar, Springfield House, Water Lane, Wilmslow, Cheshire SK9 5AX Tel 0625 535711. And if ambiguity should set in, then it is probably safer to pay the small registration fee rather than risk being fined.

Paradox 3.5: An Overview of Changes

During the preparation of this book Version 3.5 of Paradox was announced in September 1990, with the following additional features:

- ❑ Compatible with Paradox SQL-Link product
- ❑ Adoption of Borland's VROOM (Virtual Runtime Object Oriented Memory Manager) technology for improved performance and increased memory for PAL applications
- ❑ Utilisation of Borland's TurboDrive technology: Built-in 286/386 Protected Mode support; able to use up to 16 Mb of Extended memory on 286, 386 or 486- based machines

- ❑ Support of most PAL functions within calculated fields in forms and reports

- ❑ Additional or enhanced PAL commands and functions:

  RMEMLEFT
  SAVETABLES
  FORMTYPE
  RECORDSTATUS
  CALCDEBUG
  RESYNCKEY
  UNDO
  Ctrl E enhancement (incremental menus; dual mode operation)

- ❑ Optimisation of procedure libraries. NB: earlier versions of Paradox cannot use procedure libraries created by Version 3.5

- ❑ Better error handling for low memory conditions

- ❑ New diagnostic, tuning and colour setting systems in the Custom Configuration Program

- ❑ Multi-table forms now allow up to nine linked detail tables (up from five in Version 3)

- ❑ Support for 3Com 3+Open networks

- ❑ Export and Import for QuatroPro

- ❑ New installation procedures. Files are unzipped at installation reducing the number of disks included in the product. Paradox disks are now read only to protect users from potential viruses.

System requirements are substantially similar to those for Version 3, so Paradox users may well find it worthwhile to upgrade to Version 3.5

Index

P

Q

R

S

T

An Invitation

Sigma Press is the largest independent publisher of computer books in the United Kingdom, and also has a very active leisure publishing division. Marketing and distribution of our computer books has been handled for 10 years by John Wiley & Sons Ltd, the UK subsidiary of a major US publisher.

We always welcome proposals for new books, and can ensure a rapid and informed response. In addition to mainstream computer topics, we particularly welcome book proposals in specialist areas, sometimes too difficult for larger publishers to grapple with.

Books on software or hardware developed mainly in the UK and Europe are also a speciality, as we are closer to these markets than our US competitors.

To assess your proposal, we need:

- ❑ a contents list
- ❑ a sample chapter (if available)
- ❑ an estimate of the final length of the book
- ❑ an estimated completion date
- ❑ a list of competing books – with an indication of why yours is necessary
- ❑ where relevant – names of two experts in your area from whom we can ask an opinion about your book

If you have any questions, or would like to discuss your proposal informally, contact:

Graham Beech
Commissioning Editor
Sigma Press
1 South Oak Lane
Wilmslow
Cheshire SK9 6AR

Phone: 0625 – 531035 Fax: 0625 – 536800